CAPE TOWN

Forthcoming titles include

Baltic States • Chicago • Corfu
First-Time Round the World • Grand Canyon
Philippines • Skiing & Snowboarding in North America
South America • The Gambia • Walks Around London

Forthcoming reference titles include

Chronicle series: China, England, France,
India • Night Sky

read Rough Guides online

www.roughguides.com

Rough Guide Credits

Text editor: Clifton Wilkinson
Series editor: Mark Ellingham
Production: Julia Bovis, James Morris and Michelle Bhatia
Cartography: Maxine Repath and Kingston Presentation
Graphics
Proofreading: Jennifer Speake

Publishing Information

This second edition published June 2002
by Rough Guides Ltd,
62–70 Shorts Gardens, London, WC2H 9AH

Distributed by the Penguin Group:

Penguin Books Ltd, 80 Strand, London WC2R ORL.
Penguin Putnam, Inc. 375 Hudson Street, New York 10014, USA
Penguin Books Australia Ltd, 487 Maroondah Highway,
PO Box 257, Ringwood, Victoria 3134, Australia
Penguin Books Canada Ltd, 10 Alcorn Avenue,
Toronto, Ontario, Canada M4V 1E4
Penguin Books (NZ) Ltd,
182–190 Wairau Road, Auckland 10, New Zealand

Typeset in Bembo and Helvetica to an original design by Henry Iles.
Printed in Spain by Graphy Cems.

© Tony Pinchuck and Barbara McCrea, 2002
384pp, includes index
A catalogue record for this book is available from the British Library.

ISBN 1-85828-841-X

THE ROUGH GUIDE TO

CAPE TOWN

by Tony Pinchuck
and Barbara McCrea

ROUGH
GUIDES

We set out to do something different when the first Rough Guide was published in 1982. Mark Ellingham, just out of university, was travelling in Greece. He brought along the popular guides of the day, but found they were all lacking in some way. They were either strong on ruins and museums but went on for pages without mentioning a beach or taverna. Or they were so conscious of the need to save money that they lost sight of Greece's cultural and historical significance. Also, none of the books told him anything about Greece's contemporary life – its politics, its culture, its people, and how they lived.

So with no job in prospect, Mark decided to write his own guidebook, one which aimed to provide practical information that was second to none, detailing the best beaches and the hottest clubs and restaurants, while also giving hard-hitting accounts of every sight, both famous and obscure, and providing up-to-the-minute information on contemporary culture. It was a guide that encouraged independent travellers to find the best of Greece, and was a great success, getting shortlisted for the Thomas Cook travel guide award, and encouraging Mark, along with three friends, to expand the series.

The Rough Guide list grew rapidly and the letters flooded in, indicating a much broader readership than had been anticipated, but one which uniformly appreciated the Rough Guide mix of practical detail and humour, irreverence and enthusiasm. Things haven't changed. The same four friends who began the series are still the caretakers of the Rough Guide mission today: to provide the most reliable, up-to-date and entertaining information to independent-minded travellers of all ages, on all budgets.

We now publish more than 150 titles and have offices in London and New York. The travel guides are written and researched by a dedicated team of more than 100 authors, based in Britain, Europe, the USA and Australia. We have also created a unique series of phrasebooks to accompany the travel series, along with an acclaimed series of music guides, and a best-selling pocket guide to the internet and World Wide Web. We also publish comprehensive travel information on our website: **www.roughguides.com**

Help us update

We've gone to a lot of trouble to ensure that this Rough Guide is as up to date and accurate as possible. However, things do change and all suggestions, comments and corrections are much appreciated. We'll send a copy of the next edition (or any other Rough Guide if you prefer) for the best letters.

Please mark letters **"Rough Guide Cape Town Update"** and send to:

Rough Guides, 62–70 Shorts Gardens, London, WC2H 9AH, or Rough Guides, 4th Floor, 345 Hudson St, New York NY 10014.

Or send email to: mail@roughguides.co.uk
Online updates about this book can be found on Rough Guides' website (see opposite).

Acknowledgements

Barbara and Tony would like to thank:
Our editor, Clifton Wilkinson, for his precision editing, his awe-inspiring eye for detail and for being a pleasure to work with. Thanks too, to: our mothers for their support, especially Lily for many afternoons of child-minding; Stephen Watson for his comments and additions to the literature section; Dave Bristow for his ever-cheerful and well-informed advice; Stanley Singer for help with restaurants; Ida Cooper; Hugh Tyrell; Ben Maclennan; Guy Berger; Steve Jaffe for information about the theatre scene; Dr Debbie Young at the MTN Centre for Dolphin Studies and all the unmentioned friends and readers who gave us their time and information.

Readers' Letters

CONTENTS

Introduction

Cape Town's setting, on the Cape Peninsula, is simply stunning. A rugged tail of land washed by two oceans and dominated by iconic **Table Mountain**, the peninsula culminates dramatically at the sea-pounded cliffs of **Cape Point**. Generally, when locals talk about Cape Town, they mean the whole peninsula and to really get to grips with the city you need to spend time outdoors. Walking (or taking the cable car) up Table Mountain, catching the train down the False Bay coast to the 150km of sandy beaches that fringe the peninsula, or heading inland for hiking and picnicking in the many gardens and forests are the best ways for visitors to capture the essence of the city.

Though Cape Town is the legislative capital of South Africa, it is the least "African" city in the country, with black Africans making up less than a quarter of its population. The city's unique feature is the Creolized **coloured culture**, which evolved from the interaction between Europeans and slaves brought from East Africa and the Far East. Mosques in the Bo-Kaap quarter, adjacent to the city centre, add spice to the colonial streetscape; **Cape cuisine** combines local ingredients with Eastern flavours; and **Cape jazz** is heard in the coloured townships of the Cape Flats as well as city-centre clubs. Over fifty percent of Capetonians are **coloured**, while about 27 percent are **white**, descended mainly from Dutch and British settlers. To complicate matters, language fails to line up conveniently with ethnicity, and **Afrikaans**, the city's most widely spoken language, is used by a large proportion of coloureds and many whites. The city's minority African population predominantly speak **Xhosa**, one of South Africa's nine official African languages, but **English** is the effective lingua franca, and will get you by 99 percent of the time. For more on coloured culture, and the complex dynamics of race in Cape Town, see p.328.

This **ethnic diversity**, along with high standards of accommodation, smart restaurants, slick clubs, laid-back cafés and a vibrant gay scene, makes visiting Cape Town a truly cosmopolitan experience. Most visitors only see the areas that were classified under apartheid as "white" and still remain relatively safe and salubrious: radiating out from the city centre, the largely affluent suburbs cling to the slopes of Table Mountain or perch at the edge of the peninsula's two coasts. But for most Capetonians, living in the crowded **townships** and **shantytowns** on the **Cape Flats**, just getting on with their lives is set against the harsh reality of sky-high crime rates. These areas, to the east of the city, can be visited on guided tours, and if you really want to get under the skin of the African areas you can now enjoy the hospitality of staying in one of several B&Bs in a Xhosa home.

Table Mountain, frequently mantled by its "tablecloth" clouds, is the solid core of Cape Town, dividing the city into distinct zones, with public gardens, wilderness, forests, hiking routes, vineyards and desirable residential areas.

To its north lies the **city centre**, an attractive collage of Georgian, Cape Dutch and Victorian architecture, built on the foundations of the **slave society** that occupied it for the first half of its 350-year existence. Eyed by the Portuguese, Dutch and English in their turn, it became the place where Europe, Asia and Africa met. Today the centre is as much a cultural melting pot as ever, where coloured families from the Cape Flats do their shopping, young whites hang out in hip coffee bars, Muslims pray, street kids loiter on corners, buskers play to passing crowds and Africans converge from across the continent to hawk crafts.

A stone's throw from the centre, the **V&A Waterfront** is Cape Town's most popular spot for shopping, eating and drinking in a highly picturesque setting among the piers and quays of a working harbour, and is also the embarkation point for catamarans to **Robben Island**, the notorious site of Nelson Mandela's incarceration. The rocky shore west of the Waterfront is occupied by the inner-city suburbs of **Green Point** and **Sea Point**, whose main drag is lined with some of the peninsula's oldest and best restaurants, while their back streets are crammed with backpacker lodges, B&Bs and hotels. Equally good for accommodation, but leafy and upmarket in comparison, the **City Bowl suburbs** gaze down from the Table Mountain foothills across the central business district to the ships in Duncan Dock.

South from Sea Point, a coastal road traces the chilly **Atlantic seaboard** under the heights of the Twelve Apostles and past some of Cape Town's most expensive suburbs and spectacular beaches at Clifton, Camps Bay and Bakoven. Further south, past Hout Bay, the road merges with the precipitous **Chapman's Peak Drive**, ten dramatically snaking kilometres of Victorian engineering carved into the western cliffsides of the Table Mountain massif, high above the crashing waves. To the east, across Table Mountain, the exceptionally beautiful **Kirstenbosch National Botanical Gardens** creep up the lower slopes, as do the **Constantia Winelands** a little further south, while the middle-class **southern suburbs** stretch down the peninsula as far as Muizenberg. The Metrorail line, the only viable public transport down the length of the peninsula, cuts through these suburbs and continues along the **False Bay seaboard**, passing through villagey **Kalk Bay**, with its intact harbour and working fishing community, and **Fish Hoek**, which has the best bathing beach along the eastern side of the peninsula, before the final stop at the historic settlement of **Simon's Town**.

Away from the city, an hour's drive east of the Cape Flats into the Western Cape interior are the beautiful **Winelands**, with elegant examples of Cape Dutch architecture, wonderful wines and excellent restaurants. South of Cape Town you can take the picturesque coastal route, winding around massive sea-cliffs, to reach Hermanus, the largest settlement on the **Whale Coast**, and a fabulous spot for shore-based whale-watching.

When to visit

Cape Town and the Western Cape coastal belt have a **Mediterranean climate** (contrary to expectations, it's not tropical), and the warm dryish summers are balanced by cool wet winters. Cape Town is a windy city and it can gust throughout the year; although seasons are reasonably well defined, the weather is notoriously changeable. Come prepared for hot days in winter and cold snaps in summer: pack at least one short-sleeved garment during the cooler months and a jumper and jacket whatever time of year you come.

For sun and swimming, the best time to come is from **October to mid-December** and **mid-January to Easter**, when it's light till well into the evening and there's an average of ten hours of sunshine a day. From mid-December to mid-January, Cape Town becomes congested as the nation takes its annual seaside holiday. This is major party time: the annual minstrel carnival and the Mother City Queer Project, a gay extravanganza, are staged during the festive season, while the Summer Sunset Concert season in Kirstenbosch National Botanical Gardens also starts its four-month run in December. If you plan to visit at this time, book your accommodation and transport well in advance.

Despite its shorter daylight hours, the **autumn** period, from April to mid-May, has a lot going for it: the south-easter (see box below) has dropped but air temperatures remain pleasantly warm and the light is sharp and bright. For similar reasons the **spring** month of September can be very agreeable, with the added attraction that following the winter rains the peninsula tends to be at its greenest, with much of the fynbos (see p.107) in flower. Although spells of heavy rain occur in **winter** (June and July), it tends to be relatively mild, with temperatures rarely falling below 6°C. Glorious sunny days with crisp blue skies are common, and you won't see bare wintry trees either: indigenous vegetation is evergreen, and gardens flower year round. It's also in July that the first migrating whales begin to appear along the Cape Peninsula, usually staying till the end of November.

THE CAPE DOCTOR

The southeaster, the cool summer wind that blows in across False Bay, forms a major obsession for Capetonians. Its fickle moods can singlehandedly determine what kind of day you're going to have, and when it gusts at over 60kph you won't want to be outdoors, let alone on the beach. Conversely, its gentler incarnation as the so-called Cape Doctor brings welcome relief on humid summer days, and lays the famous cloudy tablecloth on top of Table Mountain.

CAPE TOWN'S CLIMATE

	F°		C°		RAINFALL	
	AVERAGE DAILY		AVERAGE DAILY		AVERAGE MONTHLY	
	MAX	MIN	MAX	MIN	IN	MM
Jan	79	60	26	16	0.6	15
Feb	80	60	27	16	0.7	17
March	78	58	25	14	0.8	20
April	73	53	23	12	1.6	40
May	69	49	20	9	2.7	69
June	65	46	18	8	3.7	93
July	65	45	18	7	3.2	82
Aug	65	46	18	8	3.0	77
Sept	67	48	19	9	1.6	40
Oct	70	51	21	11	1.2	30
Nov	74	56	24	13	0.6	15
Dec	77	59	25	15	0.7	17

BASICS

Getting there

Though a cruise provides the most memorable means of getting to Cape Town, the cheapest and most practicable way is to fly. There are direct flights from the UK and the US, while from Canada choices are more limited and from Australia and New Zealand the best option can often be a round-the-world ticket, or a flight via Johannesburg.

FROM THE UK AND IRELAND

Frequent **direct flights** (11hr 30min) connect London Heathrow with Cape Town; South African Airways (SAA), British Airways (BA) and Virgin Atlantic all cover this route. However, more flights go to **Johannesburg**, the country's principal gateway and the busiest hub in Africa: domestic connections between the two cities are excellent. There are no direct flights from UK airports other than Heathrow.

You can also often pick up competitive deals on flights with European airlines (including KLM, Lufthansa and Air France) or African carriers (Air Zimbabwe and Air Namibia amongst others) which entail **changing planes** in their national hubs and some involve a stopover in Johannesburg (although you won't have to change planes

3

there). On such flights you'll often be allowed to break your journey at little or no extra cost – an attractive option if you want to take a breather on the long-haul route and take in another city. There are no direct flights **from Ireland** to South Africa; you need to change in London or, for example, Amsterdam, if you're flying with KLM.

FARES

Most of the discount and specialist travel agents listed opposite can quote fares on scheduled flights. Check out the ads in the travel pages of the weekend newspapers, London's listings magazine *Time Out* for special deals and the latest prices. Websites, where available, are listed below – it's worth checking out these sites for **"online specials"** available via internet auctions. It's invariably cheaper to buy tickets through agents (see opposite) than through airlines themselves.

High season for travel to Cape Town is always December to mid-January, Easter and August, coinciding with European peak holiday periods. The medium-priced **shoulder seasons** run from mid-January to March and September to November, while the **low season** is from April to July. It's always worth enquiring when the seasons begin and end as these vary from airline to airline and year to year; changing your departure date by a day can sometimes make a real difference to the price. Discounted return fares to Cape Town start around £530 for a direct flight and under £400 for flights via Europe. Another option is a **round-the-world** (RTW) ticket: an RTW including Cape Town will start at around £900 for a one-year open ticket.

Airlines

Air France UK ☎020/8742 6600, Ireland ☎01/844 5633; ⓦwww.airfrance.fr.

Air Zimbabwe UK ☎020/7491 0009; ⓦwww.airzim.co.zw.

Alitalia UK ☎020/7602 7111, Ireland ☎01/677 5171; ⓦwww.alitalia.co.uk.

British Airways UK ☎0845/773 3377, Ireland ☎0141/222 2345; ⓦwww.britishairways.com.

Iberia UK ☎020/7830 0011, Ireland ☎01/677 9846; ⓦwww.iberia.com.

KLM UK ☎08705/074 074, Northern Ireland ☎0990/074 074, Republic of Ireland ☎0345/445 588; ⓦwww.klmuk.com.

Lufthansa UK ☎0845/737 7747, Ireland ☎01/844 5544; ⓦwww.lufthansa.com.

Olympic UK ☎0870/606 0460, Ireland ☎01/608 0090; ⓦwww.olympic-airways.co.uk.

South African Airways UK ☎020/7312 5000; ⓦwww.flysaa.com.

Virgin Atlantic UK ☎01293/747 747, Ireland ☎01/873 3388; ⓦwww.virginatlantic.com.

Flight agents

Bridge the World UK ☎020/7911 0900; ⓦwww.bridgetheworld.com.

Cheap Flights ⓦwww.cheapflights.com.

Deck Chair ⓦwww.deckchair.com.

Expedia ⓦwww.expedia.co.uk.

Flightbookers UK ☎020/7757 2444; ⓦwww.ebookers.net.

Flynow UK ☎020/7835 2000; ⓦwww.flynow.com.

Last Minute ⓦwww.lastminute.com.

The London Flight Centre UK ☎020/7244 6411; ⓦwww.topdecktravel.co.uk.

North South Travel UK ☎01245/608 291; ⓦwww.northsouthtravel.co.uk.

STA Travel UK ☎0870/160 6070; ⓦwww.statravel.co.uk.

Trailfinders UK ☎020/7628 7628, Ireland ☎01/677 7888; ⓦwww.trailfinders.com.

Travel Bag UK ☎0870/900 1350; ⓦwww.travelbag.co.uk.

Travel Cuts UK ☎020/7255 2082; ⓦwww.travelcuts.co.uk.

FARES

PACKAGE TOURS

If time is short and you're keen on seeing the major sights, you might want to join a **package tour**. You can pick up five-day/six-night guided tours of Cape Town for around £400 (excluding meals and flights). Virgin Holidays offers a pick-and-mix range of **self-drive packages** that includes seven-night two-centre packages; their Cape Town and Durban option starts at £1200 (excluding flights) and you'll pay an extra £300 if you combine Cape Town with Vic Falls instead of with Durban.

Tour operators

Abercrombie and Kent ☎0845 0700 610;
ⓦwww.abercrombiekent.co.uk.

Africa Travel Centre
☎020/7387 1211;
ⓦwww.africatravel.co.uk.

Art of Travel ☎012/8565 0011;
ⓦwww.artoftravel.co.uk.

Cox & Kings ☎020/7873 5000;
ⓦwww.coxandkings.co.uk.

Kuoni Worldwide ☎01306/747 002; ⓦwww.kuoni.co.uk.

Rainbow Tours ☎020/7226 1004;
ⓦwww.rainbowtours.co.uk.

Thomas Cook Holidays
☎0870/750 0512;
ⓦwww.thomascook.co.uk.

Virgin Holidays ☎01293/617 181;
ⓦwww.virginholidays.co.uk.

Worldwide Journeys and Expeditions ☎020/7386 4646;
ⓦwww.worldwidejourneys.co.uk.

FROM THE US AND CANADA

From North America, the only **direct flights** to Cape Town are with South African Airways (SAA), flying from Atlanta and taking just under fourteen hours. SAA's alliance partner, Delta Air, provides connections with 134 US cities. SAA also has direct flights from New York to Johannesburg, with convenient onward connections to Cape Town.

Most travellers get from North America to Cape Town **via Europe**, changing planes there. Daily flights are operated by SAA, British Airways and Virgin Atlantic Airways via London; Air France via Paris; and KLM/Northwest via Amsterdam – see "From the UK and Ireland" for more details. Check the waiting time between connecting flights to avoid a long layover. There are no direct flights to South Africa **from Canada**; you have to fly via the US or Europe.

FARES

Keep an eye out for **special offers** but, barring these, the cheapest of the airlines' published fares is usually an **Apex** ticket, which will carry certain restrictions. You have to book – and pay – at least 21 days before departure and spend a minimum of seven days abroad (maximum stay three months) and you tend to get penalized if you change your schedule.

Many airlines offer youth or student fares to **under–26s**; a passport or driving licence is sufficient proof of age. These tickets are subject to availability and can have eccentric booking conditions.

You can normally cut costs further by going through a **specialist flight agent**: either a consolidator, who buys up blocks of tickets from the airlines and sells them at a discount; or a discount agent, who in addition to dealing with discounted flights may also offer special student and youth fares and other travel-related services, such as insurance, car rental and tours. See p.8 for a list of agents.

Fares for travel from North America to South Africa are highest between mid-June and mid-September, and early December to mid-January. The rest of the year is low season (most airlines have no shoulder season). Sample standard Apex fares to Cape Town in low season start at around $1400 from Atlanta and New York, while you'll pay in the region of $1800 from Los Angeles.

Airlines

Air France US ☎1-800/237-2747, Canada ☎1-800/667-2747; ⊛www.airfrance.com.

British Airways US ☎1-800/247-9297, Canada ☎1-800/668-1059; ⊛www.britishairways.com.

Delta US ☎1-800/241-4141; ⊛www.delta.com.

Northwest/KLM US ☎1-800/447-4747; ⊛www.nwa.com.

South African Airways US ☎1-800/722-9675; ⊛www.flysaa.com.

Virgin Atlantic Airways 1-800/862-8621; ⊛www.virginatlantic.com.

Discount agents and consolidators

Air Brokers International US ☎1-800/883-3273 or 415/397-1383; ⊛www.airbrokers.com.

Cheap Tickets
⊛www.cheaptickets.com.

Council Travel US ☎1-800/226-8624 or 617/528 2091; ⊛www.counciltravel.com.

Educational Travel Center US ☎1-800/747-5551 or 608/256-5551; ⊛www.edtrav.com.

Expedia ⊛www.expedia.com.

High Adventure Travel US ☎1-800/350-0612 or 415/912-5600; ⊛www.airtreks.com.

Hotwire ⊛www.hotwire.com.

Priceline ⊛www.priceline.com.

Sky Auction ⊛www.skyauction.com.

STA Travel US ☎1-800/777-0112 or ☎1-800/781 4040; ⊛www.sta-travel.com.

Travel Cuts Canada ☎1-800/667-2887 or ☎416/979-2406; ⊛www.travelcuts.com.

Travelocity ⊛www.travelocity.com.

PACKAGE TOURS

- -

As well as being convenient, package tours can throw open specialist activities that would otherwise be difficult to coordinate. One option is an eleven-day trip with Backroads, which includes exploration of the Cape Peninsula and Winelands on foot as well as big game adventures in northern South Africa: it costs from around US$5000.

Tour operators

Abercrombie and Kent
☎1-800/323-7308;
ⓦwww.abercrombiekent.com.

Adventure Center ☎1-800/228-8747 or 510/654-1879;
ⓦwww.adventure-center.com.

Adventures Abroad
☎1-800/665-3998 or 604/303-1099; ⓦwww.adventures-abroad.com.

AfricaTours ☎1-800/235-3692;
ⓦwww.africasafaris.com.

Backroads ☎1-800/462-2848 or 510527 1555;
ⓦwww.backroads.com.

Cox & Kings ☎1-800/999-1758;
ⓦwww.coxandkingsusa.com.

Europe Train Tours ☎1-800/5512085 or 914/758 1777;
ⓦwww.ettours.com.

Global Exchange
☎1-800/497 1994;
ⓦwww.globalexchange.org.

Goway Travel ☎1-800/387 8850 or 416/322-1034;
ⓦwww.goway.com.

International Gay and Lesbian Travel Association
☎1-800/448-8550;
ⓦwww.iglta.com.

Questers Worldwide Nature Tours ☎1-800/468 8668;
ⓦwww.questers.com.

REI Adventures ☎1-800/622 2236.

Saga Holidays ☎1-887/265-6862;
ⓦwww.sagaholidays.com.

FROM AUSTRALIA AND NEW ZEALAND

South Africa is an expensive destination for travellers from Australia and New Zealand. A ticket to Europe with a stopover in South Africa, or even a round-the-world (RTW) ticket, generally represents better value than a straightforward return.

There are no nonstop flights to Cape Town from Australia or New Zealand, but there are **direct flights** to

Johannesburg from both the eastern states and Western Australia, taking around fourteen hours from Sydney, with good onward connections to Cape Town. From **New Zealand** you fly via Sydney to Johannesburg. South African Airways (SAA) and Qantas have direct flights along this route; some of the Asian airlines (Air Lanka, Malaysia Airlines, Singapore Airlines and Thai Airways) tend to be less expensive, but their routings often entail more stopovers.

FARES

Whatever kind of ticket you're after, your first call should be to one of the specialist flight agents listed opposite; staff can fill you in on all the latest **fares** and special offers. All the fares quoted are for travel during low or shoulder seasons; flying at peak times (primarily mid-May to Aug and Dec to mid-Jan) can add substantially to these prices. The best return fares you're likely to find are around A$2300 from the eastern states and A$2000 from Western Australia. From New Zealand, fares start at NZ$2500. If you plan to visit Cape Town en route to **Europe**, you can expect to pay in the region of A$2500/NZ$3200.

Round-the-world tickets (RTW) that take in South Africa are worth considering. Possible itineraries include: starting from either Melbourne, Sydney or Brisbane, flying to Johannesburg, then travelling overland to Cape Town, before flying to London, and taking in Amsterdam, New York and San Francisco on the way back home (from A$2500); or, starting from Perth, flying to Denpasar, Casablanca, Istanbul, Nairobi, then down to Cape Town and Johannesburg on the return leg to Perth (from A$2500).

From New Zealand, you could fly from Auckland to Sydney, Bangkok and London, returning via Cape Town, Johannesburg and Perth to Auckland. Fares for this route start at NZ$3200.

Airlines and flight agents

Air New Zealand Australia ℡13 2476, New Zealand ℡09/357 3000; ℗www.airnz.com.

British Airways Australia ℡02/8904 8800, New Zealand ℡09/356 8690; ℗www.britishairways.com.

Malaysia Airlines Australia ℡13 2627, New Zealand ℡09/373 2741 or toll-free ℡0800/657 472; ℗www.malaysiaair.com.au.

Qantas Australia ℡13 1211, New Zealand ℡09/357 8900 or ℡0800/808 767; ℗www.qantas.com.au.

Singapore Airlines Australia ℡13 1011, New Zealand ℡09/303 2129; ℗www.singaporeair.com.

South African Airways Australia ℡02/9223 4402; ℗www.saairways.com.au.

Thai Airways Australia ℡1300/651 960, New Zealand ℡09/377 3886; ℗www.thaiair.com.

Flight agents

Anywhere Travel Australia ℡02/9663 0411 or ℡018 410 014; ℮anywhere@ozemail.co.au.

Budget Travel New Zealand ℡09/366 0061 or ℡0800/808 040.

Destinations Unlimited New Zealand ℡09/373 4033.

Flight Centres Australia ℡13 1600, New Zealand ℡09/358 4310.

STA Travel Australia ℡13 1776, New Zealand ℡09/309 0458; ℗www.statravel.com.au.

Thomas Cook Australia ℡1800/801 002, New Zealand ℡09/379 3920; ℗www.thomascook.com.au.

Trailfinders Australia ℡02/9247 7666.

Travel Shop ℗www.travelshop.com.au.

Unique Travel ℗www.uniquetravel.com.au.

PACKAGE TOURS

Package holidays from Australia and New Zealand to South Africa tend to be either expensive or of the extended overland variety, although airlines are beginning to put together bargain fly-drive options as demand increases.

PACKAGE TOURS

Drive Away Holidays offers flights with SAA to Cape Town via Jo'burg, including ten days' car rental, from Sydney, Melbourne, Brisbane and Adelaide for around A$2300 and around A$2100 from Perth. You can also buy off-the-peg tours, which you can add on to your independent holiday: Contiki offers a three-day "Cape Town Jaunt" which takes in the city highlights and the Winelands, starting at A$400.

Tour operators

Abercrombie and Kent
Australia ℡03/9699 9766 or ℡1800/331 429, New Zealand ℡9/579 3369; ⓦwww.abercrombiekent.com.au.

Africa Travel Centre Australia ℡02/9249 5444 or ℡1800/000 447, New Zealand ℡09/520 2000; ⓦwww.travel.com.au.

Birding Worldwide Australia ℡03/9899 9303; ⓦwww.birdingworldwide.com.au.

Contiki Holidays Australia ℡02/9511 2200 or ℡1300/301 835; ⓦwww.contiki.com.

Drive Away Holidays ℡1300/363 500; ⓦwww.driveaway.com.au.

Peregrine Adventures Australia ℡03/9662 2700 or ℡1300 655 433; ⓦwww.peregrine.net.au.

Visas and red tape

EU nationals, as well as those of the US, Canada, Australia and New Zealand, need only a valid **passport** and sufficient funds to stay for up to six months in South Africa. All visitors need a valid **return ticket**; if you try to enter South Africa without one, you may be required to deposit the equivalent of your fare home with customs (the money will be refunded to you after you have left the country).

For longer stays, **extensions** (around R390) may be granted in the Aliens Control Section at the Department of Home Affairs (56 Barrack St ☏021/462 4970), where you will be quizzed about your intentions and your funds. Rampant unemployment means that your chances of finding work in South Africa are slim, but if you are offered a job you'll need to apply for a **work permit** through a South African diplomatic mission in your home country – a slow and cumbersome process.

At present, the per person **duty free** allowance in South Africa is two litres of wine and one litre of spirits, 400 cigarettes, fifty cigars and 250g of tobacco.

Arrival

One of the world's most majestic moments of **arrival** is cruising into Table Bay on a luxury liner. For most, however, the approach is much less picturesque – indeed, it can be something of a shock. Whether you come in by air or road, there's small chance of avoiding the grey, industrial sprawl and the miles of squatter camps that line the N2 into town.

BY AIR

Cape Town International Airport is on the Cape Flats, 22km east of the city centre. Two **shuttle bus** companies, Legend Tours (℡021-936-2814) and Dumalisile (℡021-934-1660) have desks in the international arrivals hall outside the baggage reclaim area and run a door-to-door service. Although they don't operate to a strict schedule since they try to take three or four passengers travelling on the same route, you shouldn't have to wait more than fifteen minutes for your minibus to leave. The fare from the airport into the city centre is R110 for the first person and R20 for each additional passenger; to Fish Hoek on the southern section of the Cape Peninsula it's R220 for the first person and R20 per each additional person. Note that the fares are divided equally amongst the group. An alternative is the similarly priced Magic Bus (℡021-934-5455), which must be **prebooked** a day ahead, will meet you at the airport and take you anywhere on the peninsula.

Metered **taxis** operated by Touch Down Taxis, the company officially authorized by the airport, rank in reasonable numbers outside both terminals and cost about R150 for the trip into the city. Inside the international terminal, you'll find the **car rental** desks of Alamo, Avis, Budget, Europcar, Hertz, Imperial, Khaya, National, Sizwe and Tempest (see p.251). Prebooking a vehicle is recommended as they do run out of available cars, especially during the week when there is a big demand from domestic business travellers. There are no trains from the airport. A **bureau de change** is open to coincide with international arrivals.

BY BUS AND TRAIN

Greyhound, Intercape and Translux intercity **buses** and mainline **trains** from other provinces all terminate in the centre of town around the interlinked central complex that also includes the **Golden Acre** shopping mall, at the junction of Strand and Adderley streets. The Golden Acre shopping complex can be a slightly confusing place, but if you use public transport at all, you're bound to find yourself here at some stage of your stay. Everything you need for your next move is within two or three blocks. There's a **left-luggage** facility next to platform 24 at the train station (Mon–Fri 7am–4pm).

Information and maps

The best source of information about the city is **Cape Town Tourism** (ⓦwww.cape-town.org), which has two excellent **information bureaux**: the **city Visitors' Centre** (March–Nov: Mon–Fri 8am–6pm, Sat 8.30am–1pm & Sun 9am–1pm; Dec–Feb: Mon–Fri 8am–7pm, Sat 8.30am–1pm & Sun 9am–1pm; ☏021-426-4260, ℻021-426-4266), at the corner of Burg and Castle streets, a five-minute walk two blocks northwest of the station; and the **Clocktower Precinct Visitors' Centre** (daily 9am–9pm; ☏021-405-4500) in a fabulous office at the V & A Waterfront next to the Nelson Mandela Gateway to Robben Island overlooking the harbour. Both centres operate comprehensive accommodation and activity booking services, have a swanky coffee shop, a bookshop and cybercafé as well as lots of brochures and very cheap city maps.

The best sources for weekly **events listings** are the *Top of the Times* supplement in Friday's *Cape Times*, and the *Good Weekend* pullout in the *Saturday Argus*, while the *Mail & Guardian*, which comes out on Fridays, injects some attitude into its reviews and listings supplement. *Cape Review*, a monthly listings magazine with a passing resemblance to London's and New York's *Time Out*, gives a broad range of information on food, wine, gay venues, nightlife and sporting events.

CAPE TOWN ON THE INTERNET

Cape Peninsula National Park
ⓦwww.cpnp.co.za
Official site of the national park that forms the remarkable backdrop to Cape Town, including Cape Point, Table Mountain and the penguin colony at Boulders Beach, with solid background information on its natural history as well as practical information.

Cape Town Events
ⓦwww.capetownevents.co.za
Comprehensive guide to what's on in South Africa's legislative capital.

Cape Town Metropolitan Tourism
ⓦwww.gocapetown.co.za
Site of one of the several bodies that promotes tourism in Cape Town and a good complement to the Cape Town Tourism site.

Cape Town Tourism
ⓦwww.cape-town.org
The largest and most useful of

the several official sites that seek to promote tourism to Cape Town.

Getaway
ⓦwww.getawaytoafrica.com
Online presence of South Africa's biggest travel magazine with daily tourism news and a searchable database of destinations, accommodation and activities throughout South Africa.

Independent Online
ⓦwww.iol.co.za
South African news from the country's biggest newspaper group, sister to the London *Independent*, with links to the *Cape Times* and *Cape Argus*, Cape Town's morning and afternoon dailies.

Q-online ⓦwww.q.co.za
The definitive South African gay website, with information on clubs and nightlife as well as useful contacts.

Township Crawling

ⓦwww.townshipcrawling.com

Despite being the commercial site of Thuthuka Tours, this is one of the best introductions to the history of Cape Town's African townships with background history, information on nightlife, food, customs and lifestyle. Also contacts for overnight stays, craft markets and eateries.

Western Cape Nature Conservation

ⓦwww.capenature.org.za

Information about the numerous wilderness areas and nature reserves in the Western Cape within striking distance of Cape Town.

ZA@PLAY

ⓦwww.mg.co.za/mg/art/artmenu.htm

Comprehensive listings of what's on in South Africa's major cities, including daily updates on exhibitions, film, theatre and gigs.

MAPS

The inexpensive **maps** available from Cape Town Tourism are adequate for the centre and surrounding areas, but if you're planning to explore beyond the confines of the city centre, you'll need to invest in a detailed **street atlas**, found at most bookshops, including the ubiquitous CNA chain. MapStudio's *A to Z Streetmap* is the cheapest and is fine for the centre and most of the suburbs, although it doesn't cover Simon's Town. Most comprehensive of the lot is MapStudio's *Cape Town Street Guide*, which covers the entire Cape Peninsula as well as the Winelands towns of Paarl, Stellenbosch and Somerset West in detail.

Cape Town's best bookshops are listed on p.207.

MAPS

Transport

For visitors, the most useful municipal transport is the Metrorail **train line** that cuts through the southern suburbs then along the False Bay coast to Simon's Town, and the frequent daytime **bus service** connecting the five-kilometre strip that takes in the city centre, Waterfront and Sea Point. These are the best areas to stay if you don't want to rely on a rented car.

Central Cape Town is compact enough to walk around, but much of what you'll want to see is spread along the considerable length of the Peninsula, so to make the most of your visit you'll need to rent a vehicle or get to grips with reasonably priced **tourist shuttle buses**, **minibus taxis**, **metered taxis** or organized tours. Apart from the Simon's Town train and Sea Point buses, municipal public transport in Cape Town is poor. Most middle-class Capetonians have never used it, preferring to get around in private cars.

Taking municipal buses, minibus taxis or trains after dark is not recommended; use one of the metered taxi or shuttle services listed on pp.22–3.

BUSES

The only frequent and reliable **bus** services are those from the centre to the Waterfront and Sea Point; buses also go down the Atlantic seaboard to Camps Bay and Hout Bay. Don't, however, attempt to catch a bus to the southern sub-urbs: the train is much quicker and more efficient. All the principal terminals are around Adderley Street and Golden Acre (see opposite).

Tickets are sold on buses by the driver, and if you're planning on using them frequently, consider buying a **Ten-Ride Clip Card**, which from the city costs R22 to Sea Point, and R35 to Camps Bay. Valid for fourteen days, the card will save you around 25 percent on the price of indi-vidual tickets, (a single ticket to Sea Point costs around R3, and about R5 to Camps Bay). For **timetables**, enquire at the Golden Arrow **information booth** (toll-free ☎0801/212111, ⓦwww.gabs.co.za) at the Grand Parade central bus terminal. It's always advisable to check bus times and points of departure at the booth, as these can change inexplicably.

The official open-top bus tour of Cape Tourism, **the Cape Town Explorer**, is also an extremely useful, if slightly expensive (a flat rate of R60 per person per day), means of transport for negotiating the city-centre sights and the Atlantic Seaboard beaches. There are two buses and you can hop on and off throughout the day wherever you please along the route (but you should tell the driver where you want to get on and off). **Departures** are hourly (April–Sept 9.40am–1.40pm, Oct & March 9.40am–2.40pm, Nov–Feb 9.40am–4.40pm,) from the **V & A Waterfront** Visitors' Centre in Dock Road. It gets to the **Cape Town Tourism office** on the corner of Burg and Castle streets fifteen minutes later. From here it goes past the **City Hall**, the **Castle of Good Hope**, **District Six**, **Parliament**, the

South African Museum, the **Bo-Kaap**, **Kloofnek Road**, **Signal Hill**, **Sea Point** and the **Atlantic Seaboard** beaches as far as Camps Bay.

BUS INFORMATION

City bus terminals

Cape Town Station Adderley St: buses to Waterfront.

Golden Acre Bus Terminus Off Strand St, wedged between Golden Acre Shopping Centre, the station and the Grand Parade: buses to Green Point, Sea Point, Camps Bay and Hout Bay.

Useful bus services

Buses are designed for commuters; consequently services start at 6.30am weekdays and finish by 6 or 6.30pm. The exception are the Waterfront buses which start at 6am and end around 11pm. Note that the buses aren't numbered; you identify them from the destination on the front.

City to:

Hout Bay Golden Acre Terminal–Lower Plein St–Darling Rd–Adderley St–Main Rd, Green Point–Sea Point–Victoria Rd, Camps Bay–Hout Bay Beach–Hout Bay Harbour. Mon–Sat 6 daily to Hout Bay, Sun 3 daily to Hout Bay.

Sea Point Golden Acre Terminal–Mouille Point–Main Rd, Green Point–Main Rd, Sea Point. Mon–Sat at least 13 daily.

Waterfront Cape Town Station–Riebeeck St–Buitengracht St–Waterfront. Mon–Sat every 10min, Sun every 15min.

V & A Waterfront to:

City V & A Waterfront–Cape Town Station. Mon–Sat every 10min, Sun every 15min.

Sea Point V & A Waterfront–Mouille Point–Green Point–Three Anchor Bay–Beach Rd, Sea Point. Daily every 20min.

TAXI SERVICES

Metered taxis, regulated by the Cape Town Municipality, don't cruise up and down looking for fares; you'll need to go to the taxi ranks around town, including the Waterfront, the train station and Greenmarket Square. Alternatively, you can phone to be picked up: Marine Taxi Hire (℡021-434-0434) is the most reliable company. Taxis must have the driver's name and identification clearly on display and the meter clearly visible. Fares work out at around R10 per kilometre, which is expensive compared with other forms of transport, but worth it at night when metered taxis are the safest way of getting around.

The term "taxi" is ambiguous in Cape Town as elsewhere in South Africa: it's used to refer to conventional metered cars, jam-packed minibuses and their more upmarket cousins, Rikki's.

MINIBUS TAXIS

Minibus taxis are cheap, frequent and race up and down the main routes at tearaway speeds. As well as crazed driving, be prepared for the pickpockets who work the taxi ranks. Minibus taxis can be hailed from the street or boarded at the central taxi rank, adjacent to the train station. Once you've boarded, pay the *guardjie* (assistant), who sits near the driver. Fares should be under R4 for most trips.

SHUTTLE BUSES

A growth area in Cape Town is **shuttle buses**, which are physically indistinguishable from minibus taxis, the difference being that they have to be booked, and they can pick you up from your accommodation. Generally they are minibuses, which in some cases run to a schedule or alternatively are chartered. They tend to be cheaper than metered taxis but are more expensive than minibus taxis. One of the most useful services runs on demand in co-operation with Cape Town Tourism during the bureau's opening hours, going from their office to Kirstenbosch National Botanical Gardens (R35 one way), and also to the Lower Cable Station and other points of interest.

Reliable operators you can charter include: Sun Tours & Shuttle (☎021-696-0596, 021-697-0488 or 083-270-5617 ⒺSuntours@iafrica.com), which offers a 24-hour service between any two points on the Peninsula including the city to the airport (R140 for the first three, then R30 per additional passenger); and the similarly priced Boogey Bus (☎082-495-5698), which specializes in taking passengers to clubs, including those on the Cape Flats.

RIKKI'S

Rikki's are more visitor-friendly versions of minibus taxis, carrying not more than eight passengers, and aimed principally at tourists. They are small open-backed vehicles, which you need to book by telephone. In Cape Town, Rikki's (7am–7pm; ☎021-423-4892) are restricted to the City Bowl, the Waterfront and the Atlantic seaboard as far as Camps Bay – they don't go into the suburbs. There is also a regular Rikki's service in Simon's Town, operating between the station and other points in the village on request. Fares are kept down by picking up and dropping off passengers along the way (R6–15). Rikki's also operate mini-tours to destinations that include Cape Point and Stellenbosch, for which they charge R60–80 an hour for a whole vehicle.

RIKKI'S

TRAINS

Cape Town's **train** service (timetable information ☎0800-656-463) is a relatively reliable if slightly rundown urban line that runs from Cape Town central station, through the southern suburbs and all the way down to Simon's Town. Highly recommended as an outing in its own right, and undoubtedly one of the great urban train journeys of the world, it reaches the False Bay coast at Muizenberg and continues south, sometimes so spectacularly close to the ocean that you can feel the spray and peer into rock pools. By far the nicest way to travel is in the **Biggsy's buffet car** (five times a day in each direction Mon–Fri, and four times Sat & Sun) which serves light snacks, beers and other refreshments.

Trains run overground, and there are no signposts to the stations on the streets, so if you're staying in the southern suburbs ask for directions at your accommodation; otherwise look at a map or ask around. Tickets must be bought at the station before boarding. You're best off in the reasonably priced first-class carriages; curiously, there's no second class, and third class is not recommended – it's often full, less comfortable, and you'll be very conspicuous as a visitor. A first-class single from Cape Town to Muizenberg is R10. Suburban trains tend to run pretty close to the **timetable**, with departures from the central station to the southern suburbs as far as Retreat leaving roughly every ten minutes at peak times (Mon–Fri 5.10–8.40am & 3.30–6pm). Services are slightly less frequent as far as Fish Hoek (about every 20 mins Mon–Fri 5.10am–7.30pm & Sat 5.20am–6pm; every hour Sun 7.30am–6.30pm) and Simon's Town (about every 40 mins Mon–Fri 5.10am–7.30pm & Sat 5.20am–6pm; every hour Sun 7.30am–6.30pm). From mid-December to the end of March there are additional Sunday trains.

Three other lines run east from Cape Town to Strand (through Bellville) and to the outlying towns of

Stellenbosch and **Paarl**; however, unless travelling to these destinations, the journeys aren't recommended as they run through some less safe areas of the Flats.

The main stations on the Cape Town–Simon's Town Metrorail line are shown on map 2.

DRIVING

Cape Town has good roads and several fast **freeways** that can whisk you across town in next to no time, except at peak hours (7–9am & 4–5.30pm). Take care approaching: the on-ramps frequently feed directly into the fast lane, and Capetonians have no compunction in exceeding the speed limits.

The obvious landmarks of Table Mountain and the two seaboards make orientation straightforward, particularly south of the centre, and there are some wonderful journeys, the most notable being Chapman's Peak Drive (see p.122), a narrow winding cliff-edge route with the Atlantic breaking hundreds of metres below.

Foreign **licences** are valid in South Africa for up to six months provided they are printed in English. If you don't have an English-language licence, you'll need to get an International Driving Permit before arriving (available from national motoring organizations). When driving, keep your licence and passport on you at all times.

In this former British colony, driving is on the **left-hand side**, and **speed limits** range from 60kph in built-up areas to a maximum of 120kph on highways. Note that traffic lights are called **robots** in South Africa. Roundabouts are rare; instead you'll find **four-way stops**, where the rule is that the person who got there first leaves first, and you are not expected to give way to the right.

DRIVING

25

ROAD SAFETY

South Africa has among the world's worst **road accident statistics** – the result of recklessness, drunk driving and defective and overloaded vehicles. Keep your distance from cars in front, as pile-ups are common. On national and provincial roads, watch out for **overtaking traffic** coming towards you; overtakers frequently assume you'll pull into the hard shoulder to get out of their way and drivers coming up from behind will also expect you to temporarily drive in the hard shoulder while they overtake. This is perfectly legal, and dangerous, especially in a country where it is common for pedestrians and animals to walk along the hard shoulder.

An unwritten rule of the road on the Peninsula is that **minibus taxis** have the right of way. Don't mess with them: their vehicles are bigger than yours, they often carry handguns and will routinely run through amber lights as they change to red – as will many Capetonians.

A number of places around the Cape Peninsula have both Afrikaans and English names (Cape Town itself is known to Afrikaners as Kaapstad). Road signs tend to alternate between the two, making it worth familiarizing yourself with both versions if you're driving; see glossary of Afrikaans signs on p.357.

VEHICLE RENTAL

Given Cape Town's scant public transport, renting a vehicle is the only convenient way of exploring the Cape Peninsula and it needn't break the bank: there are dozens of competing **car rental** companies to choose from (see p.251). To find out who's currently operating and to get the best deal, either pick up one of the brochures at the Cape Town Tourism offices or look in the Yellow Pages phone book. For one-way rental (to drive down the Garden Route and fly out of Port Elizabeth, for example), you'll have to rely on one of the bigger and pricier nationwide companies (see p.251).

For **motorbike rental**, Le Cap Motorcycle Hire, 3 Carisbrook St (℡021-423 0823), can provide all the necessary gear and they rent out serious bikes (from R220 daily, plus 80c/km). African Buzz, 220 Long Street, in the city centre (℡021-423-0052) rents out 100cc **scooters** with all the gear you need for a fully inclusive R160 for 24 hours. They also provide a map of the Cape Peninsula with suggested routes and points of interest.

One of the most popular, and hair-raising, road routes for cyclists is along the narrow hairpins of Chapman's Peak Drive (see p.122), which offer stupendous views of the Atlantic. There are also a number of dedicated mountain-biking routes in the peninsula's nature reserves. See p.250 for rental outlets.

TOURS

Guided tours enable you to orientate yourself quickly and get to the highlights in a hurry. A growing number of smaller companies offer niche cultural tours, the most popular of which are **townships visits**, which can safely get you around the African and coloured areas that were created under apartheid. Apart from these, a number of other outfits, listed on pp.28–30, can help you scratch beneath Cape Town's surface.

CITY CENTRE AND PENINSULA SIGHTS

Cape Town Explorer Cape Town Tourism ☎021-426-4260; Topless Tours ☎021-556-0700, ⓦwww.ticketweb.co.za. Cape Town Tourism's official bus tour is a two-hour circular ride in an open-top double-decker bus that follows a fixed route around the main central sights with a running commentary. It's also a useful, if expensive, form of transport for getting around the centre. See "Bus information" on p.21 for times and route details. Booking not necessary; R60. They also run an all-day tour of the whole Peninsula as far as Cape Point that leaves Cape Tourism's city-centre office on the corner of Burg and Castle streets on Tues, Thurs & Sat at 9.30am and returns at about 6pm. Booking essential; R210.

City Walking Tour ☎021-426-4260. Operated by Cape Town Tourism (Mon–Fri 11am), this departs from their visitor centre, on the corner of Burg and Castle streets. The roughly two-hour strolls don't go into any of the sites, but are good for orientation. R50.

Day Trippers ☎021-531-3274, ⓦwww.daytrippers.co.za. Cycling from Scarborough into the Cape of Good Hope Nature Reserve with hikes down to Cape Point, as well as tours to the usual sights such as the Winelands. From R265.

Hylton Ross Tours ☎021-511-1784, ⓦwww.hyltonross.co.za. Cover all the popular sights along the Cape Peninsula and also have scheduled guided daytrips to Hermanus (Wed & Sun), which cost R260.

Mother City Tours ☎021-448-3817, ⓕ021-448-3844. Half- and full-day tours of the city, Cape Point, Table Mountain and the Winelands. Half day from R245, full day R335. They also run whale-watching trips in season (R350).

CULTURAL AND TOWNSHIP TOURS

AfriCultural Tours ☎021-423-3321. Comprehensive look at Cape Town's "other side", not just the townships, but also a "Slave Route" tour, a tour of San rock art sites and visits to traditional music makers, dancers and artists. For a chance to experience the upbeat side of Cape Flats nightlife, join their "Vibey Jazz" tour. Half day R200, full day R280.

Grassroute Tours ☎021-706-1006, ⓦwww.grassroutetours.co.za. An alternative take on the traditional tour packages includes a township tour that takes in the African and coloured townships. They also do walking tours of the Bo-Kaap, including the *kramats* (Muslim shrines). Half day R220, full day R380.

Muse-Art Journeys ☎021-919-9168 or 082-921-1126, ⓔmuse-art@iafrica.com. Exciting portfolio of cultural tours of which their music outings (Wed & Fri eve; R350) that take in two or three nightclubs are the most popular. They also go on a craft route that visits township craftworkers who recycle materials and do special interest tours on request.

Our Pride ☎021-531-4291 or 082-446-7974, ⓔourpride@mweb.co.za. Highly recommended interactive tours, where you get to meet the people of the Bo-Kaap, District Six as well as the African townships and squatter camps. They also do jazz outings in which you go to two clubs, and a "Township by Night" trip, which includes supper at a township restaurant and a visit to a shebeen. Half day R220.

Thuthuka Tours ☎021-439-2061 or 082-979-5831, ⓦwww.townshipcrawling.com. Outstanding range of scheduled township tours geared to individual interests, including Xhosa rituals, authentic consultations with a traditional healer and night-time music outings. Half-day departures are Mon–Fri

9am–12.30pm and 1.30–4.30pm and cost R180. The full-day tour, costing R360, runs Mon–Fri 1.30–10pm and incorporates nightlife into the tour. On Saturday afternoons they take a half-day Xhosa Folklore tour, in which you witness traditional rituals that are still alive in the townships.

Western Cape Action Tours
ⓣ021-461-1371,

ⓦwww.dacpm.org.za. Led by former Umkhonto weSizwe (ANC armed wing) activists from Cape Town, tours focus on the fight against apartheid and the post-apartheid scene. Visitors go to the townships and see sites of political resistance, as well as visiting a traditional healer, housing projects and township markets. Half day R200, full day R400.

Money, costs and banks

Cape Town is the most expensive city in South Africa, but visitors coming from Europe, North America or Australia and New Zealand will still find it generally cheaper than home. Backpackers staying in hostels, eating cheap meals or self-catering and using trains, buses or minibus taxis can live on R250 per person a day. Staying in an en-suite room in a good B&B or guest house, eating at moderate restaurants, using a couple of taxis a day and paying for the odd tour or museum expect to pay around R500–600 per person a day. For not a lot more than R600 you can live it up, and for R1200 per person a day you can stay at a top hotel, eat at the best restaurants and rent a car.

CURRENCY

South Africa's currency is the **rand** (R), divided into 100 cents. Notes come in R10, R20, R50, R100 and R200 denominations and there are coins for R1, R2 and R5 as well as 1c, 2c, 5c, 10c, 20c and 50c. The rand lost thirty percent of its value against major currencies during 2001

For the most current exchange rates, consult the useful currency converter Ⓦ www.xe.net/currency

---

(and this depreciation is expected to continue for the foreseeable future, but at a slower rate), meaning that at the time of writing, the **exchange rate** stood at around R16 to the pound sterling, R10 to the euro, R11 to the US dollar and R6 to the Australian dollar.

CREDIT CARDS, ATMS AND TRAVELLERS' CHEQUES

Bank cards, usable at cash machines or **automatic teller machines** (ATMs) throughout South Africa, are the most convenient way to carry your funds. Visa, Mastercard and most international ATM cards (check with your bank before departing) can be used to withdraw money at ATMs 24 hours a day. Ask your bank which option you should choose for your card when the machine asks for the account type (cheque, savings, transmission or credit). Remember that all cash advances are treated as loans, with interest accruing daily from the date of withdrawal, and there may be a transaction fee on top of this. **Credit cards** are also very handy for hotel bookings and for paying for upmarket tourist facilities, and are essential for car rental. Visa and Mastercard are most widely accepted.

Many **debit cards** can also be used to make withdrawals from ATMs in South Africa. These are not liable to interest payments, and the flat transaction fee is usually quite small – your bank will able to advise on this. Make sure you have a personal identification number (PIN) that's designed to work overseas.

Travellers' cheques make a useful backup as they can be replaced if lost or stolen. American Express, Visa and

Be aware that ATMs are favourite hunting grounds for conmen and ATM scams are a part of South African life. See "Safety tips", p.38 for further advice.

Thomas Cook are all widely recognized. However, they'll be useless if you're heading into remote areas, where you'll need to carry **cash**, preferably in a very safe place, such as a leather pouch under your waistband. The usual fee for travellers' cheque sales is one or two percent, though this fee may be waived if you buy the cheques through a bank where you have an account. It pays to get a selection of denominations. Make sure to keep the purchase agreement and a record of cheque serial numbers safe and separate from the cheques themselves. If cheques are lost or stolen, the issuing company will expect you to report the loss immediately to their office in South Africa; most companies claim to replace them within 24 hours. Both dollar and sterling cheques are accepted in South Africa.

BANKS AND EXCHANGE

Most **banks** have foreign currency counters and there are branches in the city centre, the V & A Waterfront and at most of the suburban shopping malls. You'll also find bureaux de change in the major tourist areas of town, which often operate extended hours. Outside banking hours some hotels will change money, although you can expect to pay a fairly hefty commission. You can also change money at branches of American Express and Rennies Travel.

Opening hours and holidays

The working day starts and finishes early in South Africa: most **shops** and **businesses** open on weekdays from 8.30am until around 5pm; on Saturdays many shops close for the day at lunchtime and are closed all day on Sunday. However, these patterns have changed since the collapse of apartheid, and you'll find a growing number of retailers that remain open on Sundays and as late as 9pm every night; this applies particularly to the larger malls and shopping centres (see pp.201–203).

Banking hours are Monday to Friday 9am to 3.30 or 4pm, and Saturday 9am to 11am, while some **bureaux de change** stay open until 7pm. **Post offices** are open 8.30am to 4.30pm on weekdays and Saturdays 8am to 11.30am, and **government departments** weekdays from 8am until 4pm.

HOLIDAYS

School holidays in South Africa can disrupt your plans, especially if you want to stay in cheaper accommodation (self-catering, cheaper B&Bs and so on), all of which are likely to be booked solid. If you do travel to Cape Town over the school holidays, book your accommodation well in advance.

The longest and busiest holiday period is **Christmas** (summer), which for schools stretches roughly from mid-December to mid-January; this is also when accommodation prices peak. Flights and train berths can be hard to get from December 16 to January 2, when many businesses and offices close for their annual break. You should book your flights – long-haul and domestic – as early as six months in advance for the Christmas period. The provinces stagger their school holidays but, as a general rule, they cover the following periods: Easter, March 20–April 15; winter, June 20–July 21; and spring, Sept 19–Oct 7.

Public holidays

New Year's Day January 1	**Youth Day** June 16
Human Rights Day March 21	**National Women's Day** August 9
Good Friday	**Heritage Day** September 24
Easter Sunday	**Day of Reconciliation**
Easter Monday	December 16
Freedom Day April 27	**Christmas Day** December 25
Workers' Day May 1	**Day of Goodwill** December 26

Crime and the police

Despite horror stories of sky-high **crime** rates, most people visit Cape Town without incident. This is not to minimize the problem – crime is probably the most serious difficulty facing South Africa. However, **safety** in central Cape Town has greatly improved over the past few years as a result of the deployment of a force of privately funded tourist police and the installation of 24-hour surveillance cameras. The greatest proportion of violent crime takes place in the poorer areas – predominantly townships.

POLICE

Generally, **police** presence is almost non-existent, and the police have a rather poor image. It's best simply to be reasonably cautious. In the unlikely event of your being robbed, don't expect too much crime-cracking enthusiasm (and don't expect to get your property back), but you will need to report the incident to the police, who should give you a case reference for insurance purposes. A crime must be reported in the district in which it occurs and you should phone before trawling out to confirm which the correct police station is. Charge offices are listed in the blue National Government section at the end of the White Pages telephone directory, under "Police Service (SA)".

GUNS AND MUGGINGS

Guns, both licensed and illicit, are an everyday part of life, routinely and openly carried by police – and some citizens. In many high streets you'll spot firearm shops rubbing shoulders with places selling clothes or books, and you'll come across notices asking you to deposit your weapon before entering the premises. If you fall victim to a **mugging**, you should take very seriously the usual advice not to resist.

SAFETY TIPS

Although you should take care in Cape Town, don't allow paranoia to mar your stay. Be aware that you are more exposed in some places, such as the Cape Flats townships, than others, for example the V & A Waterfront or Kirstenbosch National Botanical Gardens (which are both pretty safe), and act accordingly. If in doubt, ask for advice at Cape Town Tourism's office or at your accommodation.

In general
- Try not to look like a tourist.
- Dress down: don't wear jewellery and expensive watches.
- Don't carry a camera or video openly.
- Remain calm and co-operative if you are mugged.
- Don't leave valuables exposed (on a seat or the ground) while having a meal or drink.
- Be aware of what people in the street around you are doing – especially groups.

On foot
- Grasp bags firmly under your arm.
- Don't carry excessive sums of money on you.
- Don't put your wallet in your back trouser pocket.

After dark
- Use taxis rather than public transport.
- Avoid wandering around alone in the city centre – especially off the main drags.

On the road
- Lock car doors.
- Have rear windows sufficiently rolled up to keep out opportunistic hands.
- Never leave anything worth stealing in view when your car is unattended; take items indoors or lock them in the boot.

At cash machines
- Never help anyone who claims to be having problem with a cash machine, no matter how well-spoken, friendly or distressed they seem – tell them to contact the bank.
- Never accept help from strangers if you have a problem at a cash machine.
- Don't allow people to crowd you while withdrawing money – if in doubt, go to another machine.
- Never allow anyone to see you punch in your personal identification number (PIN).
- If your card gets swallowed, report it without delay.

SAFETY TIPS

THE GUIDE

THE GUIDE

The city centre

Cape Town's city centre is the most historically intense district in the country and the oldest urban area in Southern Africa. It has a stunning physical setting, dominated by the omnipresent Table Mountain to the south and the pounding Atlantic to the north. While the prime attractions lie elsewhere, the city centre has some interesting museums, and its streets still pulse with the cultural fusion that has been Cape Town's hallmark since its founding in 1652.

The area covered in this chapter is shown on colour map 4.

Adderley Street, connecting the main train station in the north to St George's Cathedral in the south, is the obvious orientation axis and one (with the harbour at one end and Table Mountain rearing up from the other) you'd struggle to lose your way on.

South of Adderley Street where it takes a sharp right into Wale Street, you'll find the symbolic heart of Cape Town (and arguably South Africa), with the **Houses of Parliament**, museums, historic buildings, archives and De Tuynhuys, the Western Cape office of the President, arranged around the **Gardens**. Adderley Street continues as the oak-lined pedestrianized **Government Avenue**, which cuts through the Gardens and terminates at Orange Street, the hectic route to the southern suburbs that marks the boundary between the city centre and the salubrious inner-city suburbs of Gardens, Tamboerskloof, Oranjezicht and Vredehoek.

West of Adderley Street is the closest South Africa gets to a European quarter – a tight network of streets with cafés, buskers, bookshops, street stalls and antique shops congregating around the pedestrianized **St George's Mall** and **Greenmarket Square**. Parallel to St George's Mall, **Long Street**, the quintessential Cape Town thoroughfare, is lined with colonial Victorian buildings that house pubs, bistros, nightclubs, backpacker lodges, bookshops and antique dealers, whose wrought-iron balconies afford glimpses of Table Mountain and the sea. The **Bo-Kaap**, or Muslim quarter, three blocks further west across Buitengracht (which means the Outer Canal, but is actually a street), exudes a piquant contrast to this, with its minarets, spice shops and cafés selling curried snacks.

The telephone code for Cape Town is ☎021
and must be dialled before all numbers

East of Adderley Street, and close to each other near Cape Town station, lie three historically loaded sites. The oldest building in South Africa, the **Castle of Good Hope** is an indelible symbol of Europe's colonization of South Africa, a process whose death knell was struck from nearby **City Hall**, the attractive Edwardian building from which Nelson Mandela made his first speech after being released. Southeast of the castle lie the poignantly desolate remains of **District Six**, the coloured inner-city suburb that was razed in the name of apartheid.

Strand Street marks the edge of Cape Town's original beachfront (though you'd never guess it today); all urban

CAPE TOWN'S TOP NEW MUSEUMS...

Some of Cape Town's best central museums are part of a new wave of the past five years, characterized by their specific focus and great design. There are several, equally compelling exhibitions that have been around for some time, but in general most of the rest of the museums are seriously underfunded and you shouldn't expect the levels of sophistication found in Europe or North America.

District Six Museum (p.73). Fascinating and moving tribute to the people of the Cape Town inner-city suburb whose destruction became an international cause célèbre.

Gold of Africa Museum (p.74). Antiquities and exquisite small artworks wrought from gold, mostly from West Africa, constituting the most important collection of its kind in the world.

Nelson Mandela Gateway and Robben Island Museum (p.86). Cape Town's only World Heritage Site, Robben Island is totally unmissable for its notorious prison which became the symbol of apartheid South Africa – "the imprisoned society".

South African Jewish Museum and Holocaust Exhibition (p.56, p.59). Two brilliantly designed exhibits, telling the story of South Africa's Jewish population.

...and the best of the rest

Castle of Good Hope (p.71). South Africa's oldest colonial building, with a fine collection of seventeenth- to nineteenth-century domestic objects used at the Cape.

South African National Gallery (p.55). One of the most important showcases of contemporary South African art.

Two Oceans Aquarium (p.85). Outstanding oceanarium that can hold its own next to the world's best. Devoted to the denizens of the Indian and Atlantic oceans that wash South Africa's shores, its highlights include a kelp forest and sharks.

THE CITY CENTRE

development on the **Foreshore** to its north stands on reclaimed land, though there's little to see apart from **Duncan Dock**, where tankers and large passenger ships drop anchor.

ADDERLEY STREET

Map 4, D2–4. Cape Town station.

Adderley Street, once lined with centuries' worth of handsome buildings, still merits a stroll today for what grand architecture remains. The attractive streetscape has

THE NAMING OF ADDERLEY STREET

Although the Dutch used Robben Island (see p.86) as a political prison, the South African mainland only narrowly escaped becoming a second Australia, a penal colony where British felons and enemies of the state could be dumped. By the 1840s, "respectable Australians" were lobbying for a ban on the transportation of criminals to the Antipodes, and the British authorities responded by trying to divert convicts to the Cape.

In 1848, the *Neptune* set sail from Bermuda with a cargo of 282 prisoners headed for Cape Town, where the news of its departure was met with outrage. Five thousand citizens gathered on the Grand Parade the following year to hear prominent liberals denounce the British government, an event depicted in *The Great Meeting of the People at the Commercial Exchange* by Johan Marthinus Carstens Schonegevel, which hangs in the Rust-en-Vreugd Museum (see p.54). When the ship docked in September 1849, governor Sir Harry Smith forbade any criminal from landing, while, back in London, politician Charles Adderley successfully addressed the House of Commons in support of the Cape colonists. In February 1850, the *Neptune* set off for Tasmania,

been blemished by large 1960s shopping centres and office blocks, but just minutes away from its crowded malls, among the streets and alleys around Greenmarket Square, you can still find some human scale and historic texture.

Adderley Street was formerly the Heerengracht (Gentlemen's Canal): a waterway that ran from the Company's Gardens down to the sea. Low-walled channels, ditches, bridges and sluices once ran through Cape Town and earned it the name Little Amsterdam. However, during the nineteenth century the canals were buried underground, and in 1850 Heerengracht was renamed Adderley Street (see

and grateful Capetonians renamed the city's main thoroughfare **Adderley Street**.

In 2001, there was a postscript to all this with yet another attempt to rename Adderley Street, this time by the populist National Party mayor **Peter Marais**. Marais announced that he wanted to alter its name to **Nelson Mandela Street** and the adjoining Wale Street, which runs through the Bo-Kaap, to **F.W. de Klerk Street** after South Africa's last National Party president. Most of the coloured residents of the Bo-Kaap were less than delighted about having their main street named after a former proponent of apartheid. Marais ran a purported "consultation exercise" which delivered a huge number of signatures in favour of the change. When later it turned out that many had been signed by the same hand, the renaming was shelved, Marais was sacked and the Democratic–National Party coalition that ran Cape Town and the Western Cape collapsed. In the strangest twist in the tale, the National Party formed a coalition with the ANC – its once bitterest enemies (see "A brief history of Cape Town" pp.325–7) – and Marais was promoted to premier of the province.

ADDERLEY STREET

box on p.44). There's little evidence of the canals today, except in name – one section of the street is still called Heerengracht and a parallel street to its west is called Buitengracht (sometimes spelled Buitengragt), meaning the Outer Canal. Apart from the **Slave Lodge**, **Groote Kerk** and **St George's Cathedral**, all at the southwest end of the street, the only notable building is the **First National Bank**, completed in 1913, which was the last South African building designed by Sir Herbert Baker. Inside the banking hall, a solid timber circular writing desk, its original inkwells still in place, resembles an altar to capitalism.

The Groote Kerk

Map 4, D4. Daily 9.30am–4.30pm; free.

Sometimes described as "Cape Gothic" in style, the **Groote Kerk** (Great Church), diagonally opposite the First National Bank in Adderley Street, is essentially a Classical building with Gothic and Egyptian elements. The soaring space created by its vast vaulted ceiling and the magnificent **pulpit**, a masterpiece by sculptor Anton Anreith and carpenter Jan Jacob Graaff, are worth stepping inside for. Supported on a pair of sculpted lions with gaping jaws, the pulpit was carved by Anreith when his first proposal, featuring Faith, Hope and Charity, was rejected by the church council for being "too Popish".

Designed and built between 1836 and 1841 by **Hermann Schutte** (see p.333), a German who became one of the Cape's leading early nineteenth-century architects, the church replaced an earlier Baroque one that had become too small for the swelling ranks of the Dutch Reformed congregation at the Cape. The beautiful freestanding **clock tower** adjacent to the newer building is a remnant of the original church.

The Slave Lodge

Map 4, D4. ℡021-461-8280, ⓦwww.museums.org.za/slavelodge;
Mon–Sat 9.30am–4.30pm; R7.

Previously known as the Cultural History Museum, the
Slave Lodge houses an eclectic collection of antiquities
and artefacts from around the world as well as good displays
on the Cape. The museum was renamed on Heritage Day,
1998, and is currently in the process of reinventing itself to
portray South African social history, especially the blood-
stained story of slavery.

For 186 years, more than half its existence as an urban settlement, Cape Town's economic and social structures were
built on slavery (see box on p.48), and the Slave Lodge was
built in 1679 for the Dutch East India Company to house its
human chattels. The Company was the largest single owner
of slaves at the Cape; by the 1770s, almost a thousand of
them were held at the Lodge. Under Company administration the Lodge also became the Cape Colony's main brothel, its doors thrown open to all comers for an hour each
night. Following the British takeover and the auctioning of
the slaves, it became the Supreme Court in 1810, and
remained so until 1914. From 1914 the building was used as
government offices, and in 1966 became a museum.

A couple of small but interesting displays can be found
on the ground floor, to the left of the entrance hall. The
first deals with **Khoisan hunter-gatherers**, the original
inhabitants of the Cape (and South Africa), focusing on
their knowledge of plants and herbs, many of which are still
in use today. An adjacent room houses "**186 Years of
Slavery**", centred around a model of the lodge as it was
300 years ago. A poignant memorial plaque on one wall
lists, by first name only, the slaves who endured the
appalling conditions of the fortress-like structure, and a map
on another wall refers to sites in the city centre with slave

connections: where they worked, worshipped, were sold, punished and executed.

SLAVERY AT THE CAPE

Slavery was officially abolished at the Cape in 1838, but its legacy lives on in South Africa: the country's coloured (mixed race; see p.328) inhabitants, who make up fifty percent of Cape Town's population, are largely descendants of slaves, and some historians argue that apartheid was a successor to slavery. Certainly, domestic service, still widespread throughout South Africa, and certain labour practices such as the "*dop* system", in which workers on some farms are partially paid in rations of cheap plonk, can be directly traced back to slavery.

By the end of the eighteenth century, the almost 26,000-strong slave population of the Cape exceeded that of free burghers. Despite the profound impact this had on the development of social relations in South Africa, until the publication of a number of studies on slavery in the 1980s, it remained one of the most neglected topics of the country's history. There's still a reluctance on the part of most coloureds to embrace their slave origins.

Few if any slaves were captured at the Cape for export, making the colony unique in the African trade. Paradoxically, while people were being captured elsewhere on the continent for export to the Americas, the Cape administration, forbidden by the VOC from enslaving the local indigenous population, had to look further afield. Of the 63,000 slaves who were imported to the Cape before 1808, most came from East Africa, Madagascar, India and Indonesia, representing one of the broadest cultural mixes of any slave society. This diversity initially worked against the establishment of a unified group identity, but eventually a creolized culture emerged which, among other things, played a major role in the development of the Afrikaans language.

You pass through a couple of rooms devoted to a smattering of Greek and Roman antiquities to the "**Cape Kaleidoscope**" exhibition, occupying two large galleries – well worth taking in for the crash course it offers on the political and economic development of Southern Africa's first European settlement. Bizarrely, four rooms of artefacts from China, Japan, Tibet and Indonesia, followed by displays of African and Oriental weapons, interrupt the flow before you once again return to galleries relating to Cape Town, which occupy the entire southwest wing. The collection includes some intriguing items: the **padrãos** (stone crosses) left by sixteenth-century Portuguese mariners; engraved **postal stones** that marked the arrival of passing ships at Table Bay; and some historic **postage stamps**. However, the selection may prove a little too random to hold your interest for long.

Behind the Slave Lodge, on the traffic island in Spin Street, a simple and inconspicuous plinth marks the site of the Old Slave Tree, under which slaves were auctioned.

St George's Cathedral

Map 4, C4.
Diagonally opposite the Slave Lodge, at the south end of Adderley Street as it turns into Wale Street, **St George's Cathedral**, built in the early twentieth century, is more interesting for its history than for Herbert Baker's Victorian Gothic design. The previous Anglican church on the same site had been an impressive structure based on the Greek Revival St Pancras church in London, but was considered too "pagan" for a Christian place of worship, and was pulled down.

It was against the doors of the present St George's that **Desmond Tutu** hammered on September 7, 1986, symbolically demanding to be enthroned as South Africa's first black archbishop. Three years later, he heralded change by leading 30,000 people from the Cathedral to the Grand Parade, where he coined his now famous slogan of multi-racialism, telling the crowd: "We are the rainbow people! We are the new people of South Africa!" The fact that this was the first mass demonstration in the city since 1960 allowed to go ahead without police disruption hinted that the final days of apartheid were at hand.

The walk from the Slave Lodge to Bertram House is sometimes referred to as "Museum Mile" because it provides access to around a dozen significant sites, including the flagship institutions of the National Gallery, the Holocaust Centre, the South African Museum and the Planetarium, covered in detail below.

GOVERNMENT AVENUE AND THE GARDENS

Map 4, D5–7. Cape Town station.

Government Avenue is the pedestrianized southern extension of Adderley Street, an oak-lined boulevard and one of the most serene walks in central Cape Town.

Looming on your right as you enter the north end of the avenue, the **South African Library** (Mon–Fri 9am–6pm, Sat 9am–1pm; free) houses one of the country's best collections of antique historical and natural history books covering Southern Africa. Built with revenue from a tax on wine, it opened in 1822 as one of the first free libraries in the world.

Continuing along Government Avenue from the South African Library, past the rear of parliament, you can peer through an iron gate to see the grand buildings and tended flowerbeds of **De Tuynhuys**, the office (but not residence) of the president. Built in 1700 as the guest house for visiting VOC (Dutch East India Company) dignitaries, the building was subjected to additions and alterations by the Dutch throughout the eighteenth century. Under the governorship of Lord Charles Somerset during the nineteenth-century British occupation, extensive changes were made, and the wings, visible from the Gardens, were built, with verandahs covered by elegantly curving awnings typical of the Colonial Regency style. To peer into the gardens of Tuynhuys, stand on the walkway leading up to its locked gates; the ditches to either side of you are all that remain visible of Cape Town's former **canal system**. One party of tourists, during Mandela's presidency, stood amazed here as the great man, renowned for his common touch, strolled across the lawns for a friendly chat.

A little further along, the tree-lined walkway opens out into a formal gravel square with ponds and statues, around which are sited Cape Town's most important museums, covered from p.54.

The Gardens

Stretching from here to the South African Museum and Avenue Road, the **Gardens** (aka the Cape Town, Botanical or Company's Gardens) were the initial *raison d'être* for the Dutch settlement at the Cape. Established in 1652 to supply fresh greens to the VOC, whose ships traded between the Netherlands and the East, the Gardens were initially worked by imported slave labour. This proved too expensive, as slaves had to be shipped in, fed and housed, so the Company phased out its own farming and granted land to free burghers, from whom it bought fresh produce (see p.313). At the end of the seventeenth century, the gardens were turned over to botanical horticulture for Cape Town's growing colonial elite, with ponds, lawns, landscaping and a crisscross web of oak-shaded walkways being introduced. Today they are full of local plants, the result of long-standing interest in Cape botany; European scientists have been sailing out since the seventeenth century to classify and name specimens.

Cecil Rhodes certainly thought the gardens a pleasant place to meander – it was during a stroll here that he plotted the invasion of Matabeleland and Mashonaland, both of which became amalgamated into Rhodesia and subsequently Zimbabwe. Rhodes also introduced an army of small, furry colonizers to the gardens: North American grey squirrels. There's a statue of Rhodes here, as well as an unexceptional outdoor **café**.

THE HOUSES OF PARLIAMENT

Map 4, D5. Tours Mon–Fri 9am–1pm on the hour; booking essential ☎021-403-2201; free. Cape Town station.

South Africa's **Houses of Parliament** back onto Government Avenue, with their entrance on Parliament Street. Not one building but a complex of interlinking ones, its labyrinthine corridors connect hundreds of offices and debating chambers.

One-hour **tours** take in the old and new debating chambers, the library and museum, and should be booked at least two weeks ahead (two months ahead during school holidays) through the Tours Section (see above); you must provide your identity number or passport number, when booking. Arriving for the tour bring the letter confirming you've booked, as well as your identity document or passport.

For day tickets to watch the **debating sessions** – the most interesting of which is question time (Wed 3pm onwards), when you can hear ministers being quizzed by MPs if parliament is sitting – contact the Public Relations office on ☎021-403-2460 or 021-403 2461. Members of the ANC sit to the right of the speaker, so if you want to see them you should enter the gallery at the rear via the right entrance; minority parties sit opposite. You're most unlikely to see the president, who is not a member of parliament and rarely attends sittings. When he does, for the opening of parliament or for visits by foreign leaders, seats are invariably snapped up very quickly.

Completed in 1885, the original building is in imposing Victorian Neoclassical style, and first served as the legislative assembly of the Cape Colony. After the Boer republics and British colonies amalgamated in 1910, it became the parliament of the Union of South Africa. This is the old parliament, where more than seven decades of repressive legislation, including apartheid laws, were passed. It's also where **Hendrik Verwoerd**, the arch-theorist of apartheid, met his bloody end, not at the hand of a political activist, but stabbed to death by a parliamentary messenger who committed the act because, as he told police, "a tapeworm ordered me to do it." Due to his mental state the assassin escaped the gallows to outlive apartheid – albeit in an institution. Verwoerd's portrait, depicting him as a man of vision and gravitas, once hung over the main entrance to the dining room; in 1996 it was removed, ostensibly for "cleaning", along with paintings of generations of white parliamentarians. The new chamber was built in 1983 as part of the **tricameral parliament**, P.W. Botha's attempt to avert majority rule by trying to co-opt Indians and coloureds – but in their own separate debating chambers (see p.323). This chamber has become the **National Assembly**, where you can watch sessions of parliament (see above).

RUST-EN-VREUGD

Map 4, E5. Mon–Sat 9am–4pm; R5. Cape Town station.

The most beautiful of Cape Town's house museums, **Rust-en-Vreugd**, a couple of blocks east of the Gardens at 78 Buitenkant Street, was once surrounded by countryside, but now stands along a congested route that brushes past the edge of the central business district.

Designed by architect **Louis Michel Thibault** and sculptor **Anton Anreith**, the two-storey facade features a pair of stacked balconies, the lower one forming a stunning portico fronted by four Corinthian columns carved from teak. Framed by teak pilasters, the front door is a real work of art, rated by architectural historian de Bosdari as "certainly the finest door at the Cape". Above the door, the fanlight is executed in elaborate Baroque style.

The house was built in 1778 for **Willem Cornelis Boers**, the colony's Fiscal (a powerful position akin to the police chief, public prosecutor and collector of taxes rolled into one), who was forced to resign in the 1780s following allegations of wheeler-dealing and extortion. Under the British occupation, it was the residence of **Lord Charles Somerset** during his governorship (1814–1826).

You can park inside the grounds of Rust-en-Vreugd, which is fortunate given the jammed roadsides of Buitenkant and the surrounding streets; to do so, temporarily leave your car in front of the museum while you ask at reception to be let in through the gates.

Inside, the William Fehr Collection of **artworks on paper** occupies two ground-floor rooms and includes illustrations by important documentarists such as **Thomas Baines**, who is represented by hand-coloured lithographs and a series of watercolours recording a nineteenth-century expedition up Table Mountain. **Thomas Bowler**, another prolific recorder of Cape scenes, painted his striking landscape of Cape Point from the sea in 1864, showing dolphins frolicking in the foreground.

A tranquil escape from the busy street, the **garden** is a reconstruction of the original eighteenth-century semi-formal one, laid out with herbaceous hedges, gravel walkways and a lawn with a gazebo, the property being defined by a boundary of bay trees.

THE SOUTH AFRICAN NATIONAL GALLERY

Map 4, D6. Tues–Sun 10am–5pm; R5. Cape Town station.

Not far from the southern end of Government Avenue, on the corner of tiny Gallery Lane, is the **South African National Gallery**, which contains a fine permanent collection of contemporary South African art.

As the number of items far exceeds the capacity of its exhibition space, displays regularly change, but one of the few pieces almost invariably on display is **Jane Alexander**'s powerfully ghoulish plaster, bone and horn sculpture, *The Butcher Boys* (1985–86), created at the height of apartheid repression. It features three life-size figures with distorted faces that exude a chilling passivity, expressing the artist's interest in the way violence is conveyed through the human figure. Alexander's work is representative of "**resistance art**", which exploded in the 1980s, broadly as a response to the growing repression of apartheid. Resistance art, produced by committed people from all ethnic groups, was inspired by the idea that artists had a responsibility to engage politically; it spanned a wide range of subject matter, styles and media. **Paul Stopforth**'s powerful graphite and wax triptych, *The Interrogators* (1979), featuring larger-than-lifesize portraits of three notorious security policemen, is a work of monumental hyper-realism.

Many other artists, unsurprisingly for a culturally diverse country, aren't easily categorized; while works have tended to borrow from Western traditions, their themes and execution are uniquely South African. The late **John Muafangelo** employed biblical imagery in works such as *The Pregnant Maria* (undated), producing highly stylized, almost naive black and white linocuts, while in *Challenges Facing the New South Africa* (1990), **Willie Bester** used paint and found shanty-town objects to depict the melting pot of the Cape Town squatter camps.

Since the 1990s, and especially in the post-apartheid period, the gallery has engaged in a process of redefining what constitutes contemporary **indigenous art** and has embarked on an acquisitions policy that "acknowledges and celebrates the expressive cultures of the African continent, particularly its southern regions". Material that would previously have been treated as ethnographic, such as a major **bead collection** as well as carvings and **craft objects**, is now finding a place alongside oil paintings and sculptures.

In the vicinity of the Gardens, the best place for snacks and refreshments is the National Gallery's café (opening hours same as gallery), which serves light lunches, coffees and cakes; there's also a small shop selling art books, postcards, artwork and crafts.

THE SOUTH AFRICAN JEWISH MUSEUM AND THE GREAT SYNAGOGUE

Map 4, D7. Mon–Thurs & Sun 10am–5pm, Fri 10am–2pm; R20.
Cape Town station.

Partially housed in South Africa's first synagogue, built in 1863, the **South African Jewish Museum** at 84 Hatfield

Street, to the south of the National Gallery, is one of Cape Town's most ambitious permanent exhibitions. It tells the story of South African Jewry from its beginnings 150 years ago to the present – a narrative which starts in the Old Synagogue from which visitors cross, via a gangplank, to the upper level of a new two-storey building, symbolically re-enacting the arrival by boat of the first Jewish immigrants at Table Bay harbour in the 1840s. Employing multimedia interactive displays, models and Judaica artefacts, the exhibition follows three threads: "**Memories**", looking at the roots and experiences of the immigrants; "**Reality**", covering their integration into South Africa; and "**Dreams**", examining a diversity of views about the role of Jews in South Africa, their relationship to Israel and their position in the world. Other displays examine anti-Semitism, apartheid and the Jews who opposed it, as well as Nelson Mandela's relationship with the Jewish community.

Drawing parallels between Judaism and the ritual practices and beliefs of South Africa's other communities, the "**Culture among Cultures**" display covers topics such as birth, marriage, circumcision and death. The **basement level** houses a walk-through reconstruction of a Lithuanian *shtetl,* or village (most South African Jews have their nineteenth-century roots in Lithuania), as well as the **Discovery Centre**, an interactive computer with a genealogy bank, a searchable database on Jewish life and culture and a "glimpse into Israel". A restaurant, shop and an auditorium are also housed in the museum complex.

The Great Synagogue

Map 4, D7.

One of Cape Town's outstanding religious buildings, the **Great Synagogue**, adjacent to the Jewish Museum, faces onto the Gardens. Designed by Scottish architects, it was

THE SOUTH AFRICAN JEWISH MUSEUM AND THE GREAT SYNAGOGUE

completed in 1905 and features an impressive dome and two soaring towers after the style of central European Baroque churches. To see the arched interior and the alcove decorated with gilt mosaics, you need to ask at the Holocaust Centre (see opposite), and you may be asked to provide some form of identification.

JUDAISM IN SOUTH AFRICA

Today there are around twenty thousand Jews in Cape Town, the majority descended from Eastern European refugees who fled discrimination and pogroms during the late nineteenth and early twentieth centuries.

Since 1795, when the occupying British introduced freedom of worship at the Cape, Jews in South Africa have faced few legal impediments. However, there were instances of semi-official anti-Semitism during the twentieth century, the most notable being in the policy of the Nationalist Party while in opposition during the 1940s. Before World War II, elements in the party came under the influence of Nazi ideology, which was being poured into South Africa by the German foreign and propaganda offices, and they began to attribute all the ills facing Afrikanderdom to a "British-Jewish capitalist" conspiracy. In 1941, the party adopted and touted a policy of ending Jewish immigration and even repatriating "undesirable immigrants", as well as placing stronger controls over naturalization and the introduction of a "vocational permit" system to protect "the original white population against unfair competition". Ironically, on the eve of taking power in 1947, the party of apartheid turned its back on anti-Semitism: one of its first acts after winning the 1948 election was to recognize the newly created state of Israel, with which it maintained links until it relinquished power in 1994.

THE CAPE TOWN HOLOCAUST CENTRE

Map 4, D7. Sun–Thurs 10am–5pm, Fri 10am–1pm; free. Cape Town station.

Opened in 1999, the **Holocaust Exhibition** constitutes one of the most moving and brilliantly executed museums in Cape Town. Housed upstairs in the Holocaust Centre, in the same complex as the Jewish Museum, the centre resonates sharply in a country that only recently emerged from an era of racial oppression – a connection that the exhibition makes explicitly. A densely layered narrative is related through text, photographs, artefacts (such as a concentration camp uniform), film clips, soundtracks, multimedia and interactive video, while the design uses modulated lighting, cobblestones reminiscent of the ghettos and pieces of barbed wire and railway track to evoke the death camps.

Exhibits trace the history of anti-Semitism in Europe, culminating with Nazism and the Final Solution; they also look at South Africa's Greyshirts, who were motivated by Nazi propaganda during the 1930s and were later absorbed into the National Party. There are accounts of heroism, often tragic, including acts of resistance by Jews, and a touch screen portrays many individuals in Europe who risked their lives to protect or rescue the victims of Nazism. To conclude, a twenty-minute video tells the story of survivors who eventually settled in Cape Town.

THE SOUTH AFRICAN MUSEUM AND PLANETARIUM

Map 4, D7. Daily 10am–5pm; museum R8 (Wed free), planetarium R10, combined R15. Cape Town station.

The nation's premier museum of natural history and human sciences, the **South African Museum**, west of Government Avenue and across the Gardens from the National Gallery at 25 Queen Victoria Street, has cultural and wildlife displays that will satisfy both adults and kids (see p.233).

Downstairs, the **ethnographic galleries** include some good displays on the traditional arts and crafts of several African groups, some exceptional examples of **rock art** (entire chunks of caves sitting in the display cases), and casts of stone birds found at Great Zimbabwe, across South Africa's border. Upstairs, the **natural history galleries** display mounted mammals, dioramas featuring prehistoric Karoo reptiles, a slightly old-fashioned but appealing dinosaur display and Table Mountain flora and fauna. The highlight is the four-storey "**whale well**", in which a collection of beautiful marine mammal skeletons hang like massive mobiles, accompanied by the eerie strains of their song. Free one-hour screenings of natural history films take place in the museum's **T.H. Barry Auditorium** (Wed 1pm, Sat & Sun 1, 2 & 3pm).

**The BP Mindspaces exhibition at the museum has
ten computers with internet access for R8 per half-hour –
the cheapest surfing in town.**

The display at the attached **Planetarium** (shows Mon–Fri 1pm, Sat & Sun noon, 1pm & 2.30pm, Tues also at 8pm) depicts the southern sky in all its glory. In addition, a changing programme of exhibits covers topics such as San sky myths, as well as special shows for kids. Leaflets at the museum provide a list of forthcoming attractions and you can buy a monthly chart of the current night sky, which is especially handy if you're staying outside the city.

BERTRAM HOUSE

Map 4, D7. Tues–Sat 9.30am–4.30pm; R5. Cape Town station.

At the top (southernmost) end of Government Avenue,

you'll come upon **Bertram House**, whose beautiful two-storey brick facade looks out across a fragrant herb garden. Built in the 1840s, the museum is significant as the only surviving brick Georgian-style house in Cape Town, and it displays typical furniture and objects of a well-to-do colonial British family in the first half of the nineteenth century.

The site was bought in 1839 by John Barker, an attorney from Yorkshire who came to the Cape in 1823. He named the house after his wife, Ann Bertram Findlay, who died in 1838, and it's believed that he was responsible for building it. Declared a National Monument in 1962, Bertram House was extensively restored to its current state between 1983 and 1984. Imported face brick and Welsh slate were used to recreate the original facade, while the interior walls were redecorated in their earlier dark green and ochre, based on the evidence of paint scrapings. Reception rooms are decorated in the Regency style, while the porcelain is predominantly nineteenth-century English, although there are also some very fine Chinese pieces.

For more on Cape architecture, see p.332.

AROUND ST GEORGE'S MALL

Map 4, C4. Cape Town station.

Southwest of, and parallel to, Adderley Street, pedestrianized **St George's Mall** runs from Thibault Square, near the railway station, down to Wale Street. It's a less hectic route between the station and the Company's Gardens, with coffee shops, snack bars, street traders, buskers, dancers, drummers, choirs and painters adding a certain buzz.

Church Street (which crosses the mall towards its southern end) and the surrounding area abound with antique dealers, and on the pedestrianized section at its northeastern end you'll find an informal antique market. Prices are competitive and you may pick up unusual jewellery, bric-a-brac, Africana and old sheet music.

Nearby **Greenmarket Square**, surrounded by Art Deco buildings, is worth at least a little exploration to soak up the vaguely European atmosphere, with cobbled streets, cafés and grand buildings. As its name implies, the square started as a vegetable market, though it spent many ignominious years as a car park. Human life has returned and it's now a flea market, selling crafts and jewellery.

The Old Town House

Map 4, C4. Mon–Sat 10am–5pm; ℡021-424-6367; R5.

On the southwestern side of Greenmarket Square are the solid limewashed walls and small shuttered windows of the **Old Town House**, entered from Longmarket Street. Built in 1755, this charming example of Cape Dutch architecture with its fine interior has seen duty as a guard house, a police station and Cape Town's city hall, and these days houses the **Michaelis Collection** of seventeenth-century Dutch and Flemish paintings.

Referred to as the Dutch "Golden Age", the seventeenth century was one of great prosperity for the Netherlands, during which it threw off the yoke of its Spanish colonizers and sailed forth to establish colonies of its own in the East Indies, and of course at the Cape. The wealth that trade brought to the Netherlands stimulated the development of the arts, with paintings reflecting the values and experience of Dutch Calvinists. A notable example is **Frans Hals'** *Portrait of a Woman*, hanging in the upstairs gallery. Executed in shades of brown, relieved only by the merest hint of red, it reflects the Calvinist aversion to ostentation.

The sitter for the picture, completed in 1644, would have been a contemporary of the settlers who arrived at the Cape some eight years later. Less dour, and showing off the wealth of a middle-class family, is the beautiful *Couple with Two Children in a Park*, painted by **Dirck Dirckz Santvoort** in the late 1630s, in which the artist displays a remarkable facility for portraying sensuous fabrics, which glow with reflected light; you can almost feel the texture of the lace trimming.

In the eighteenth century, the portico of the Town House was known as the "slaves' portico" because in rainy weather slaves would take refuge there and, according to a commentator who visited the Cape in 1805, "talk over the hardships of life in slavery".

Other paintings, most of them quite sombre, depict mythological scenes, church interiors, still lifes, landscapes and seascapes, the latter being very close to the seventeenth-century Dutch heart, often illustrating vessels belonging to the Dutch East India Company or the drama of rough seas encountered by trade ships. A tiny **print room** on the ground floor has a small selection of works by Daumier, Gillray and Cruikshank, as well as one of **Goya**'s most famous works, *El Sueño de la Razón Produce Monstruos* (The Sleep of Reason Produces Monsters).

Small visiting exhibitions also find space here, and good evening classical concerts are a regular thing. You can pick up the Town House's quarterly newsletter, which lists forthcoming events, or watch the press (*The Good Weekend* entertainment supplement in *Saturday Argus* being a good source). Tickets are available on the door immediately prior to the event.

AROUND ST GEORGE'S MALL

LONG STREET

Map 4, C2–6. Ⓦwww.longstreet.co.za. Cape Town station.

Parallel to Adderley Street and one block northwest of Greenmarket Square, **Long Street** aptly runs the full length of the city centre and continues as lively Kloof Street, which cuts through the City Bowl suburbs to Kloofnek, a junction that splays out to the Lower Cable Station, Sea Point, the Atlantic seaboard and Signal Hill. The buzzing artery itself is one of Cape Town's most interestingly diverse thoroughfares – a great place for some leisurely exploration, with views of Table Mountain, Signal Hill and Lion's Head, as well as glimpses of the sea.

When it was first settled by Muslims some three hundred years ago, Long Street marked Cape Town's boundary; by the 1960s it had become a sleazy alley of drinking holes and whorehouses. Miraculously it's all still here, but with a whiff of gentrification. Mosques still coexist with bars, brothels above old-fashioned locksmiths, pawnbrokers alongside porn shops. Gun shops sit next to delicatessens, antique dealers, craft shops and cafés. Several excellent secondhand bookshops feature, and there are more **backpacker lodges** per square metre than on any other street in Cape Town, with a growing number of student travel agencies, cheap car-rental outfits and adventure-activity outlets appearing to service them.

For details on Long Street accommodation see p.142, for eating see p.174.

The Palm Tree Mosque

Map 4, C5.

An unmistakable landmark at no. 185, along the upper reaches of Long Street, the **Palm Tree Mosque** (not open to the public) is fronted by a lone palm tree, its fronds caressing the upper storey. Significant as the only surviving eighteenth-century house in a street that was once full of them, it was erected in 1780 by Carel Lodewijk Schot as a private dwelling. The house was bought in 1807 by Frans van Bengal, a member of the local Muslim community, and a freed slave, Jan van Boughies, who became its imam, turning the upper floor into a mosque, which it remains, and the lower into his living quarters.

The Pan African Market

Map 4, C4. Mon–Fri 9am–5pm, Sat 9am–3pm; ☎021-424-2957.
One of Cape Town's most intriguing places for African crafts is also one of the easiest to miss. The inconspicuous frontage of the **Pan African Market** at 76 Long Street belies the three-floor warren of passageways and rooms, which burst at the hinges with traders selling vast quantities of art and artefacts from all over the continent. Hidden amongst less inspiring offerings you'll find terrific masks from West Africa, brass leopards from Benin as well as textiles, contemporary South African art, CDs, musical instruments, leathersmiths, tailors, hair braiders and a drum instructor.

The South African Missionary Meeting-House Museum

Map 4, C3. Mon–Fri 9am–4pm; free.
Towards the harbour end of Long Street at no. 40, the **South African Missionary Meeting-House Museum** is an exceptional building with one of the most beautiful frontages in Cape Town. Broken into three bays by four slender Corinthian pilasters sürmounted by a gabled pediment, its facade gives the remarkable appearance of being

LONG STREET

all window. Inside, an impressive Neoclassical timber **pulpit** perches high above the congregation on a pair of columns, framing an inlaid image of an angel in flight. Completed in 1804 by the South African Missionary Society, it was the first missionary church in the country, where slaves were taught literacy and instructed in Christianity.

The Society itself was founded in 1799 by Reverend Vos in alarmed response to the fact that many slave owners were neglecting the religious education of their slaves. Owners believed that, once baptized, their slaves' emancipation became obligatory – a misunderstanding of the law, which merely stated that Christian slaves couldn't be sold. Vos, himself a slave owner, saw proselytization to the bonded as a Christian duty and even successfully campaigned to end the prohibition against selling Christian slaves, which he believed was "a great obstacle in this country to the progress of Christianity", because it encouraged owners to avoid baptizing their human chattels.

An interesting permanent set of display boards covers the work of the early missionaries and mission stations throughout the Western Cape.

THE BO-KAAP

Map 4, A3–6. Cape Town station.

Minutes from parliament on the slopes of Signal Hill, the **Bo-Kaap** is one of Cape Town's oldest and most attractive residential areas, brightly painted nineteenth-century Dutch and Georgian terraces concealing a network of alleyways that are the arteries of the **Muslim community**. The Bo-Kaap harbours its own strong identity, made all the more unique by the destruction of District Six, with which it had much in common. A particular dialect of Afrikaans is spoken here, although it is steadily being eroded by English, which has a higher social status and lacks the associations with apartheid.

Bo-Kaap residents are descended from dissidents and slaves imported here by the Dutch in the sixteenth and seventeenth centuries. They became known collectively as "**Cape Malays**", a term you'll still hear, even though it's a misnomer: fewer than one percent of slaves actually came from Malaysia.

The Bo-Kaap is most easily reached by foot along Wale Street, which trails up from the south end of Adderley Street and across Buitengracht to become the district's main drag.

The Bo-Kaap's charming facades and quiet cobbled streets give it a deceptively quaint feel; apart from Wale Street and the Museum, this is not a good place to wander alone. The safest way to get under the skin of the area is on one of the several tours that take in the museum and walk you around the district, the best (and cheapest) of these being the two-hour walk run by Bo-Kaap Guided Tours (bookings on ☏021-422-1554 or 082-423-6932; R55), operated by residents of the area.

The Bo-Kaap Museum

Map 4, A4. Mon–Sat 9.30am–4.30pm; R5; ☏021-424-3846, ⓦwww.museums.org.za/bokaap.

A good place to find out about the Muslim quarter is the **Bo-Kaap Museum**, 71 Wale Street, near the Buitengracht end. The museum consists mainly of the house and effects of Abu Bakr Effendi, a religious leader brought out from Turkey by the British authorities in 1862 as a mediator between feuding Muslim factions. He stayed and became an important member of the community, started an Arabic school and wrote a book in the local vernacular – possibly the first book to be published in what can be recognized as Afrikaans. Exhibits also explore a local brand of Islam, which has its own unique traditions and nearly two dozen *kramats* (shrines) dotted about the peninsula.

Architecturally, the museum is typical of the modest single-storey houses of the Bo-Kaap, employing a raised *stoep* (verandah) to accommodate the extreme slope of the site. Like many of the earlier buildings, some of which date as far back as the 1780s, it has sash windows, a fan-light above the door, a flat roof and a decorative wavy parapet.

The Auwal Mosque

Map 4, A5.
One block south of the museum, on Dorp Street, is the **Auwal**, South Africa's first official mosque, founded in 1797 by the highly influential Imam Abdullah ibn Qadi Abd al-Salam (commonly known as Tuan Guru or Master Teacher), a Moluccan prince and Muslim activist who was exiled to Robben Island in 1780 for opposing Dutch rule in the Indies. While on the island he transcribed the Koran from memory and wrote several important Islamic commentaries, which provided a basis for the religion at the Cape for almost a century. On being released in 1792, he began offering religious instruction from his house in Dorp Street, before founding the Auwal nearby.

The Auwal Mosque can only be visited as part of an organized Bo-Kaap **tour** (see p.67). Ten more mosques in the Bo-Kaap, whose minarets give spice to the quarter's skyline, now serve its ten thousand residents.

CITY HALL AND THE GRAND PARADE

Map 4, E3–4. Cape Town station.
Built in 1905 in an Italian Renaissance style, the **City Hall**, south of the station on the corner of Parade and Darling streets, is typical of the British colonial town halls erected throughout the Empire in the late nineteenth and early

twentieth centuries. One of the most photogenic buildings in Cape Town, it presents a pleasingly self-confident Edwardian facade dominated by a huge clock tower, with the unparalleled backdrop of Table Mountain.

As well as being frequently snapped, the hall can probably also claim to be the most televised South African building: **Nelson Mandela** stood on its balcony on a sweltering February day in 1990 to give his first public speech in decades, an audience of a hundred thousand supporters having waited for hours on the **Grand Parade**, across Darling Street, for their hero to arrive from Victor Vester Prison.

Usually the Parade is a desolate square, in the shadow of the station, but it livens up on Wednesdays and Saturdays when it becomes the site of a non-touristy flea market where you can buy spicy foods and an array of bits and pieces, including secondhand clothes.

Stand on the Grand Parade to snap the City Hall, and you'll not only capture the building and Table Mountain, you'll get the foreground of palm trees on the north side of Darling Street: a classic Cape Town image.

THE CASTLE OF GOOD HOPE

Map 4, F3–G3. Daily 9am–4pm; R15, free tours daily at 11am, noon & 2pm; ⓦwww.museums.org.za/wfc. Cape Town station.

From the outside, South Africa's oldest building looks a trifle desolate due its position behind the train station and city bus terminal, between busy Strand and Darling streets. Nevertheless, the **Castle of Good Hope** is well worth the entrance fee, having enjoyed a meticulous ten-year restoration that has returned the decor to the British Regency style introduced in 1798. Built in accordance with seventeenth-century European principles of fortification, the castle has strong bastions from which it could be protected by cross-fire. Finished in 1679, complete with the essentials of a moat and torture chamber, it replaced Van Riebeeck's earlier mud and timber fort, which stood on the site of the Grand Parade. For 150 years, until the early nineteenth century, the castle was the symbolic heart of the Cape administration, and the centre of the city's social and economic life.

Inside, there's a strong sense of order in the castle's pentagonal plan, though ironically there was nothing ordered about its construction, which lasted over thirteen years, with work constantly coming to a standstill because of either labour shortages or insufficient materials, and being regularly revived by the outbreak of various wars in Europe. The original seaward entrance had to be moved to its present landward-facing position because the spring tide sometimes came crashing in – a remarkable thought given that due to land reclamation it's now almost a kilometre inland.

The current **entrance gate** displays the coat of arms of the United Netherlands and those of the six Dutch cities in which the VOC Chambers were situated; the bell, cast in 1697 by Claude Fremy in Amsterdam, was used variously as an alarm signal and a summons to residents to receive pronouncements, and still hangs from its original wooden beams in the tower above the entrance. Inside the walls, the **courtyard** is sliced in half by a defensive twelve-metre-high defensive structure, or *kat*, from which cannons could be fired. Providing entry to the *kat*, the exquisite ceremonial **Kat Balcony** from which ordinances were pronounced is flanked by two shallow curving staircases, its portico supported on six fluted Ionic columns carved out of solid teak.

There's a tranquil tea shop in the castle courtyard, where you can enjoy the Cape Dutch architecture and take in the view of Table Mountain.

Free tours are useful for orientation around the castle and include the prison cells and dungeons, with centuries-old graffiti painstakingly carved on their walls. The castle is also home to the Defence Force's Western Province Command, and you may catch a glimpse of armed soldiers marching in and stepping across the elegant courtyard, Table Mountain peeking over the west wall.

The William Fehr Collection

Elaborately carved double doors at the rear of the castle's Kat Balcony open onto four interleading rooms that were the heart of VOC government at the Cape and now house the bulk of the excellent **William Fehr Collection**, one of the country's most important exhibits of decorative arts. The contents, acquired by businessman William Fehr from the 1920s, were sold and donated to the government in the 1950s and 1960s and continue to be displayed informally as Fehr preferred, instead of being arranged thematically.

Galleries are filled with items found in middle-class Cape households from the seventeenth to nineteenth centuries, with some fine examples of elegantly simple **Cape furniture** from the eighteenth century. Early colonial views of Table Bay appear in a number of **paintings**, including one by Aernot Smit that shows the castle in the seventeenth century, right on the shoreline. Among the fascinating items of antique oriental **ceramics** are a blue-and-white Japanese porcelain plate from around 1660, displaying the VOC monogram, and a beautiful polychrome plate from China dating to about 1750, which depicts a fleet of Company ships in Table Bay against the backdrop of a very oriental-looking Table Mountain.

DISTRICT SIX

The apocalyptic sound was complete when the first buildings toppled. They fell down, the facades, the inside walls, in clouds of dust that in the end were just a single cloud . . . of resentment.

Coloured poet Adam Small,
recalling the destruction of District Six

South of the castle, in the shadow of Devil's Peak, is a vacant lot shown on maps as the suburb of Zonnebloem. Before being torn apart by the apartheid regime during the Sixties and Seventies, it was District Six, an impoverished but lively community of 55,000 people, predominantly coloured. Once known as the soul of Cape Town, this inner-city slum harboured a rich cultural life in its narrow alleys and crowded tenements. Along the cobbled streets, hawkers rubbed shoulders with prostitutes, gangsters, drunks and gamblers, while craftsmen plied their trade in small workshops. After its demise, the district became mythologized as a rich place of the South African imagination, inspiring novels, poems, jazz and the blockbuster musical *District Six*.

In 1966, P.W. Botha (then Minister of Community Development – a title that carries a measure of Orwellian irony) declared District Six a White Group Area, meaning that Africans, Indians and coloureds were prohibited from living there. The bulldozers moved in, taking fifteen years to drive its presence from the sky-line, leaving only mosques and churches.

In the wake of the demolition gangs, international and domestic outcry was so great that the area was never developed, apart from a few luxury town houses on its fringes and the hefty Cape Technikon, a college that now occupies nearly a quarter of the former suburb. After years of negotiation, the original residents are being allowed to move back under a scheme to develop low-cost housing in the district.

THE DISTRICT SIX MUSEUM

Map 4, F4; Mon–Sat 10am–4.30pm; donation; ☎021-461-8745, ⓦwww.districtsix.co.za. Cape Town station.

Located at 25a Buitenkant Street, on the corner of Albertus Street, the **District Six Museum** is one of Cape Town's most compelling museums, particularly for anyone interested in South Africa's recent history. A highly creative and moving exhibit, it provides a memorial to the predominantly coloured residents of the vibrant down-at-heel inner-city suburb (see box opposite) that stood southeast of here until it was erased from the map under apartheid. The museum occupies the former **Central Methodist Mission Church**, which offered solidarity and ministry to the victims of forced removals right up to the 1980s, and was a venue for anti-apartheid gatherings. Today the church houses a series of excellent displays that include artefacts and documentary photographs, which evoke the lives of the individuals who made their home here. A huge map of District Six as it was before the bulldozers moved in occupies most of the floor and has been annotated by former residents, who describe their memories, reflections and incidents associated with places and buildings that no longer exist. There's also an almost complete collection of original street signs secretly retrieved at the time of demolition by the man entrusted with dumping them into Table Bay.

There are few places in Cape Town that speak more eloquently of the effect of apartheid on the day-to-day lives of ordinary people.

STRAND STREET AND THE LOWER CITY CENTRE

Map 4, A–C, 1–3. Cape Town station.

A major artery from the N2 freeway to the central business district, **Strand Street** neatly separates the more respectable Upper from the aptly named Lower city centre. Between the mid-eighteenth and mid-nineteenth centuries, Strand Street, because of its proximity to the shore, was one of the most fashionable streets in Cape Town, a fact that's now only discernible from the handful of quietly elegant National Monuments left standing amid the roar of traffic: Martin Melck House, which accommodates the **Gold of Africa Museum**, the **Evangelical Lutheran Church** and **Koopmans–De Wet House**.

For centuries, the **Lower City Centre**, stretching north of Strand Street to the shore and taking in the still-functional **Duncan Dock**, has been a marginal area between Cape Town and the sea. In the mid-nineteenth century, the city's middle classes viewed this seedy but vibrant quarter with a mixture of alarm and excitement – a tension that remains today.

Lower Long Street divides the area just inland from the docklands into two. To the east is the Foreshore, an ugly post–World War II wasteland of grey corporate architecture, among which is the **Artscape Centre** (previously the Nico Theatre), Cape Town's prestige arts complex. To the west, in sharp contrast, is the city's densely packed clubbing and pubbing district.

Gold of Africa Museum

Map 4, B3. Daily 10am–5pm; R20; ☎021-405-1540, Ⓦwww.goldofafrica.co.za.

Since gold was discovered around Johannesburg in the late nineteenth century, South Africa has been closely associated in the mind of the West with the precious metal and the riches it represents. But the outstanding **Gold of Africa Museum** at 96 Strand Street focuses on a completely different side to gold – the exquisite **artworks** crafted by nineteenth and twentieth century **African goldsmiths** mainly from Mali, Senegal, Ghana and the Ivory Coast. Arguably the most important such collection in the world, it was acquired in 2001 from the Barbier-Meuller Museum in Geneva, and is now housed in the beautifully restored **Martin Melck House**. The museum has historical background on the artefacts it contains and also traces Africa's ancient gold routes, but it's the several hundred beautiful items – precious masks, crocodiles, birds, a gold crown and human figures – that are the stars of the show. The highlight is the sculpted **Golden Lion** that is the symbol of the museum and is housed up some steep stairs in the last remaining *dakkamer* (roof gazebo) in Cape Town – a dark room with gilt walls. The museum also has a small auditorium with a continuous **film show**, a **wine cellar**, where you can have a snack, a coffee and quaff a glass of Cape wine in a beautiful courtyard garden, a **studio** where goldsmiths practise their art and a **shop** where you can buy gold leaf, postcards and beautiful little souvenirs.

Evangelical Lutheran Church

Map 4, B3. Mon, Wed & Fri 9am–noon; free.

Next door to the Gold of Africa Museum, at the corner of Buitengracht, which marks the eastern boundary of the Bo-Kaap, and Strand Street, the **Evangelical Lutheran Church** now stands dwarfed by office blocks, but was once a Cape Town skyscraper, its spire towering over a one- and two-storey roofscape. Converted by **Anton Anreith** in 1785 from a barn, its facade includes Classical details such as a broken pediment perforated by the clock tower, as well as Gothic ones, such as the pointy arched windows. Inside, the magnificent **pulpit**, supported on two life-size Herculean figures, is one of Anton Anreith's masterpieces; the white swan perching on top of the canopy is a symbol of Lutheranism.

STRAND STREET AND THE LOWER CITY CENTRE

The establishment of a Lutheran church in Cape Town struck a significant blow against the extreme **religious intolerance** that pervaded under VOC rule. Prior to 1771, when permission was granted to Lutherans to establish their own congregation, not only was Protestantism the only form of worship allowed, but the Dutch Reformed Church held an absolute monopoly over saving people's souls. The Lutheran Church's congregation was dominated by Germans, who at the time constituted 28 percent of the colony's free burgher population.

Koopmans-De Wet House

Map 4, C3. Tues–Sat 9.30am–4.30pm; R5; ✆021-424-2473, Ⓦwww.museums.org.za/koopmans.

Sandwiched between two office blocks, **Koopmans-De Wet House**, 35 Strand Street, is an outstanding eighteenth-century pedimented Neoclassical town house and museum, accommodating a very fine collection of antique furniture and rare porcelain. An inexpensive **guide** booklet gives interesting contextual background to the house and its history, while a separate brochure describes items in the collection: both are available at the entrance.

The building's **facade** has been attributed to Louis Thibault and Anton Anreith, but there's no proof of this. Whoever was responsible, the house represents a fine synthesis of Dutch elements – sash windows and large entrance doors – with the demands of local conditions, including the front *stoep* (verandah) framed at either end by a plastered masonry seat. Huge rooms, lofty ceilings and shuttered windows also take account of high summer temperatures.

The earliest sections of the house were built in 1701 by **Reyner Smedinga**, a well-to-do goldsmith who imported the building materials from Holland. The house changed hands more than a dozen times over the following two centuries, with minor additions made in the 1760s and a second storey added between 1774 and 1790. In 1806 it came into the hands of the de Wet family, eventually becoming the home of **Marie Koopmans-De Wet** (1834–1906), a prominent figure on the Cape social and political circuit.

The lantern in the fanlight of the entrance of Koopmans-De Wet House was a compulsory feature of all Cape town houses in the eighteenth and early nineteenth centuries, its purpose being to shine light onto the street and thus hinder slaves from gathering at night to plot.

West of Lower Long Street: clubland

Map 4, A–B2.
For as long as the docks have existed, there's been life after dark west of Lower Long Street, particularly along **Waterkant Street** and at the northern ends of **Bree** and **Loop streets**, where they intersect Waterkant. Frequented by sailors, dockers and sex workers, Cape Town's red-light district used to be a hard-drinking, drugged-up, apartheid-free zone where some of the city's best jazz was played and raids by the police were a regular part of the scene. These days, with a high density of **nightclubs** and **pubs**, the area has become the best place in Cape Town to club-crawl – one of the few where you're guaranteed action seven nights a week.

For Lower City Centre club details, see "Clubs, bars and live music" from p.191.

STRAND STREET AND THE LOWER CITY CENTRE

The Foreshore

Map 4, E–G1.

The Foreshore, an area of reclaimed land north of Strand Street stretching to the docks and east of Lower Long Street, is a clumsy postwar development which was intended to transform Cape Town's harbour into a symbolic gateway to Africa, but instead turned out as a series of large concrete boxes surrounded by acres of windswept parking lots.

Heerengracht, a truncated two-lane carriageway running from Adderley Street to the harbour and punctuated at either end by massive roundabouts, each solemnly guarded by statues of Jan Van Riebeeck and Bartholomeu Dias, was meant to be the ceremonial axis through this grand scheme, joining the city to the sea. But the road never quite makes it to the water, coming to a disappointing standstill at the dock perimeter fence before bearing east under the dismal shadow of the N1 and N2 flyovers. Cape Town's major performance venue is the **Artscape Centre** (Map 5, I5), on D.F. Malan Street just east of Heerengracht. Incorporating the large Main Theatre, it also houses the small Arena Theatre and an opera house.

For more about the Artscape Centre, see "Theatre and cinema" on p.215.

Duncan Dock

Map 3, F2–F3.

North of the Foreshore, **Duncan Dock** is Cape Town's working harbour and presents a forbidding industrial landscape of large ships and towering cranes, cut off from the city by an enormous perimeter fence. Work started on the dock in 1938, swallowing the city beachfronts at Woodstock and Paarden Island to cater for the growing supertanker traffic that was outstripping the capacity of the Victoria and Alfred Basins (see p.81). It's a fabulous place to take moody photographs of gigantic hulks against Table Mountain, but you won't want to linger here alone.

The Waterfront and Robben Island

The Victoria and Alfred Waterfront (see map, p.82, also colour map 5), usually known simply as the Waterfront, adjoins the west of Duncan Dock and is Cape Town's original Victorian harbour. Now the most popular attraction on the peninsula, it was only after two decades of stagnation that it began to be redeveloped at the beginning of the 1990s, and has become the city's central shopping area, its most fashionable eating and drinking venue, the site of an excellent aquarium and the embarkation point for trips to Robben Island, one of Cape Town's most interesting and essential excursions. Period buildings, imitation Victorian shopping malls, piers with waterside walkways and a functioning harbour complement the wide range of restaurants, outdoor cafés, pubs, clubs, cinemas, museums and outdoor entertainment, with magnificent Table Mountain rising beyond.

Arguments raged throughout the first half of the nineteenth century over the need for a proper dock. The Cape was often known as the **Cape of Storms** because of its vicious weather, which left Table Bay littered with wrecks.

Many makeshift attempts were made, including the construction of a lighthouse in 1823, and work was begun on a jetty at the bottom of Bree Street in 1832. Clamour for a harbour grew with the expansion of sea traffic arriving at the Cape in the 1850s, and reached its peak in 1860, when the Lloyds insurance company refused the risk of covering ships dropping anchor in Table Bay.

The British colonial government eventually decided that potential profits superseded the shipwrecking risks, and on a suitably stormy September day in 1860, at a huge ceremony, the teenage Prince Alfred tipped the first batch of stones into Table Bay to begin the **Breakwater**, the westernmost arm of the harbour, which was subsequently completed with convict labour. In 1869, the dock – consisting of two main basins – was completed, and the sea was allowed to pour in.

Thirty-two information boards are arranged around the Waterfront to create an excellent self-guided historical tour that starts at the Visitor Centre, where you can buy an illustrated booklet covering the same route.

THE VICTORIA AND ALFRED BASINS

Map p.82, also Map 5, E1–4 & F1–4. Waterfront shuttle bus.
Victoria Basin, the smaller **Alfred Basin** to its west, and the **Marina** beyond, create the Waterfront's geography of piers and quays, with most of the activity concentrated around the northwest side. The **Waterfront Visitor Centre**, set back from the Victoria Basin on Dock Road (℡021-408-7600, ⓦwww.waterfront.co.za), provides maps and bookings for tours and taxis. They also have an office in the Clock Tower, adjacent to the Nelson Mandela Gateway.

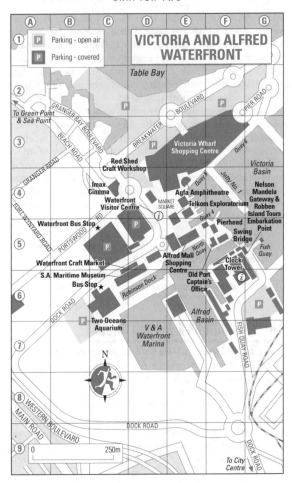

VICTORIA AND ALFRED WATERFRONT

P Parking - open air

P Parking - covered

Table Bay

To Green Point & Sea Point

GRANGER BAY BOULEVARD

BREAKWATER BOULEVARD

PIER ROAD

BEACH ROAD

GRANGER ROAD

FORT WYNYARD ROAD

PORTSWOOD RD

Red Shed Craft Workshop

Imax Cinema

Waterfront Visitor Centre

MARKET SQUARE

Victoria Wharf Shopping Centre

Quay 6

Victoria Basin

Quay 5

Agfa Amphitheatre

Telkom Exploratorium

Quay 4

Nelson Mandela Gateway & Robben Island Tours Embarkation Point

Pierhead

Swing Bridge

Fish Quay

Waterfront Bus Stop

Waterfront Craft Market

S.A. Maritime Museum Bus Stop

Alfred Mall Shopping Centre

North Quay

Robinson Dock

Old Port Captain's Office

Clock Tower

DOCK ROAD

Two Oceans Aquarium

V & A Waterfront Marina

Alfred Basin

FISH QUAY ROAD

N

WESTERN BOULEVARD

MAIN ROAD

DOCK ROAD

DOCK ROAD

To City Centre

0   250m

North of the Visitor Centre, the outdoor action centres around **Market Square** and the **Agfa Amphitheatre**, where you can sometimes catch free rock or jazz performances and occasionally hear the Cape Town Symphony Orchestra (details from the Visitor Centre). The shopping focus of the Waterfront is **Victoria Wharf**, an enormous flashy mall on two levels, extending along Quays Five and Six northeast of the amphitheatre. Inside the mall, you could be in any large city in the world, but the restaurants and cafés with outdoor seating on the mall's east side have fabulous views of Table Mountain across the busy harbour. On the west side of Victoria Wharf, the rather contrived **Red Shed Craft Workshop** (Mon–Sat 9am–9pm, Sun 10am–9pm) brings together craft-workers such as glass blowers, leatherworkers, township artists and jewellery makers under one huge roof.

Head west from Market Square (away from the water) and you'll find yourself on Dock Road; 100m north along here is the **Imax Cinema** (information ☎021-419-7365, booking via Computicket ☎083-915-8000, ⓦwww.computicket.com) at the BMW Pavilion on the corner of Portswood Road. It shows nature documentaries on topics such as African elephants, the Grand Canyon and the Amazon.

Adjacent to the Visitor Centre is one of Cape Town's best wine shops, Vaughan Johnson's (see p.211) and, to the east, the **Telkom Exploratorium** (see p.234) in Union Castle Building, a small hands-on science museum that's a winner with kids. Southwest of here along the Alfred Basin's North Quay, **Alfred Mall Shopping Centre** is a complex of fifteen touristy curio shops, boutiques and restaurants. Further west is the **South African Maritime Museum** (daily 9am–5pm; R7), really only worth visiting if you have a specialist interest and want to see its large collection of model ships. It's better to keep going for a further 200m and conserve your energies for the quite exceptional **Two Oceans Aquarium** (see p.85).

THE VICTORIA AND ALFRED BASINS

WATERFRONT TRANSPORT

The Waterfront is one of the easiest points to reach in Cape Town by **public transport**. Waterfront shuttle buses leave from outside the train station in Adderley Street every ten to fifteen minutes (daily 6am–11pm) and from Beach Road in Sea Point every twenty minutes (daily 6.30am–10.30pm), and terminate in Dock Road, at the back of the Waterfront Visitor Centre. Arriving by **car**, you'll find yourself well catered for, with several car parks and garages. If you want to leave by **taxi**, head for the taxi rank on Breakwater Boulevard.

East of the Alfred Shopping Mall, the Pierhead is dominated by the **Old Port Captain's Office**, a gabled Arts and Crafts building erected in 1904, with an imposing presence that reflected its status as the nerve centre of the harbour in the early twentieth century. It's now the headquarters of the Victoria and Alfred Waterfront Company. From the Pierhead you can use the **swing bridge** to cross to **Fish Quay** and the **Nelson Mandela Gateway** (see p.86), a museum and the embarkation point for ferries to Robben Island. As its name suggests, the swing bridge pivots to allow ships to pass through the narrow channel that connects the Victoria and Alfred basins. Rising up from Fish Quay, the **Clock Tower**, which houses a branch of the Waterfront Information Centre, is Cape Town's finest architectural folly. Built as the original Port Captain's office in 1882, this strange-looking octagonal structure with Gothic windows consists of three stacked rooms with a stairwell

Restaurants, cafés, pubs and takeaway joints by the score are dotted around the Waterfront, many of them along the quayside. Recommendations for eating are given on pp.175–6, 181–4 and for nightlife on p.196.

THE VICTORIA AND ALFRED BASINS

running through its core. The mirror room on the second floor enabled the Port Captain to survey all the activities of the harbour without leaving his office.

TWO OCEANS AQUARIUM

Map p.82, C6. Daily 9.30am–6pm; adults R45, children R20; ℗021-418-3823, ⓦwww.aquarium.co.za. Waterfront shuttle bus.

An unquestionable Waterfront highlight, the **Two Oceans Aquarium** on Dock Road at the Marina's North Wharf showcases the Cape's unique marine environment, where the warm waters of the Indian Ocean and the cold Atlantic mingle. It's all great fun, with lots of appeal for adults and kids, and is a major reason to visit the Waterfront.

Although you're not obliged to follow it, a designed route takes in the nine major galleries in sequence, starting on the **Ground Floor** with the **Indian Ocean**, where you'll see tank after tank of psychedelic fish. One of the most beautiful displays is of scores of small gossamer-like jellyfish floating gently in their ultra-violet cylindrical tank like parachutists. To its rear, the **Diversity Hall**, as its name implies, contains an astonishing variety of strange marine creatures, including giant spider crabs, octopuses, sea horses and the deadly devil firefish, whose lacy beauty disguises lethal spines. Also on the ground floor, the **Agfa Auditorium** shows videos on South Africa's marine life and related topics (such as underwater photography).

The **Basement** houses the **Alpha Activity Centre**, another good place to keep kids occupied, with free organized activities such as puppet shows and face painting, and computers which allow youngsters to explore marine ecology. The Centre is combined with the **Diving Animals** display, where you can watch a group of resident Cape fur seals frolicking under water.

> One of the aquarium highlights is the shark feeding every Sun
> at 3.30pm, when you can watch the raggies – ragged-toothed
> sharks – being hand-fed by divers. Smaller sharks, stingrays
> and turtles get their turn on Mon, Wed and Fri at 3.30pm.

The **Top Floor**, reached via a ramp, accommodates the
Story of Water, which, in glorious reconstruction, traces
the course of a river from its mouth, through a salt marsh
and lagoon, to its source. Not to everyone's taste, it features
a small colony of African penguins (which you can see in
their natural state at Boulders; see p.133), while captive sea
birds fly about the rafters. In the **Kelp Forest** in an adjacent gallery, a dense jungle of giant seaweed sways hypnoti-
cally with the rhythmic surge of the water; you can sit in
the small amphitheatre and gaze at beautiful shoals of silvery
fish shimmering through sunlit sea. From here a ramp takes
you in a gentle downward spiral through the **Predators**
exhibit, for many visitors the most compelling attraction of
all. A massive tank, open to the ocean, houses some large
resident ragged-toothed sharks, which glide past as you
walk through a glass underwater tunnel; other species con-
fined here include rays and giant turtles.

An **aquarium shop**, off the entrance foyer, with its plastic sharks, fluffy dolphins and souvenirs, can't help seeming
slightly banal, but you'll also find some interesting natural
history books, CDs and videos.

ROBBEN ISLAND AND THE NELSON MANDELA GATEWAY

Map 1, B1–2. Inclusive ferry fare, island entry fee and three-and-a-
half hour tour R100. Waterfront bus then Robben Island ferry; hourly
ferry departures 9am–3pm daily; bookings ☏021-419-1300,
Ⓦwww.robben-island.org.za.

A deeply atmospheric place, only a few kilometres from the commerce of the Waterfront, **Robben Island** is suffused by a meditative, otherworldly silence. This key site of South Africa's liberation struggle was intended to silence apartheid's domestic critics, but instead became an international focus for opposition to the regime. A flat and windswept island – which for nearly two decades was "home" to Nelson Mandela – it measures six square kilometres and is sparsely vegetated by low scrub. In December 1999 the entire island was declared a **UN World Heritage Site**.

There are a number of vendors at the Waterfront selling tickets for cruises. While some of these may go close to the island, only the official ones sold at the Nelson Mandela Gateway will get you onto it.

The only way to get to Robben Island is from the Waterfront on an official **tour**. Departures are from the **Nelson Mandela Gateway** where you buy tickets for the ferry and island tours. The Gateway (daily 7.30am–9pm; free), a two-storey building, which looks out from its fabulous vantage point across the water to the island, incorporates a restaurant with a great view and a small museum with hi-tech interactive displays including a history of Robben Island, the voices of prisoners and resistance songs. The last area you go through before heading down the ramp to the ferry aptly deals with the emotions of prisoners before they embarked for the island.

The island

Catamarans to the island take thirty minutes. After arrival at the tiny Murray's Bay harbour, you are taken around the island on a bus before a **tour of the prison**.

ROBBEN ISLAND AND THE NELSON MANDELA GATEWAY

The **bus trip** gives a strong sense of the island's windswept, strangely forlorn environment, and stops off at several historical landmarks, the first of which is the **kramat**, a beautiful shrine built in memory of Tuan Guru, a Muslim cleric from present-day Indonesia who was imprisoned here by the Dutch in the eighteenth century. On his release, he helped to establish Islam among slaves in Cape Town, where it has flourished ever since. You will also pass a **leper grave-yard** and **church** designed by Sir Herbert Baker, both of which are quiet reminders that the island was a place of exile for leprosy sufferers in the early twentieth century.

Robert Sobukwe's house is a place that seems to echo with loneliness, and is perhaps the most affecting relic of incarceration on the island. It was here that Sobukwe, leader of the Pan Africanist Congress (a radical offshoot of the ANC; see p.321) was held in solitary confinement for nine years. He was initially sentenced to three years, but was regarded as so dangerous by the authorities that they passed a special law – the "Sobukwe Clause" – to keep him on Robben Island for a further six years. No other political prisoners were allowed to speak to him, but he would sometimes gesture his solidarity with other sons of the African soil by letting sand trickle through his fingers as they walked past. After his release in 1969, Sobukwe was restricted to Kimberley under house arrest, until his death from cancer in 1978.

Another stopoff is the **lime quarry** where Nelson Mandela and his fellow inmates spent countless hours of hard labour. The soft, pale stone is extremely bright under the summer sun, as a result of which Mandela and others have in later years suffered eye disorders. As the years passed, the lime quarry became a place of furtive study among the prisoners, with the help of sympathetic warders.

The bus tour also takes in a stretch of coast dotted with shipwrecks and abundant seabirds, including the elegant

Egyptian sacred ibis. You may also spot some of a recently expanded population of **antelope**: springbok, eland and bontebok.

The Maximum Security Prison

The **Maximum Security Prison**, a forbidding complex of unadorned H-blocks on the edge of the island, is introduced with the **Footsteps of Mandela** tour through the famous **B-Section**; you'll be guided by a former inmate, after which you're free to wander. B-Section is a small compound full of tiny rooms that has become legendary in South African history; initially a place of defeat for the resistance movement, it ironically came to incubate and concentrate the energies of liberation. **Mandela's cell** is marked with fine understatement, but the rest have been left locked and empty.

In the nearby **A-Section**, the "Cell Stories" exhibition skilfully suggests the sparseness of prison life; the tiny isolation cells contain personal artefacts loaned by former prisoners (including a functional saxophone made of found objects), plus quotations, recordings and photographs. There is a powerful minimalism to this exhibit; take your time, and let the recent past envelop you.

Towards the end of the 1980s, cameras were sneaked onto the island, and inmates took snapshots of each other, which have been enlarged to almost life size and mounted as the **Smuggled Camera Exhibition** in the D-Section communal cells. The jovial demeanour of the prisoners indicates their knowledge that the end was conceivably within sight; moreover, the warm camaraderie that evidently connects them suggests how people endured so many years of captivity. Another good option during the prison visit is the **Living Legacy** tour in F-Section, in which ex-political prisoner guides describe their lives here and answer your questions. **Overnight visits** are planned.

"WE SERVE WITH PRIDE"

Nelson Mandela may have been the most famous Robben Island prisoner, but he certainly wasn't the first. Established in the seventeenth century, it was a place of banishment for those who offended the political order – first for the Dutch, later the British and most recently the Afrikaner Nationalists. The island's first prisoner was the Strandloper leader Autshumato, who became an emissary of the British. After the Dutch settlement was established, he was jailed on the island in 1658 by Jan van Riebeeck. The rest of the seventeenth century saw a succession of East Indies political prisoners and Muslim holy men exiled here for opposing Dutch colonial rule (the latter going on to establish Islam at the Cape).

During the nineteenth century, the British used Robben Island as a dumping ground for deserters, criminals and political prisoners. Captured Xhosa leaders who defied the Empire during the Frontier Wars of the early to mid-nineteenth century were transported by sea from the Eastern to the Western Cape to be imprisoned, and many ended up on Robben Island. In 1846, the island's brief was extended to include a whole range of the socially marginalized, and criminals and political detainees were joined by vagrants, prostitutes, lunatics and the chronically ill – all endured a regime of brutality and maltreatment, even in hospital. In the 1890s, a leper colony was established alongside the social outcasts. The mentally ill were removed in 1921, and the lepers in 1930. During World War II, the Defence Force took over the island to set up defensive guns against a feared Axis invasion, which never came.

Robben Island's greatest era of notoriety began in 1961, when it was taken over by the Prisons Department. Prisoners arriving at the island prison were greeted by a slogan on the gate that read: "Welcome to Robben Island: We Serve with Pride." By 1963, when Nelson Mandela arrived, it had become a maximum security prison, and all the warders – and none of the prisoners – were white; inmates were only allowed to send and receive one letter every six months, and common-law and political prisoners were housed together, until 1971, when they were separated in an attempt to further isolate the politicals. Harsh conditions, including routine beatings and forced hard labour, were exacerbated by geography; there's nothing but sea between the island and the South Pole, with icy winds blowing in from across the Atlantic, and inmates were made to wear shorts and flimsy jerseys. Like every other prisoner, Mandela slept on a thin mat on the floor (until 1973, when he was given a bed because he was ill), and was kept in a solitary confinement cell measuring two metres square for sixteen hours a day.

The prisoners' ways of protesting – hunger strikes, legal action and go-slows – won improved conditions over the years. The island also became a university behind bars, where people of different political views and generations communed; it was not unknown for prisoners to give academic help to their warders. The last political prisoners were released from Robben Island in 1991, and the remaining common-law prisoners were transferred to the mainland in 1996. On January 1, 1997, control of Robben Island was transferred from the Department of Correctional Services to the Department of the Arts, Culture, Science and Technology, which established it as a museum.

Robben Island became the central focus of South Africa's millennium celebrations. Two hours before midnight, Mandela, President Mbeki and six former political prisoners walked to Mandela's former cell, where the octogenarian liberation hero handed a lighted candle to his successor. "It symbolizes that the freedom flame can never be put down by anybody," Mandela said. "There are good men and women around that will always keep it alight."

Table Mountain

T he icon that announces Cape Town to seafarers, Table Mountain (1086m), a flat-topped massif with dramatic cliffs and eroded gorges, dominates the northern end of the peninsula. Its north face overlooks the city centre, with the distinct formations of Lion's Head and Signal Hill to the west and Devil's Peak to the east. The west face is made up of a series of gabled formations known as the Twelve Apostles. The southwest towers over Hout Bay, and the eastern face looks down over Cape Town's suburbs.

Table Mountain is a compelling feature in the middle of the city, a wilderness where you'll find wildlife and 1400 species of **flora**. Indigenous mammals include baboons, dassies (hyraxes) and porcupines, while the animals that resemble mountain goats are Himalayan tahrs, descended from specimens introduced by Cecil Rhodes onto his estate, which escaped to flourish on the mountain.

A popular source of recreation for Capetonians, Table Mountain has suffered under the constant pounding of **hikers**, though the damage isn't always obvious – certainly not from the dizzying summit. If you plan on tackling one of the hundreds of walks and climbs on its slopes, go properly prepared (see box on p.96); you might also like to consider the services of a guide (see "Sports and outdoor activities" on p.223). One common difficulty is people losing the track (often due to sudden mist falling) and ending up stranded and lost.

DASSIES

The outsized fluffy guinea pigs you'll encounter at the top of Table Mountain are dassies, or hyraxes (*Procavia capensis*), which, despite their appearance, aren't rodents at all, but the closest living relatives – some way back – of elephants. Their name (pronounced like "dusty" without the "t") is the Afrikaans version of *dasje*, meaning "little badger", given to them by the first Dutch settlers. Dassies are very widely distributed, having thrived in South Africa with the elimination of predators, and hang out in suitably rocky habitat all over the country.

Like reptiles, dassies have poor body-control systems and rely on shelter against both hot sunlight and the cold. They wake up sluggish and first thing in the morning seek out rocks where they can catch the early morning sun – this is one of the best times to look out for them. One adult stands sentry against predators and issues a low-pitched warning cry in response to a threat. Dassies live in colonies of a dominant male and eight or more related females and their offspring.

THE CABLE CAR

Map 3, C6–7. May to Oct R68 return; Nov to Apr R85 return. Shuttle bus from Cape Town Tourism; or minibus taxi. Free car parking along the road leading to the Cable Car Station.

The **cable-car** journey up Table Mountain is a Cape Town must, and to cope with half a million visitors annually a state-of-the art Swiss system was installed in 1997. The floor of the fishbowl-shaped car is designed to complete a 360-degree rotation on its way to the top, giving passengers

THE CABLE CAR

a full panorama. Cars leave from the **Lower Cable Station** on Tafelberg Road (daily every 10–20 min: Feb–Mar 8.30am–9pm; April 8.30am–7.30pm; May–Oct 8.30am–6pm; Nov 7.30am–9pm; Dec–Jan 8am–10pm; ☎021-424-5148 or 021-424-8181).

The trip takes you to the **Upper Cable Station** at the northeastern end of the Western Table, a height of 1073m. From here you can walk along a circular paved path to get spectacular views of Table Bay on one side and the Atlantic seaboard on the other. An overpriced but pleasant **tea room** has fine views, plus there's a classier bistro and a gift shop.

TABLE MOUNTAIN WALKS

Walking up the mountain will give you a greater sense of achievement than being ferried up by the cable car, but proceed with extreme caution: the **weather** is subject to rapid changes, both in general and in small localized areas, the main hazards being sun, mist and violent winds. Unless you're going with a knowledgeable guide, attempt only the simplest routes as outlined below.

The *Approved Paths on Table Mountain* map is published by the Mountain Club of South Africa, and is available from Cape Union Mart at the Waterfront or Cavendish Square Shopping Centre in Claremont (R15).

Signal Hill and Lion's Head

Map 3, C3 & B5. Signal Hill Road to Lion's Head, 2hr; Lion's Head ascent, 2hr.

From the roundabout at the junction of Kloof Nek and Tafelberg roads, where you'll find the Kloof Nek bus terminus, a road leads all the way along **Signal Hill** to a car park and lookout with great views over Table Bay, the docks and the city. A cannon was formerly used for sending signals to ships at anchor in the bay, and the Noon Gun, still fired from the viewpoint at the top, sends a thunderous rumble through the Bo-Kaap below. Halfway along the road is a sacred Islamic *kramat* (shrine), one of several dotted around the Peninsula.

You can also walk up **Lion's Head**, an unstrenuous and popular hike that seems to bring out half of Cape Town every full moon. Heading north from Kloof Nek for about 500m along Signal Hill Road, you'll come to a car park. An obvious jeep track, which becomes a path, leads west from here up the head.

Platteklip Gorge and Maclear's Beacon

Map 3, D7. Tafelberg Road to Platteklip Gorge, 2–3hr.

The first recorded ascent of Table Mountain was by the Portuguese captain, Antonio de Saldanha, in 1503. He wisely chose **Platteklip Gorge**, the gap visible from the central front table (the north side) which, as it turned out, is the most accessible way up. It's a very steep slog though, which takes two to three hours from the foot to the summit, if you're reasonably fit. A short and easy extension will get you to Maclear's Beacon (1086m, Map 2, D3), the highest point on the mountain. Taking the Platteklip route, you end up at the Upper Cable Station, so you can hop on a car to get back down.

The route starts out at the Lower Cable Station, to which you can take the tourism shuttle bus. From here, walk east for 1.5km along Tafelberg Road until you see a high embankment built from stone and maintained with wire netting (or drive the 1.5km and park on the roadside); just beyond and to the left of a small dam is a sign pointing to Platteklip Gorge. A steep fifteen-minute ascent brings you onto the **upper contour path**. Head east along this for about 25m, then take the path heading up the mountain indicated by a sign reading "Contour Path/Platteklip Gorge". Zigzagging from here onwards, the path is very clear. Once on top, turn right and ascend the last short sec-

TABLE MOUNTAIN SAFETY

Make sure you . . .
- Don't climb alone.
- Inform someone you're going up the mountain, tell them your route, when you're leaving and when you expect to be back.
- Leave early enough to give yourself time to complete your route during daylight.
- Don't try to descend via an unknown route – if you get lost in poor weather, seek shelter, keep warm and wait for help.
- Never leave litter on the mountain.
- Never make fires – no cooking (even on portable stoves) is allowed.

Wear . . .
- Good footwear – boots or running shoes are recommended.
- A broad-rimmed hat to keep the sun off.

Take . . .
- A backpack.
- A water bottle – allow two litres per person.
- Enough food – sandwiches, glucose sweets, nuts, raisins, juice.
- A warm jersey.
- A waterproof windbreaker.
- Sunglasses.
- High-factor sunscreen.
- Plasters for blisters.
- Money for the cable car.

tion onto the **front table**, for a breathtaking view of the city. A sign points the way to the Upper Cable Station – a fifteen-minute walk along a concrete path, which is usually thronged with visitors.

Maclear's Beacon is about 2km (45min) from the top of the Platteklip Gorge on a path leading eastward, with waymarks – white squares on little yellow footsteps – guiding you all the way. The path crosses the front table with Maclear's Beacon visible at all times. From the top you'll look out over False Bay and the Hottentots Holland Mountains to the east.

The Pipe Track

Map 3, C5–B7. Kloof Nek bus terminus; up to 3hr each way.

One of the most rewarding and easiest walks along the mountainside is along the **Pipe Track**, a service road that leads from Kloof Nek along the west flank of Table Mountain. The route begins at some stone steps opposite the Kloof Nek bus terminus, just to the west of the Tafelberg Road turnoff (if you're driving, park on Tafelberg Road). Steps lead up alongside forestry staff houses before the path levels off under some pines. On the level for roughly 7km, the track runs beneath the Twelve Apostles and follows the mountain's contours, offering fantastic views of the Atlantic.

The route intersects several climbs up the mountain. The first, after about 45 minutes, is indicated by a sign to **Blinkwater Ravine** (closed to the public due to rockfalls). A further ten to fifteen minutes brings you to the Kasteelspoort ascent (signposted under gum trees), followed by **Woody Ravine** and the last, roughly 25 minutes after Kasteelspoort, at **Slangolie Ravine**, where the path ends. The rock bed on Slangolie is steep, unstable and to be avoided. Turn back when you see the first of the Woodhead

TABLE MOUNTAIN WALKS

Tunnel danger signs. The Pipe Track isn't a circular route, so you can turn back at any point; the walk takes two to three hours each way.

Skeleton Gorge and Nursery Ravine

Map 2, D4. Skeleton Gorge ascent, 2hr 30min; Nursery Ravine descent, 2hr 30min.

You could make an ascent of Table Mountain via one route and descend down another, beginning and ending at the Kirstenbosch National Botanical Gardens' **restaurant** for tea; the entire walk lasts about five hours. Starting at the restaurant, follow the **Skeleton Gorge** signs, which lead you onto the **Contour Path**. At the Contour Path, a plaque indicates that this is **Smuts' Track**, the route favoured by Jan Smuts, the Boer leader, statesman, philosopher, friend to the British and South African prime minister (1919–24 and 1939–48). The plaque marks the start of a broad-stepped climb up Skeleton Gorge, involving wooden and stone steps, wooden ladders and loose boulders. Be prepared for steep ravines and difficult rock climbs, and under no circumstances stray off the path as it's easy to get lost. It requires reasonable fitness, but can take as little as an hour. Skeleton can be an unpleasant way down, especially in the wet season when it gets slippery.

Nursery Ravine is recommended for the descent. At the top of Skeleton Gorge, walk a few metres to your right to a sign indicating Kasteelspoort. It's just 35 minutes from the top of Skeleton along this path to the head of Nursery Ravine; the descent returns you to the 310-metre Contour Path, which leads back to Kirstenbosch.

- -
Kirstenbosch National Botanical Gardens
are covered in detail on p.105.
- -

The southern
suburbs

The bulk of Cape Town's residential sprawl extends east into South Africa's interior away from Table Mountain and the city centre. It's here that the southern suburbs, the formerly whites-only residential areas, cut a swath from town, down the east side of Table Mountain, ending just before Muizenberg on the False Bay coast. Most of the peninsula's suburban attractions are concentrated here, including the best malls and cinemas.

From anywhere in the southern suburbs you can see Table Mountain rising above Cape Town. The area offers some quick escapes from the city heat into forests, gardens and **vineyards**, all hugging the eastern slopes of the mountain, and its extension, the Constantiaberg.

Adjacent to the southern suburbs and separated from them by the M5 freeway, the **Cape Flats** tail off to the east in a nondescript conglomeration of coloured suburbs, African townships and burgeoning shanty towns. This is where most Capetonians live, yet because of its reputation for crime and violence it's the part of the city least explored by tourists. However, conducted tours, which are the safest way of getting around, give a real insight into the other side of Cape Town.

Southern suburbs stations along the Metrorail line, from Cape Town to Simon's Town, are shown on map 2.

WOODSTOCK, SALT RIVER AND OBSERVATORY

Map 3, G4–5 & H4–5. Woodstock, Salt River & Observatory stations.

First and oldest of the suburbs as you take an easterly exit from town is **Woodstock**, leafless and windblown, but redeemed by some nice Victorian buildings, originally occupied by working-class coloureds but now largely yuppified.

To its east, **Salt River** is a harsh, industrial, mainly coloured area, built initially for workers and artisans, while **Observatory**, abutting Salt River's southern end, is generally regarded as Cape Town's bohemian hub, a reputation fuelled by its proximity to the University of Cape Town in Rondebosch and its large student population. Many of the houses here are student digs, but the narrow Victorian streets are also home to young professionals, hippies and arty types. The refreshingly unrestored peeling arcades on Observatory's Lower Main Road, and the streets off it, have some nice cafés and lively bars, as well as a wholefood store, an African fabrics shop and a couple of antiques emporiums. The huge **Groote Schuur Hospital**, which overlooks the freeway that sweeps through Observatory, was the site of the world's first heart transplant in 1967.

For party animals Observatory makes a good alternative to the city centre with nightlife (see p.197) and accommodation (see p.158) within easy walking distance of one another.

MOWBRAY AND ROSEBANK

Map 3, H6–7. Mowbray & Rosebank stations.

Heading along Station Road, away from the mountain and south of Observatory, is **Mowbray**, originally and gruesomely called Drie Koppen (Three Heads), after the heads of three slaves were impaled there in 1724; its name was changed in the 1840s. In the nineteenth century, this was the home of philologist Willem Bleek, who lived with a group of Khoisan convicts provided by the colonial authorities, so that he could study their languages and world-view. Bleek's pioneering work still forms the basis of much of what we know about traditional San (Bushman) life.

Rosebank, to Mowbray's south, has a substantial student community, some resident in the so-called Tampax Towers, the unmistakable circular blocks on Main Road. Just beyond them is the brown-brick **Baxter Theatre**, on the corner of Woolsack and Main roads, one of Cape Town's premier arts complexes (see p.216). Heading west up Woolsack Road, after about 400m the road leads to the back of **Mostert's Mill** (daily 9am–5pm; free), which incongruously faces onto the busy M3 freeway. A real Dutch-style windmill with sails, built in 1796, it harks back to the days when there were wheat fields here instead of roads.

UCT Irma Stern Museum

Map 3, H7. Tues–Sat 10am–5pm; R7. Rosebank station.

Irma Stern is acknowledged as one of South Africa's pioneering twentieth-century artists, perhaps more for the fact that she brought modern European ideas to the colonies than anything else. The **UCT Irma Stern Museum** on Cecil Road, about 100m from Mostert's Mill, was the artist's home for 38 years until her death in 1966. It's definitely worth a visit to see Stern's collection of Iberian,

African, oriental and ancient artefacts; the whole house, in fact, reflects the artist's fascination with exoticism, starting with her own Gauguinesque paintings of "native types", the fantastic carved doors she brought back from Zanzibar and the very untypical garden that brings a touch of the tropics to Cape Town with its exuberant bamboo thickets and palm trees.

Born in 1894 in the South African backwater town of Schweitzer-Reneke to German-Jewish parents, Stern studied at Germany's Weimar Academy, against whose conservatism she reacted. She adopted **expressionist distortion** in her paintings, some of which were included in the *Neue Sezession* exhibition in Berlin in 1918. Stern went on several expeditions into Zanzibar and the Congo in the 1940s and 1950s, where she found the source for her intensely sensuous paintings. One of her most famous works is the much-reproduced *The Eternal Child* (1916), a simple but vibrant portrait of a young girl, while *The Wood Carriers* (1951) uses raw ochres, browns and oranges to create an exoticized portrayal of a pair of African women.

Although Stern's work was appreciated in Europe, when she returned to South Africa after World War II, critics claimed that her style was simply a cover for technical incompetence. Indeed, her paintings shocked contemporary South Africa, but the country's art historians now regard her as the central figure of her generation.

RONDEBOSCH AND AROUND

Map 3, H7. Rosebank & Rondebosch stations.

South of Rosebank, neighbouring **Rondebosch** is home to the **University of Cape Town** (UCT), handsomely festooned with creepers and sitting grandly on the mountainside, overlooking Main Road and the M3 highway. Of passing interest on the UCT campus is **The Woolsack**, just off Woolsack Road, a "cottage in the woods for poets and artists" designed in 1900 by Sir Herbert Baker for Cecil John Rhodes, who invited **Rudyard Kipling** "to hang up his hat there" whenever he visited the Cape. Taking his friend at his word, Kipling fled the English winter every year from 1900 to 1907, bringing his family to Cape Town and spending five to six months at The Woolsack, where it's said he wrote his famous poem *If*. The house is now occupied by the University's architecture faculty.

For more on Cecil Rhodes and the history of Cape Town, see p.318.

Rhodes features big in this neck of the woods; if you continue south from The Woolsack down the M3 (known here as Rhodes Drive), you'll pass **Groote Schuur**, another house built for him. One of Herbert Baker's most celebrated South African buildings, Groote Schuur exemplifies the Cape Dutch Revival style, which combined Cape vernacular elements with ideas from the Arts and Crafts Movement, then current in Baker's native Britain: it established a basis for what became seen as a local architectural idiom. Groote Schuur became the official prime ministerial (then presidential) residence of the Cape, though Nelson Mandela preferred to stay at the adjacent **Genadendal**. Neither building is open to the public.

The Rhodes Memorial

Map 3, H6. Daily dawn to dusk; free. Rosebank station.

North of the Upper Campus of the University of Cape Town, towards the city, is **Rhodes Memorial**, built to resemble a Greek temple and grandiosely conspicuous against the slopes of Devil's Peak. The monument is reached via a signposted road that spurs northwest off the

M3 just as Rhodes Drive becomes the Princess Anne Interchange. On a site chosen by Herbert Baker and Rudyard Kipling, the temple-like structure celebrates Cecil Rhodes' energy with a sculpture of a horse rearing up wildly. The empire-builder's bust is planted at the top of a towering set of stairs, lined with reclining lions inspired by the Avenue of Sphinxes at Karnak in Egypt, a site greatly admired by Rhodes. Carved in stone beneath the bust, a ponderous inscription by Kipling reads: "The immense and brooding spirit still shall order and control."

The *Rhodes Memorial Restaurant*, is a popular and recommended venue for breakfast or lunch with terrific views of Cape Town.

Equally eye-catching are the herds of wildebeest and zebra, which nonchalantly graze in the Rhodes Estate on the slopes around the Memorial as cars fly past on the M3. From here you can walk to the King's Blockhouse, formerly a signalling station, and on to the Contour Path, one of the major Table Mountain walking routes, which follows the eastern side of the mountain, way above the southern suburbs and Kirstenbosch Gardens to Constantia Nek (see "Table Mountain walks" on p.94).

South of Rondebosch

Map 2, E3–4. Newlands & Claremont stations.

Continuing **south from Rondebosch** along the M3 (here called the Van der Stel Freeway), or along the more congested Main Road, you pass some of Cape Town's most prestigious suburbs. **Newlands**, almost merging with Rondebosch, is home to the city's famous rugby and cricket stadiums, while the well-heeled suburb of **Claremont** to its south is becoming an alternative to the city centre and the Waterfront for shopping and entertainment, with two cinema complexes and several malls. Alongside the high-quality shops, hawkers sell clothes, vegetables and herbs; closer to Claremont Station you can buy tasty *boerewors* rolls from women who cook them outdoors on *skottel braais* (gas braziers).

A little further on, **Bishopscourt**, as its name suggests, is home to the Anglican bishop of Cape Town; Archbishop Desmond Tutu lived here when it was a whites-only suburb. Partly because of its prime site next to Kirstenbosch National Botanical Gardens – some plots have views of both the forested mountainside and the sea – this is one of the most prestigious areas in Cape Town; a number of consuls occupy huge properties behind forbiddingly high walls. Further down the line, **Wynberg** is known for the open-air Maynardville Theatre (see p.216) and quaint little rows of shops and eating places.

KIRSTENBOSCH NATIONAL BOTANICAL GARDENS

Map 2, D4. April–Aug 8am–6pm, Sept–March 8am–7pm; R15.
Shuttle bus from Cape Town Tourism.

Five kilometres south of Rondebosch, on Rhodes Avenue, are the popular **Kirstenbosch National Botanical Gardens**. The gardens are magnificent, glorying in lush shrubs and exuberant blooms, which trail off into **fynbos**, covering a huge expanse of the rugged eastern slopes and wooded ravines of Table Mountain. The setting is quite breathtaking – this is a great place to have tea and stroll around gazing up the mountain, or to wander onto the paths, which meander steeply to the top.

If you don't have a car and don't want to take an organized tour, the best way to get to Kirstenbosch is on one of the **buses** operated from Cape Town Tourism (℡021-426-4266; departures on demand during visitor centre opening hours; R35 one way). Alternatively you'll have to rely on one of the local taxi services (see p.22). If you're driving, take the M5, and leave it at the signposted Rhodes Avenue turnoff. There's no train.

Kirstenbosch is the oldest and largest botanical garden in South Africa, and was created by **Cecil Rhodes** in 1895 (his camphor and fig trees still flourish). Today, over 22,000 indigenous plants, and a research unit and library, attract researchers and botanists from all over the world. There's a nursery selling local plants, while characteristic Cape plants, found nowhere else in the world, are cultivated on the slopes. Little signboards and paved paths guide you through the highlights of the gardens, with trees and plants identified by tags. One unusual route is the one created for visually impaired visitors, with labels in Braille and an abundance of aromatic and textured plants.

The cultivated gardens blend seamlessly into the mountainside, as there are no fences cutting off the way to the top of **Table Mountain**. From here, you can make your way up the mountain: two popular paths, starting from the Contour Path above Kirstenbosch, are **Nursery Ravine** and **Skeleton Gorge** (see p.98).

Kirstenbosch is wonderful for picnics; if you're in town over the summer, bring a bottle of Cape fizz to one of the Sunday evening open-air concerts held in the gardens (see p.248).
There's also a good restaurant with outdoor seating for breakfasts, lunches, teas and good coffee (see p.248).

CONSTANTIA AND ITS WINELANDS

Map 2, C5 & D4–5.

South of Kirstenbosch lie the elegant suburbs of **Constantia** and the Cape's oldest **winelands**. Luxuriating

FYNBOS AND THE CAPE FLORAL KINGDOM

Early Dutch settlers were alarmed by the paucity of good timber on the Cape Peninsula's hillsides, which were covered by nondescript, scrubby bush they described as *fijn bosch* (literally "fine bush") and which is now known by its Afrikaans name **fynbos** (pronounced "fayn-bos"). They set about planting exotics, like the oaks that now shade central Cape Town, and over the ensuing centuries their descendants established pine forests on the sides of Table Mountain in an effort to create a landscape that fulfilled the European idea of the picturesque. It's only relatively recently that Capetonians have come to claim fynbos proudly as part of the peninsula's unique natural heritage.

You'll see fynbos all over Cape Town, and especially on the mountainsides. Remarkable for its astonishing variety of plants, it makes up eighty percent of the vegetation of the **Cape Floral Kingdom**, the smallest and richest of the world's six floral kingdoms; its 8500 species make it one of the global biodiversity hot spots. The Cape Peninsula alone, measuring less than 500 square kilometres, has 2256 plant species (nearly twice as many as Britain, which is 5000 times bigger). While the other five floral kingdoms cover vast areas such as Australia or the northern hemisphere, the entire Cape kingdom stretches across a relatively narrow coastal crescent. And despite the rather unpromising grey-green appearance from afar of the Cape Town mountainsides, if you get into the fynbos at any time of year (although spring and summer are the best times) you'll encounter countless beautiful little flowering shrubs.

The four basic types of fynbos are: **proteas**, South Africa's national flower which you'll see sold in bouquets at the airport if nowhere else; **ericas**, which comprise 600 species of heather (there are just 26 in the rest of the world); **restios**, or reeds; and **geophytes**, including ground orchids and the startling flaming red disas, which flower on Table Mountain in late summer.

CONSTANTIA AND ITS WINELANDS

on the lower slopes of Table Mountain and the Constantiaberg, with tantalizing views of False Bay, the winelands are a thirty-minute drive from the centre off the M3, which runs south to Muizenberg.

The winelands started cultivated life in 1685 as the farm of **Simon van der Stel**, the governor charged with opening up the fledgling Dutch colony to the interior. Thrusting himself wholeheartedly into the task, he selected an enormous tract of the choicest land set against the Constantiaberg, the section of the peninsula just south of Table Mountain. Today, Constantia is Cape Town's oldest and most prestigious residential area, exuding the easy ambience of landed wealth, shaded by oak forests and punctuated with farm stalls, riding schools, designer Cape Dutch-style shopping centres and, of course, the vineyards.

Constantia grapes have been used for winemaking since van der Stel's first ouput in 1705. After his death in 1712, the estate was divided up and sold off as the modern **Groot Constantia**, **Buitenverwachting** and **Klein Constantia** vineyards. All three estates are open to the public and offer tastings – they're definitely worth devoting a few hours to, especially if you aren't heading further afield to the Winelands proper. Smaller in scale than Groot Constantia, Buitenverwachting and Klein Constantia both offer free wine tasting in less regimented conditions than at the bigger estate.

The Cape Winelands proper around the towns of Stellenbosch, Paarl and Franschhoek are covered on pp.280–307.

GETTING TO THE WINERIES

There is no public **transport** to Constantia, but Groot Constantia features on most organized **tours** of Cape Town or the peninsula; see p.28. To get to the estates **by car**, take the signposted Groot Constantia off-ramp from the M3 onto Ladies Mile Extension, and follow the signs to Groot Constantia. Buitenverwachting and Klein Constantia are on Klein Constantia Road, just off Ladies Mile Extension, and are clearly signposted.

Groot Constantia

Map 2, D5. Museum daily 10am–5pm; R8. Cellar tours and wine tasting (booking essential ☏021-794-5128, ⓦwww.museums.org.za/grootcon): April–Sept 11am & 3pm; Oct–March daily every hour 10am–4pm; R20. Wine tasting only: May–Nov daily 10am–4.30pm; Dec–Apr daily 9am–6pm; R14. Grounds free.

The largest Cape Town wine estate and the one most geared to tourists is **Groot Constantia**, a National Monument and satellite of the Cultural History Museum. Apart from having beautiful buildings and delightful gardens, it offers enough attractions in its museum, shop, cellar and two restaurants to justify a half-day visit.

Built in 1692, the **manor house**, a quintessential Cape Dutch building, was van der Stel's home, modified at the end of the eighteenth century, possibly by the French architect Thibault. It's thought that the magnificent gables were added in the eighteenth or early nineteenth centuries, with an allegorical figure representing Abundance recessed into a niche in the central gable. The interior forms part of the **museum** and is decorated in a style typical of eighteenth- and nineteenth-century Cape landowners, containing interesting Neoclassical as well as Louis XV and XVI furniture and Delft and Chinese ceramics.

If you walk straight through the house and down the ceremonial axis, you'll come to the so-called **cellar** (actually a two-storey building above ground), fronted by a brilliant relief pediment. Attributed to the sculptor Anton Anreith, it depicts riotous bacchanalia, featuring Ganymede in a scene that symbolizes winemaking. Inside, you can see the collection of wine-related objects dating from antiquity – such as amphoras – to the present.

Booking is essential for tours of the modern production cellar, but if you only want to taste and buy you're free to pop in to the **Bertrams Cellar** tasting room, where you should sample their flagship Governeurs Reserve, a red whose blend varies from vintage to vintage, and their Shiraz Reserve. The best whites include the Chardonnay Reserve, Sauvignon Blanc and Weisser Riesling.

The estate's informal and child-friendly *Tavern Restaurant* has outdoor seating and a kids' playground; the more formal *Jonkershuis* is described on p.178.

Buitenverwachting

Map 2, D5. Mon–Fri 9am–5pm, Sat 9am–1pm; free.

Buitenverwachting (roughly pronounced: bay-tin-fur-vuch-ting, with the "ch" as in the Scottish rendition of loch), on Klein Constantia Road, is a bucolic place in the middle of the suburbs, with sheep and cattle grazing in the fields as you approach the main buildings. Ducks, part of the environmentally friendly approach, are used for pest control – feeding on snails that prey on vines – while around the main buildings you might also spot a fine pig, contributing to the beautifully manicured gardens by nibbling at the lawns.

The **architecture** and setting at the foot of the Constantiaberg are as good reasons to come here as are the top-ranking wines. Overlooking the vineyards and backing onto the garden, the homestead was built in 1794 (the 1769 on the gable appears to be wrong) by Arend Brink, and features an unusual gabled pediment broken with an urn motif. Buitenverwachting produces some of South Africa's best **wines**, among them the classy Christine, a claret-style blend, and some excellent whites including their Sauvignon Blanc, Chardonnay and Rhine Riesling.

Despite deep historic roots, the estate is mould-breaking and has for many years provided its workers with some of the best living conditions of any South African farm. Unusual labour practices include the provision of two social workers, weekly visits by a doctor to the farm clinic and worker involvement in the selection of new staff.

This estate excels at food as well as wine and the *Buitenverwachting Restaurant* (see p.186) is a hot spot for a meal. They also do luxury picnic lunches (Nov–Apr Mon–Sat 12.30–2.30pm; R65; booking essential – contact Sue ☏021-794-2122 or 082-973-8543), which you can enjoy under the oaks in their fabulous gardens.

Klein Constantia

Map 2, C5. Mon–Fri 9am–5pm, Sat 9am–1pm; free.

Klein Constantia, Klein Constantia Road (just over a kilometre west of Buitenverwachting), has a friendly atmosphere, despite its slightly austere Cape Dutch exterior, and produces some fine wines. Something of a cult curiosity is its **Vin de Constance**, the recreation of an eighteenth-century Constantia beverage that was a favourite of Napoleon, Frederick the Great and Bismarck. It's a delicious dessert wine with a hefty price tag attached, packaged in a replica of the original bottle, and makes a novel souvenir. Apart from this, the estate shines through its **white wine** output, producing top-ranking Sauvignon Blanc, Semillon and Rhine Riesling. As well as wine, there's wildlife here: look out for the guinea fowl that roam the estate munching on beetles, and in summer you may see migrant steppe buzzards preying on unsuspecting starlings, which eat the grapes.

TOKAI

Effectively the southern extension of Constantia, forested **Tokai** is an excellent area for leafy recreation away from the centre, with some relaxed and child-friendly places for eating and drinking. To drive to Tokai from the centre of Cape Town, head south along the M3 and exit north onto Ladies Mile Road; continue for 100m before turning south into Spaanschemat River Road, which runs through the suburb.

You can easily combine Tokai with a trip to the seaside, as the suburb is fifteen minutes' drive from the False Bay seaboard. Because it's protected from the winds, it also makes a good refuge when the southeaster blows.

Tokai Forest

Map 2, C6. Daily dawn to dusk.

Most people come out to Tokai for the well-marked hiking paths and mountain biking trails in the pine plantations of the **Tokai Forest**. You can get there along the M3 or Spaanschemat River Road (which becomes Orpen Road) – then turn west from either into Tokai Road, which leads straight to the forest. About 1.2km from the M3 or 500m from Spaanschemat River Road, the road first passes through a forested section, equipped with picnic tables, though this isn't the nicest part of the forest or the best place to picnic. Instead keep on till you reach the Arboretum (see below).

A little further along the road from the picnic sites, you'll come to an opening in the forest occupied by **Tokai Manor House** (not open to the public). Designed by Louis Michel Thibault (see p.333) and built around 1795, this National Monument is an elegant gem of Cape Dutch architecture surrounded by trees, and combines the Cape Dutch style with the understated elegance of French Neoclassicism.

A hundred metres to its west lies the entrance to another National Monument, the historic plantation of trees that constitute the **Tokai Arboretum** (daily dusk to dawn; R2 donation), which has a car park and is the best place to begin rambling or have tea and scones at the thatched **café** close to the entrance gate. The arboretum is the work of Joseph Storr Lister, who was a nineteenth-century Conservator of Forests for the Cape Colony. In 1885 he experimented with planting 150 species of trees from temperate countries, with oaks and eucalyptus featuring extensively as well some beautiful California redwoods. Storr discovered that conifers were best suited to the Cape, which is why the plantation to the west of the arboretum, owned by the Safcol timber company, consists mainly of pines.

Several tracks and trails crisscross the arboretum and plantation providing easy walks and mountain biking trails (bring your own bike). There are several longer hikes, including the walk from the entrance gate to **Elephant's Eye Cave** (6km). This can easily be completed in well under three hours, and passes through beautiful moist woodland, before opening into montane fynbos that covers the slopes of the Constantiaberg, eventually leading to the

TOKAI

THE CAPE FLATS

Flat, barren and windswept, Cape Town's largest residential area, taking in the coloured districts, African townships and shanty-town squatter camps, is unavoidable as it stretches east from the former whites-only southern suburbs. Exclusively inhabited by Africans and coloureds in separate areas, the Flats can be both shocking and heartening, their abject poverty coexisting with a spirit of enterprise and stoicism.

Several projects are under way to encourage tourists into the townships but with crime a concern, the recommended way to visit is on one of the **tours** listed on p.29, operated by residents of the Cape Flats or in co-operation with local communities, and emphasizing face-to-face encounters with ordinary people. What you see depends on the interests of the tour group, but could include: visits to shebeens, nightclubs and a township restaurant; chats to residents of squatter camps and the Langa hostels; and meetings with traditional healers and music makers, township artists and craft-workers. Some tours also take in "sites of political struggle", where significant events in the fight against apartheid occurred.

African townships were set up as dormitories to provide labour for white Cape Town, not as places to build a life, which is why they had no facilities and no real hub. **Men-only hostels**, another apartheid relic, are at the root of many of the area's social problems. During the 1950s, the government set out a blueprint to turn the tide of Africans flooding into Cape Town. No African was permitted to settle permanently in the Cape west of a line near the Fish River (the old frontier between the Cape Colony and the Xhosa chiefdoms in the nineteenth century), over 1000km from Cape Town. Women were entirely banned from seeking work in the city and men prohibited from bringing their wives to join them. By 1970, there were ten men for every woman in Langa.

TOKAI

In the end, apartheid failed to prevent the influx of work-seekers desperate to come to Cape Town. Where people couldn't find legal accommodation they set up **squatter camps** of makeshift iron, cardboard and plastic sheeting. During the 1970s and 1980s, the government attempted to eradicate these by demolishing them, but they soon reappeared, and are now a permanent feature. One of the best known is **Crossroads**, whose inhabitants suffered campaigns of harassment that included killings and continuous attempts to bulldoze it out of existence. Through sheer determination – and no little desperation – its residents hung on and eventually won the right to stay. Today, the government is making attempts to improve conditions in the shanty towns by bringing in running water and sanitation: facilities are starting to improve, families are moving in and traders are beginning to operate.

Langa, east of the white suburb of Pinelands and north of the N2, is the oldest and most central township. In this grey and shapeless place, women sell sheep and goat heads, alongside entrepreneurs running state-of-the-art phone bureaux. Middle-class black families live in smart suburban houses while, in former men-only hostels, as many as three families share one room.

South of the African ghettos is **Mitchell's Plain**, a coloured area stretching down to the False Bay coast. More salubrious than any black township, Mitchell's Plain reflects how lighter skins meant better conditions under apartheid. But for coloureds the forced removals were also tragic, many being summarily forced to vacate family homes because their suburb had been declared a White Group Area. Many families were relocated here when District Six was razed (see p.72), and their communities never fully recovered, resulting in the violent gangs which have become an everyday part of Mitchell's Plain youth culture.

TOKAI

●

115

cave, which offers terrific panoramas. Ask for a map and directions at the entrance gate or, if this is unattended, at the adjacent café.

Steenberg Vineyards

Map 2, D6. Tasting and sales: March–Aug Mon–Fri 8.30am–4.30pm; Sept–Feb Mon–Fri 8.30am–4.30pm, Sat 9am–1pm; free.

In a fabulous location at the foot of Steenberg mountain, the **Steenberg Vineyards** comprise a fine Cape Dutch manor house and three other farm buildings, set around a large formal garden dating from 1695. This is South Africa's oldest wine estate: the lands were granted by Governor Simon van der Stel to the five-times widowed Catherina Michelse in 1682 and sold on in 1695 to Frederik Roussouw. That year Roussouw erected the first buildings and made the first wine on the estate. After his death, his widow Christina Diemer turned it into a highly profitable business providing hospitality to travellers and provisions to the fleet when the VOC declared Simon's Town its winter port in 1741. It is now one of Cape Town's best country hotels, using the refurbished buildings that were declared a National Monument in 1996. Of their wines, the fine Merlot is the best of their reds and, when it comes to whites, the Sauvignon Blanc and Semillon stand out.

For refreshments, the Barnyard Farmstall, just outside the winery gate, does excellent coffee and tasty snacks, and has a kids' playground (see p.240).

TOKAI

The Atlantic seaboard

able Mountain's steep drop into the ocean along much of the western peninsula forces the generally upmarket suburbs along the Atlantic seaboard to cling dramatically to the slopes. The sea washing the west side of the peninsula can be very chilly, far colder than on the False Bay seaboard, but there's consolation in the dramatic coastal roads, particularly beyond Sea Point. The coast itself consists of a series of bays and white-sand beaches, edged with smoothly sculpted rocks; inland, the series of rocky buttresses known as the Twelve Apostles gaze down onto the surf. The beaches are ideal for sunbathing or sunset picnics – it's from this side of the peninsula that you can watch the sun sink into the ocean, creating fiery reflections on the sea.

MOUILLE POINT AND GREEN POINT

Map 5. Sea Point & V & A Waterfront buses.

Just to the west of the V & A Waterfront, Mouille Point and its close neighbour, Green Point, are among the sub-

CHAPTER 5 • THE ATLANTIC SEABOARD

1.17

urbs closest to the city centre. **Mouille Point** is known principally for its squat, rectangular, Victorian Green Point lighthouse, commissioned in the 1820s, and painted, just like a children's picture-book lighthouse, with diagonal red and white stripes. The recent opening of entrances directly connecting Mouille Point with the Waterfront has helped regenerate the suburb and has integrated the Waterfront with its neighbouring suburbs and some seriously upmarket hotels along Granger Bay Street.

Mouille Point merges with the far larger suburb of **Green Point**, which continues both inland from it and west along the ragged Atlantic shore. Over the last couple of years Green Point's proximity to the Waterfront, which is an easy ten-or-so-minute walk away, and its position along the coast has turned it from a slightly alarming red-light district into a humming area of accommodation, eateries and clubs.

Inland, at the foot of Signal Hill is **De Waterkant**, a quarter of terraced Cape cottages next to the Bo-Kaap, established in the 1700s to house artisans and freed slaves. Only three blocks by three, it has now been turned into a trendy district of bright tourist accommodation, narrow streets and corner cafés. Defining its eastern edge, Somerset Road and its continuation, Main Road, in Green Point has become one of Cape Town's principal gay strips, where numerous establishments fly the multicoloured gay flag.

SEA POINT AND BANTRY BAY

Map 6. Sea Point buses.

Continuing southwest along Main Road, Green Point merges with **Sea Point**, a long-established place for great restaurants. Middle-class couples, pram-pushing mothers, street kids and drunks create an uneasy blend of respectability and seediness that dissipates as you move into Bantry

Bay and the wealthier suburbs down the Atlantic seaboard.

The closest seaside to the city centre is a block down from Main Road, although it's too rocky for swimming. Halfway along the kilometre-long beach promenade, running alongside Beach Road, you'll catch views of **Graaff's Pool**, an institutionalized and exclusively male nudist spot, while at the Olympic-sized **outdoor pool** further along the coast at the Sea Point Pavilion, you can swim alongside the crashing surf.

At the westernmost edge of Sea Point, is **Bantry Bay**, combining the density of Sea Point with the wealth of the Atlantic suburbs and consisting of large upmarket resort hotels and self-catering apartment blocks away from the sleaze of Sea Point, but close enough should you want to walk to a restaurant.

Sea Point and Green Point are the closest suburbs to both the city and the sea and are dense with accommodation, which you'll find listed on pp.154–8.

CLIFTON TO SANDY BAY

Map 2. Hout Bay bus.

Suburbia proper begins south of Sea Point at Bantry Bay. Fashionable **Clifton** (C2), on the next cove, is sheltered by Lion's Head: the sea here is good for surfing and safe for swimming, but bone-chillingly cold. Clifton is studded with fabulous seaside apartments and has four wonderful sandy beaches, full of beautiful people in the summer, and each with a different and changing character. All are reached via steep stairways, meaning that Fourth, with the fewest steps, has become the favourite for parents with kids in tow.

A little to the south, the **Camps Bay** (C3) suburb climbs

the slopes of Table Mountain and is scooped into a small amphitheatre, bounded by the Lion's Head and the Twelve Apostles sections of the Table Mountain range. This, and the high views across the Atlantic, make Camps Bay one of the most desirable places to live in Cape Town. The main drag, Victoria Road, skirts the coast and is packed with trendy restaurants, while the wide sandy beach is accessible by bus and is enjoyed by families of all colours. Lined by a row of palms and with welcome shade for picnics, Camps Bay beach positively throngs around the Christmas and Easter breaks, despite the chilly waters.

There's little development between Camps Bay and **Llandudno** (B4), a wonderful cove 17km from Cape Town along Victoria Road (not served by public transport; the small car park spills over into the suburban streets at peak periods). A steep and narrow road winds down past very smart homes to the shore, where the sandy beach is punctuated at either end by magnificent granite boulders and rock formations. This is a good sunbathing spot and a choice one for bring-your-own sundowners.

Isolated **Sandy Bay** (B5), Cape Town's main nudist beach, can only be reached via a twenty-minute walk from Llandudno. In the apartheid days the South African police went to ingenious lengths to trap nudists, but nowadays the beach is relaxed. To get there, take the path from the south end of the Llandudno car park, through fynbos vegetation (see p.107) and across some rocks to the beach. It's a fairly easy walk, but watch out for broken glass – and bring your own food supplies, as there are no facilities of any kind.

HOUT BAY

Map 2, B–C5. City–Bakoven/Hout Bay bus.

Hout Bay is at a convenient junction for the rest of the peninsula and has the highest concentration of places to stay south of Sea Point. From Cape Town it's a twenty-one-kilometre trip either along the coast or inland via Constantia.

Although not the quaint fishing village it once was, Hout Bay still has a functioning **harbour** and is the centre of the local crayfish industry. And, despite ugly modern development and a growing shanty town, the natural setting is quite awesome. Next to the harbour and car park, the little **Mariner's Wharf** waterfront development shelters the Seafood Emporium, which has an upstairs restaurant and sells fresh fish – it's a good place to pick up fresh snoek, a Western Cape speciality.

The sea off the long slender beach is no good for swimming – too cold, too close to the harbour and too prone to fish scales floating in its surf – but the beach is perfect for walking. Away from the harbour, the **Hout Bay Museum**, 4 St Andrews Road (Tues–Fri 8.30am–4.30pm; R5), offers good exhibits on the Strandlopers (Khoisan people who hunted and gathered along the shore) and the local fishing industry.

World of Birds

Map 2, C5. Daily 9am–5pm; R30, children R20; ☎021-290-2730.

Inland from Hout Bay, **World of Birds** on Valley Road offers a great chance to see unusual species such as African blue cranes and Australian cassowaries in huge walk-through aviaries. There's also a wildlife sanctuary, as well as a children's "touch" farmyard and bird-feeding sessions throughout the day. The café and restaurant serve light lunches, or you can picnic at the Flamingo Terrace.

Alternatively, go down to the estuary near the harbour to see local birds in their natural environment for free; kingfishers and blacksmith plovers are commonly sighted residents.

HOUT BAY

CHAPMAN'S PEAK DRIVE

Map 2, C6.

Continuing south from Hout Bay, **Chapman's Peak Drive** is a thrilling journey – one of the most beautiful drives in the world. For 10km the road carves into the mountainside on the one side, dropping hundreds of precipitous metres to the ocean on the other. Unceasingly spectacular views take in the breadth of Hout Bay to the 331-metre high Sentinel, which sits on a curved outcrop. **Viewpoints** are provided along the route, but take care in high winds as it can be dangerous, with occasional rockfalls, one of which forced the authorities to close the road for over two years from the beginning of 2000.

NOORDHOEK, KOMMETJIE AND SCARBOROUGH

Noordhoek (Map 2, B7), a low-key settlement at the end of the descent from Chapman's Peak Drive, consists of small-holdings in a gentle valley, its long white beach stretching 3km across Chapman's Bay to Kommetjie. The sands are fantastic for walking and horse-riding, but can be whipped up fiercely when the southeaster blows. Swimming is hazardous, though surfers relish the rough waters around the rocks to the north. For refreshment, the only place around here is the excellent *Red Herring* **restaurant** (see p.189), about ten minutes on foot from the car park as you head away from the sea, with fine views from its outdoor deck.

Although it's only a few kilometres south of Noordhoek along the beach, getting to **Kommetjie** by road involves a fifteen-kilometre haul inland up the peninsula spine south along Noordhoek Road, taking a west turn into Kommetjie Road, to descend again. The beach's small basin (*kommetjie*), which is always a few degrees above the surrounding sea temperature, is perfect for swimming. Just to its north, Long Beach is a favourite **surfing** spot used by devotees even during the chilly winter months.

Almost 10km by road from Kommetjie, the developing village of **Scarborough** is the most far-flung suburb along the peninsula. A long wide beach edges temptingly to its south just beyond Schusters River Lagoon – resist the potentially treacherous sea and stick to the lagoon. The *Camel Rock* is a decent place to stop and eat.

**For more about surfing, see
"Sports and outdoor activities" on p.224.**

NOORDHOEK, KOMMETJIE AND SCARBOROUGH

The False Bay seaboard

False Bay, on the east coast of the peninsula, is Cape Town's longest-established and most popular seaside development, its waters several degrees warmer than those on the Atlantic seaboard. A series of village-like suburbs, served by the Metrorail, backs onto the mountains – from Muizenberg down to Simon's Town. The most characterful of these places is **Kalk Bay**, which has a small working harbour, a string of intriguing shops, some good cafés and the *Brass Bell*, a great seaside pub-restaurant. Fish Hoek, otherwise drab, has a lovely bathing beach, while **Simon's Town**, one of South Africa's oldest settlements, is worth taking in as a day-trip and makes a good base for visiting the Cape of Good Hope section of the Cape Peninsula National Park and Cape Point. A wilderness area, the reserve is an excellent place to see fynbos as well as Cape wildlife (baboons, seals and antelope species such as the horse-sized bontebok), while, at dramatic Cape Point, the cliffs drop down to an angry sea.

MUIZENBERG

Map 2, E7. Muizenberg station.

Once South Africa's most fashionable beachfront, today **Muizenberg** (pronounced mew-zin-burg) has become rather tacky, although plans are in the pipeline to upgrade and restore it. Brightly coloured bathing huts are reminders of a more elegant heyday, when it was visited by the likes of Agatha Christie, who enjoyed riding its waves while holidaying here in the 1920s: "Whenever we could steal time off," she wrote, "we got out our surf boards and went surfing."

Despite the slight air of tawdriness, Muizenberg's gently shelving sandy **beach** is the most popular along the peninsula for swimming – with reason. It's safe, the water tends to be warm and there's good surfing, plus a pavilion complex around the car park featuring tea shops, a waterslide and minigolf. Along the beachfront and Main Road you'll also find shops, cafés and restaurants catering to the seaside trade.

A paved coastal path ribbons along the ocean from Muizenberg to St James (1.5km); it's a perfect way to take in the stupendous views across the bay, and conveniently passes the Natale Labia Museum (see p.127) for refreshment.

THE HISTORICAL MILE

Map 2, E7–8. Muizenberg & St James stations.

Striking out south from Muizenberg, Main Road and the railway line hug the shore all the way to Simon's Town. A short stretch, starting at Muizenberg station, is known as the **Historical Mile**, dotted with notable buildings and easily explored on foot. **Muizenberg station**, an Edwardian-style edifice completed in 1913, is now a National Monument, while further towards Simon's Town

WHALE-WATCHING SITES

Cape Town's finest whale-watching sites are on the warm False Bay side, but it's worth noting that there are more spectacular spotting opportunities east of Cape Town, especially around Hermanus (see p.260). The best time of year for sightings is August to October and you'll need binoculars to get a decent view – look out for whale signboards indicating the best places to spend time looking for them. The commonest whales along this section of coast are southern rights (see box on p.264).

Boyes Drive, running along the mountainside behind Muizenberg and Kalk Bay, provides an outstanding vantage point. To get there by car, head out on the M3 from the city centre to Muizenberg, taking a sharp right into Boyes Drive at Lakeside, from where the road begins to climb, descending finally to join Main Road between Kalk Bay and Fish Hoek. Alternatively, sticking close to the shore along Main Road, the stretch between Fish Hoek and Simon's Town is recommended, with a particularly nice spot above the rocks at the south end of Fish Hoek Beach, as you head south towards Glencairn. Boulders Beach at the southern end of Simon's Town has a whale signboard, and smooth rocky outcrops from which to gaze out over the sea. Even better vantage points are further down the coast between Simon's Town and Smitswinkelbaai, where the road goes higher along the mountainside.

Without a car, it's easy enough to go by train to Fish Hoek or Simon's Town and whale-spot from the Jager's Walk beach path that runs along the coast from the beachfront restaurant at Fish Hoek to Simon's Town.

Information on exactly where whales have been sighted in the past 24 hours is available from the Whale Watch Hotline (☏083-910-1028).

is the **Posthuys**, a rugged whitewashed and thatched building dating from 1673 and a fine example of the Cape vernacular style.

Natale Labia Museum

Map 2, E7. Tues–Sun 10am–5pm; R5; ℡021-788-4106, Ⓦwww.museums.org.za/natale. Muizenberg station.

Most idiosyncratic of the buildings along the Historical Mile is the **Natale Labia Museum**, 192 Main Road, completed in 1930 as the residence of the Italian consul. Built in eighteenth-century Venetian style, it sits incongruously in the Main Road townscape. Inside, heavy lace obscures the magnificent view, but the museum is a satellite of the South African National Gallery and often has strong exhibitions of work from their permanent collection. An excellent **restaurant** serves up breakfasts, light meals and teas in the ersatz-Baroque interior or on the Italianate patio.

Rhodes' Cottage Museum

Map 2, E7. Tues–Sun 9.30am–4.30pm; free. St James or Muizenberg station.

The **Rhodes' Cottage Museum**, to the south of the Natale Labia Museum, was the home of Cecil Rhodes, bought by him in 1899. He died at this unassuming little building in 1902 before his grander dwelling, neighbouring Rust en Vrede (closed to the public) could be completed. Rhodes' Cottage paints a distinctly rosy portrait of the man, with photographs and a model of the Big Hole in Kimberley (where Rhodes made his fortune at the diamond diggings). Also on display is a curious diorama of World's View in Zimbabwe's Matopos Hills, where Rhodes lies buried.

THE HISTORICAL MILE

February 1902 was a particularly hot month in Cape Town and the asthmatic Rhodes, finding it difficult to breath at Groote Schuur, his grand house in Newlands, asked to be moved to his cottage in Muizenberg, where he could be cooled by the sea breezes. Even Muizenberg became unbearable, and Rhodes decided to return to England on March 26 – the day he died.

ST JAMES

Map 2, D8. St James station.

St James, 2km south of Muizenberg and just one stop away by train, is far more upmarket than its northern neighbour, and its pleasing villagey feel makes it a nice place to hop off the train. The compact beach draws considerable character from its much-photographed Victorian-style bathing huts, whose primary colours catch your eye as you pass by road or rail. The rocky beaches here don't make for great sea swimming, although it's always sheltered from the wind and there's a tidal pool that is safe for toddlers and fun for bathing at high tide, when enormous breakers crash over the sea wall. If you're feeling energetic you can also wander up the steep pedestrian-only thoroughfares that connect Main Road with Boyes Drive, of which Jacob's Ladder, lined with attractive Victorian holiday houses, is particularly quaint. From Boyes Drive you can take one of the several marked routes onto the Kalk Bay and Muizenberg mountains behind the coast, and part of the Silvermine Nature Reserve.

KALK BAY

Map 2, D8. Kalk Bay station.

Kalk Bay, one of the most southerly and smallest of Cape

Town's suburbs, is a lively **working harbour** with wooden fishing vessels, mountain views and a shopping precinct packed with trendy coffee shops, antique dealers and curiosity shops.

Apart from the larger Hout Bay, Kalk Bay is the only harbour settlement still worked by coloured fishermen; the suburb somehow managed to slip through the net of the Group Areas Act, making it one of the few places on the peninsula with an intact coloured community. From the small docks you can watch the boats come in, buy fresh fish from stalls on the quayside and, for a few extra rand, have them scaled and gutted while you wait.

Perched on the harbour wall in the station building, pounded by waves, is the popular *Brass Bell* **restaurant** (see p.189), one of Kalk Bay's biggest attractions and one of the few restaurants along the peninsula where you can actually sit by the sea – and enjoy a glass of draught Guinness.

FISH HOEK

Map 2, D8. Fish Hoek station.

In contrast to Kalk Bay, the very white suburb of **Fish Hoek**, to the south, is one of the most conservative along the entire False Bay coast. A local by-law bans the sale of alcohol, boosting the town's image as the dullest retirement village on the Cape. However, it does boast the peninsula's best swimming **beach**, with a long stretch of sand: the Cape Town to Simon's Town train stops just opposite. The surprisingly good *Fish Hoek Galley* **restaurant**, located right on the beach, has outside seating.

From in front of the restaurant, picturesque **Jager's Walk** skirts the rocky shoreline above the sea as far as Sunny Cove. The walkway, which continues unpaved for 5km as far as Simon's Town, provides a good vantage point for seeing whales.

SIMON'S TOWN

Map 2, D9. Simon's Town station.

South Africa's principal naval base, **Simon's Town** is the country's third-oldest European settlement, an exceptionally pretty place with a near-perfectly preserved streetscape. It's slightly marred on the ocean side by the **naval dockyard**, but this and glimpses of naval squaddies parading behind the high walls or strolling to the station in their crisp white uniforms are what give the town its distinct character.

Trains run from Cape Town roughly every forty minutes Monday to Saturday (every hour Sunday). The trip takes an hour, the last twenty minutes from Muizenberg skirting the coast spectacularly close to the shoreline – it's worth it just for the train ride. Trains are met at Simon's Town by Rikki's, which can also be booked (☎021-786-2136) to take you on excursions to Boulders or Cape Point. There are no buses to Simon's Town.

Simon's Town accommodation is listed on pp.168–72.

Simon's Town Museum

Map 2, D9. Mon–Fri 9am–4pm, Sat 10am–4pm, Sun 11am–4pm; R5; ☎021-786-3046, ⓦwww.simonstown.com/stm.htm. Simon's Town station.

The **Simon's Town Museum** in Court Road (the first road on your left as you walk south from the station) is in the Old Residency, built in 1772 for the governor of the Dutch East India Company. It also served as the slave quarters (the dungeons are in the basement) and town brothel. The motley collection of artefacts inside includes maritime displays and an inordinate amount on Able Seaman Just

Nuisance, a much-celebrated seafaring Great Dane who was adopted as a mascot by the Royal Navy during World War II, and is reputed to have enjoyed the odd pint along with the sailors, whom he would accompany into Cape Town on the train.

SHELTER FROM THE STORM

Founded in 1687 as the winter anchorage of the Dutch East India Company, Simon's Town was modestly named by Governor Simon van der Stel after himself. Its most celebrated visitor was Lord Nelson, who convalesced here as a midshipman while returning home from the East in 1776. Nineteen years later, the British sailed into the town and occupied it as a bridgehead for their invasion of Cape Town and the first British occupation of the Cape; after just seven years they left, only to return in 1806. Simon's Town remained a British base until 1957, when it was handed over to South Africa.

There are fleeting hints, such as the odd mosque, that the town's exclusively white appearance doesn't give the whole story. In fact, the first Muslims arrived from the East Indies in the early eighteenth century, imported as slaves to build the Dutch naval base. After the British banning of the slave trade in 1808, ships were compelled to disgorge their human cargo at Simon's Town, where one district became known as Black Town. In 1967, when Simon's Town was declared a White Group Area, there were 1200 well-established coloured families descended from these slaves. By 1973 the majority had been forcibly removed, because of the Group Areas Act (see p.322), to the desolate township of Ocean View (ironically, one of the few places along the peninsula that hasn't got an ocean view). Their departure had a damaging impact, with the town's significant historic buildings being destroyed or allowed to decay.

●

The building also reputedly still houses the ghost of Eleanor, the fourteen-year-old daughter of Earl McCartney, who lived here in the closing years of the eighteenth century. Forbidden by her parents from playing on the sands with the children of coloured fishermen, Eleanor would escape to the beach through a secret tunnel she had discovered. The dankness of the tunnel supposedly gave her pneumonia, from which she tragically died.

South African Naval Museum

Map 2, D9. Daily 10am–4pm; free. Simon's Town station.

At the **South African Naval Museum**, displays – only likely to appeal if you have a special interest in the subject – include the inside of a submarine, the bridge of a ship simulating rocking and loads of official portraits of South African Navy big guns with double-barrelled names, from 1922 to the present. From the beginning of December to mid-January, the museum operates free one-hour tours (Mon–Fri 10am & 1.30pm) of the Naval Dockyard, leaving from under the palm trees in Jubilee Square.

Jubilee Square and the Marina

Map 2, D9. Simon's Town station.

In the centre of Simon's Town, a little over a kilometre south of the station, is **Jubilee Square**, a palm-shaded car park just off St George's Street, the main drag running through town. Flanked by some good cafés and shops, including a great fish and chips restaurant, its harbour-facing side has a broad walkway with a statue of the ubiquitous Able Seaman Just Nuisance (see p.131). A couple of sets of stairs lead down to the Marina, a modest development of shops and restaurants set right on the waterfront.

Long and Seaforth beaches

Map 2, D9. Simon's Town station, then Rikki taxi.

Long Beach, just north of Simon's Town station, offers no shade and is little used. However, on windless days it can be pleasant for long walks, with views of the Hottentots Holland Mountains, and its tidal pool is safe for bathing. Access is by a number of gaps in a brick wall alongside the main road and about midway along the beach (opposite Hopkirk Way). There are free changing rooms and toilets nearby, as well as fresh water.

One of the best beaches for swimming is at **Seaforth**, adjacent to and east of the Naval Museum, where clear deep waters lap around the rocks. It's calm, protected and safe, but not pretty, being bounded on one side by the looming grey mass of the naval base.

BOULDERS

Map 2, E10. Simon's Town station, then Rikki taxi.

Two kilometres from the station towards Cape Point you leave town and come to **Boulders**, the most popular local beach, with a number of places to stay. The area takes its name from the huge rounded rocks that create a cluster of little coves with sandy beaches and clear sea pools.

Boulders Coastal Park

Map 2, E10. Open 24hr; R10 entry fee 8am–5pm. Simon's Town station, then Rikki taxi.

The main reason people come to Boulders is for the **African penguins** (formerly known as jackass penguins), in the **Boulders section of the Cape Peninsula National Park**, a fenced reserve on Boulders Beach. Passing sailors used to prey on the quirky birds and their eggs, but more recently they have fallen victim to vandals and some locals who consider them pests; they are now under the protective wing of a guard. African penguins usually live on islands off the west side of the South African coast, the Boulders birds forming one of only two mainland colonies in the world. This is also the only place where the endangered species are actually increasing in numbers, and provides a rare opportunity to get a close look at them.

MILLER'S POINT AND SMITSWINKELBAAI

Map 2, E11. Simon's Town station, then Rikki taxi.

Almost 5km south of Boulders is the popular and attractive **Miller's Point** resort, which has a number of small sandy beaches and a tidal pool protected from the southeast wind. There's a **campsite** at the caravan park, with great sea views. Along Main Road, the notable *Black Marlin* seafood **restaurant** draws busloads of tourists, while the boulders around the point attract rock agama, black zonure lizards and dassies.

The last place before you get to the Cape of Good Hope section of the Cape Peninsula National Park, is **Smitswinkelbaai** (pronounced smits-vin-cull-bye), a little cove with a small beach, which is safe for swimming but feels the full blast of the southeast wind. It's not accessible by car, as local property owners fiercely guard their privacy. To get there, park next to the road and walk down a seemingly endless succession of stairs.

CAPE PENINSULA NATIONAL PARK: CAPE OF GOOD HOPE SECTION

Map 2, C10 & C11–E14. Daily: April–Sept 7am–5pm; Oct–March 6am–6pm; R25; ℡021-780-9100, ⓦwww.cpnp.co.za.

The sea and mountain scenery in the **Cape of Good Hope** section of the **Cape Peninsula National Park** are reason enough to travel the 66km from central Cape Town. Most visitors make a beeline for **Cape Point**, seeing the rest of the reserve through a vehicle window, but walking (see the box on p.137) is the best way to appreciate indigenous **Cape flora**. At first glance the landscape appears rocky and bleak, with short, wind-cropped plants, but the vegetation is surprisingly rich – there are as many plant varieties in this small reserve as in the whole of Britain. Many familiar bright blooms such as geraniums, freesias, gladioli, daisies, lilies and irises are hybrids grown from indigenous Cape plants.

The 78-square-kilometre reserve incorporates the southernmost section of the Cape Peninsula and stretches along some 40km of rocky Atlantic and False Bay coastline which converge at Cape Point. Principally a botanical reserve, it's also packed with herbivorous **game**, including grey rhebok, Cape grysbok, the rare Cape mountain zebra, bontebok, eland, red hartebeest, duiker, dassies and ostriches. Chacma baboons are frequently sighted, while less common species include the Cape fox, caracal and porcupine. Over 150 varieties of **birds** have been recorded here. The west coast extends into the sea as a **marine reserve**: Cape Point is one of the best spots in Cape Town for sighting **whales** and **dolphins**.

Though there's no public transport to the reserve, **getting there** is not too difficult. There are **tours** which will bring you down here (see pp.28, 136), or you can rent a Simon's Town **Rikki's** (℡021-786-2136; R85, seats 6 people). If travelling **by car**, take the M3 to Muizenberg, continuing on the M4 via Simon's Town to the reserve gates, where you'll be given a good **map** that marks the main driving and walking routes, as well as the tidal pools and other facilities.

Cape Point and around

Map 2, E14. Ⓦwww.capepoint.co.za.

Most people come to the reserve to see what is frequently touted as both the southernmost tip of Africa, and the place where the Indian and Atlantic oceans meet at **Cape Point**. In fact, it's the site of neither, but is nevertheless an awesomely dramatic spot, which should on no account be missed. Cape Point sits atop massive sea cliffs with huge views, strong seas and an even wilder wind, which whips off hats and sunglasses as visitors gaze southwards from the old lighthouse buttress. The continent's real tip is at Cape Agulhas, some 300km southeast of here (see p.274), but Cape Point is a lot easier to get to than Agulhas and a lot more exciting.

Navigators since the Portuguese in the fifteenth century had to contend with the treacherous rocky promontory when they "rounded the Cape" on their way to the East. Plenty of ships lie submerged off its coast, and at **Olifantsbos** on the west side of Cape Point you can walk to two wrecks: one a US vessel sunk in 1942, and the other a South African coaster, which ran aground in 1965. The **Old Lighthouse**, built in 1860, was too often dangerously shrouded in cloud, failing to keep ships off the rocks, so another was built lower down in 1914, not always successful in averting disasters but still the most powerful light beaming onto the sea from South Africa.

Numerous tours take in the peninsula highlights:
Day Trippers (☎021-531-3274) run full-day fun outings from Cape Town for R265 (including a picnic lunch), which include cycling and walking in the national park. For general tours that take in the reserve, see p.28.

From the Cape Point car park, the famous viewpoint is a steep walk, crawling with tourists, up to the old lighthouse. Alternatively, a **funicular** (R24 return) runs to the top, where there's a curio shop. The decent *Two Oceans* restaurant at the car park has outdoor seating and huge picture windows taking in the drop to the sea below.

SWIMMING AND WALKING

Several waymarked walks lead through the Cape of Good Hope Nature Reserve. If you're planning a big hike it's best to set out early, as shade is rare and the wind can be foul, especially during summer, often increasing in intensity as the day goes on. One of the most straightforward hiking routes is the signposted forty-minute trek from the car park at Cape Point to the more westerly Cape of Good Hope. For exploring the shoreline, a clear path runs down the Atlantic side from Hoek van Bobbejaan; a convenient place to join it is at Gifkommetjie, which is signposted off Cape Point Road. From the car park, several sandy tracks drop quite steeply down the slope across rocks, through bushes and milkwood trees to the shore, along which you can walk in either direction. Alternatively, take a copy of the Government Printer's *Cape Town* map (1:50,000) for some more intrepid exploration. Bring water on any walk in the reserve, as there are no reliable fresh sources.

You'll find the beaches along signposted sideroads branching out from Cape Point Road, the main route through the reserve, going from the entrance gate to the car park at Cape Point. The sea is too dangerous for swimming, but there are safe tidal pools at the adjacent Buffels Bay and Bordjiesrif, midway along the east shore. Both have *braai* stands, but more southerly Buffels Bay is the nicer, with big lawned areas and some sheltered spots to have a picnic.

LISTINGS

Accommodation

ape Town has plenty of accommodation to suit all budgets, but to guarantee the kind of place you want booking ahead is recommended, especially over the Christmas holidays (mid-December to mid-January). The greatest concentration of accommodation is in the areas that abut the city centre: the City Bowl and the Atlantic seaside strip as far as Sea Point. The City Bowl, spreading up from the centre to the slopes of Table Mountain, comprises the city centre, Kloof Nek Road, the down-at-heel and lively suburb of Gardens, as well as the desirable inner-city suburbs of Tamboerskloof and Oranjezicht, which are close to the centre, sufficiently elevated to provide sea views and are only ten minutes' drive from the stunning Atlantic coast.

There are a few accommodation **agencies** (see p.249) that may be able to help if you're stuck.

If you don't have your own transport you'll probably want to stay in the city centre or somewhere connected to it by Metrorail train: either the southern suburbs or the False Bay seaboard. The City Bowl suburb of Gardens is adjacent to the centre and is easily walkable, while the Atlantic seaboard suburbs of Green Point and Sea Point are close to the centre and the V & A Waterfront, brim with accommodation and are along the route of the only decent bus service on the Peninsula.

ACCOMMODATION PRICE CODES

Accommodation prices vary throughout the year. Rates given are those you can expect to pay **per person** in a hotel, guest house or B&B for a double room in summer (Oct to March). These types of accommodation are usually en suite and include breakfast in the rate. If you're visiting during the Christmas school holidays (Dec to mid-Jan) or Easter, expect a substantial price hike. Self-catering accommodation is usually charged per unit, but for consistency we have given a per person rate. There is no seasonal variation for backpacker lodges and the codes given represent the price per person.

❶ up to R100	❹ R200–300	❼ R500–750
❷ R100–150	❺ R300–400	❽ R750–1000
❸ R150–200	❻ R400–500	❾ over R1000

CITY CENTRE

A cluster of backpacker lodges is concentrated on **Long Street** in the city centre, with a couple of others nearby. Most of the other accommodation consists of mid-range to expensive hotels, with the odd B&B and some self-catering cottages in the **Lower City Centre**.

BACKPACKER LODGES

Carnival Court Backpackers
Map 4, C6. 255 Long St ☎ 021-423-9003,
ⓔ carnivalcourt@freemail.absa. co.za. Cape Town station. Clean, spacious and friendly establishment in an airy Victorian apartment building converted into a lodge that was completely refurbished in 2001. A buzzing bar makes this a good place for party animals. Clean but

uninspiring rooms: twelve dorms, mostly sleeping four to six people, eight doubles and four singles. **1**

Cat & Moose

Map 4, C6. 305 Long St ⓣ 021-423-7638, ⓔ cat&moose@hotmail.com. Cape Town station.

The most stylish of the Long Street lodges, housed in an eighteenth-century building a couple of doors from the steam baths at the south end of the city centre. Timber floors with Turkish-style rugs, exposed beams, earthy reds and ochres as well as some African masks imbue it with a warm ethnic feel. The six dorms, two triples and five double rooms are arranged around a small leafy courtyard, with a waterfall cascading into a plunge pool. **1**

City Slickers

Map 4, A3. Corner 25 Rose and Hout streets ⓣ 021-422-2357, ⓕ 021-422-2355. Cape Town station.

Lively lodge in the Bo-Kaap, five minutes from the city centre, whose roof garden has views to Table Mountain. Train-carriage-style rooms have only one twin bunk or a single or double bed in each. **1**

Long Street Backpackers

Map 4, C5. 209 Long St ⓣ 021-423-0615, ⓔ longstbp@mweb.co.za. Cape Town station.

The oldest Long Street backpacker lodge, on the top two floors of an unexceptional three-storey former apartment block arranged around a courtyard with dorms, doubles and singles. Quieter than some of the other lodges in the vicinity, it's a well-organized, plain but clean place with a laundry, internet facilities and a travel desk. There's also a lively bar and a kitchen. **1**

Overseas Visitors' Club Hostel

Map 4, C6. 230 Upper Long St ⓣ 021-424-6800, ⓦ www.ovc.co.za. Cape Town station.

Well-organized lodge above

some shops with high ceilings, airy spaces and off-white interiors, run more along the lines of a guest house than a hostel. Small by Long Street standards, with three dorms (each sleeping six) with balconies. The absence of a bar makes it more tranquil than most lodges in the vicinity. A TV lounge leads onto a wraparound balcony that offers views of the street. ❶

Simply the Best

Map 4, C5. 187 Long St ⓣ021-424-8223. Cape Town station. Sizeable hostel with a party atmosphere, located on the top two floors of an undistinguished three-storey converted block of flats above a bar/bistro. Fully refurbished at the end of 2001, its great attraction is that the twelve dorms (sleeping a maximum of six) and five doubles are each self-contained, with their own kitchens and bathrooms. A good budget self-catering option in the city centre. ❶

B&BS, GUEST HOUSES AND SELF-CATERING

iKhaya Lodge

Map 4, E7. Wandel St, Dunkley Square ⓣ021-461-8880, ⓦ www.ikhayalodge.co.za. Cape Town station.
Guest house three short blocks away from the Company's Gardens and museums, and walkable to all the city-centre sights. Its eleven standard rooms in the main guest house, five luxury loft suites and two self-catering apartments, done out in ethnically inspired décor, have mountain or (cheaper) city views. The lodge's patio overlooks the outdoor eateries of trendy Dunkley Square. ❹–❻

St Paul's B&B Guest House

Map 4, B6. 182 Bree St ⓣ021-423-4420 (7am–2pm), ⓕ021-423-1580. Cape Town station. Charming, well-managed and inexpensive guest house in a Georgian building (formerly a maternity hospital) in a calm street on the city-centre fringes, within easy striking distance of the sights. Attached to the lovely brick and stone St Paul's Church and its rectory, the rooms are large, comfortable and light, with huge windows. Shared bathroom facilities. Kitchen available to guests. ❷

Travellers' Inn

Map 4, C6. 208 Long St ☎021-424-9272, Ⓦ www.travellers-inn.co.za. Cape Town station. Pleasant budget accommodation in a turn-of-the-century building above a cybercafé, with a wraparound balcony dotted with pot plants overlooking Bloem and Long streets. With no bar and no backpacker scene, this could be a good bet for travellers wanting to avoid the hectic social atmosphere of the city-centre hostels. Apart from the light and spacious family rooms (twin beds and a double bunk), accommodation is small and sparsely furnished, but clean and quite adequate. Shared bathroom facilities.

Weekly and monthly discounts available. ❶

HOTELS

Cape Gardens Lodge Hotel

Map 4, C7. 88 Queen Victoria St, Gardens ☎021-423-1260, Ⓦ www.capegardenslodge.com. Cape Town station. Smart multi-storey hotel with 56 air-conditioned rooms with cable TV, baths and showers, bang in the centre, opposite the Gardens. Two minutes from the South African Museum and Art Gallery and an easy and pleasant walk through the Company's Gardens to the city centre. ❹

Cape Heritage Hotel

Map 4, B3. 90 Bree St ☎021-424-4646, Ⓦ www.capeheritage.co.za. Cape Town station. Elegant and tastefully restored hotel located in a row of houses dating back to 1771, in Heritage Square, just below the Bo-Kaap. Fifteen

ACCOMMODATION

145

spacious rooms are each furnished in a unique theme, among them African, Japanese and Dutch. A lovely courtyard makes up for the lack of garden. ❻

Tudor Hotel

Map 4, C4. 153 Longmarket St, Greenmarket Square ⓣ 021-424-1335, ⓦ www.tudorhotel .co.za. Cape Town station. Thirty en-suite B&B rooms in a reasonably priced hotel overlooking cobbled Greenmarket Square. A five-minute walk from trendy Long Street, you can't get more central than this. ❷

V & A WATERFRONT

In keeping with the gentrified ambience of the **Waterfront**, accommodation here tends to be upmarket; this is where Bill and Hillary Clinton stayed when they visited the city in 1998. There are a couple of reasonably priced places to stay if the presidential suite isn't an option.

Breakwater Lodge

Map p.82, A6. Portswood Rd, Waterfront ⓣ 021-406-1911 (ask for Lodge Reservations), ⓦ www.breakwaterlodge.co.za. Waterfront buses.
The most affordable place to stay on the doorstep of the Waterfront, this is a sparkling white hotel linked to the Graduate School of Business and partially housed in a nineteenth-century prison building, a five-minute walk from the V & A Waterfront.

Although it lacks personality, the lodge's 200 or so standard en-suite rooms are functional and come equipped with TVs and phones, while the 110 budget units share a bathroom with one other room. Rate excludes breakfast. ❸—❹

The Cape Grace

Map p.82, E6. West Quay, V & A Waterfront ⓣ 021-410-7100, ⓦ www.capegrace.co.za. Waterfront buses.
The best hotel in the world –

at least according to a readers' poll in 2000 in *Condé Nast Traveler* – and Bill and Hillary Clinton's choice when they visited Cape Town. This is undoubtedly one of South Africa's most expensive and exclusive hotels, spectacularly sited on a slender spit that overlooks the V & A Waterfront's small vessel marina to one side and the Alfred Basin to the other. The hotel's 102 rooms have either harbour or Table Mountain views and are stylishly furnished in pared-back French period style. ❾

City Lodge
Map 5, G4. Corner of Alfred and Dock roads, Waterfront ☎021-419-9450, Ⓦwww.citylodge.co.za. Waterfront buses.
Rather austere but perfectly adequate hotel, part of a national chain, poised between the V & A Waterfront and the city centre, and less than 1km from both. Rooms have TVs

and there's a small swimming pool. While not as close to the V & A action as *Breakwater Lodge*, this is still one of the few reasonably priced places this near the Waterfront. Fri–Sun nights are cheaper and you can pick up whopping discounts of up to 75 percent on their auction site Ⓦwww.bid2stay.co.za. ❹

Victoria & Alfred Hotel
Map p.82, E5. Pierhead, Waterfront ☎021-419-6677, Ⓦwww.vahotel.co.za. Waterfront buses.
Four-star squeaky clean hotel on North Quay, bang in the heart of the Waterfront. Occupying a converted turn-of-the-century dock warehouse, within spitting distance of numerous bars and restaurants, it overlooks the Alfred Basin. Some rooms have stunning views of Table Mountain. Decor is in the Cape Dutch Revival style. Mountain- and harbour-facing ❽, mall-facing ❼.

CITY BOWL SUBURBS

The **City Bowl suburbs** are popular for accommodation, and the most northerly sections are just five to ten minutes' walk from the Gardens and museums. A few backpacker lodges can be found along Kloof Street, the continuation of trendy Long Street. The further up you go the leafier the suburbs become, and you'll find the pricier and more comfortable B&Bs, guest houses and hotels along the lower slopes of Table Mountain, overlooking the city centre and Duncan Dock.

There's no public transport to the City Bowl Suburbs, but most accommodation listed here is under 3km from Cape Town station.

BACKPACKER LODGES

Ashanti Lodge and Guest House

Map 7, D1. 11 Hof St, Gardens
ⓣ 021-423-8721,
ⓦ www.ashanti.co.za.
King of the Cape Town lodges, this is a massive, superbly refurbished two-storey Victorian mansion five minutes' walk from the Gardens. Details that give it the edge are stripped timber, chic marbling and ethnic decor, soaring ceilings, a beautifully kept front garden, cosy TV lounge and a swimming pool with sun terrace. A terrific upstairs café/bar has a deck with epic views of Table Mountain. Twelve private rooms (twin or double beds) and ten dorms (sleeping six to eight) are furnished with custom-made wrought iron bunks and beds. Facilities include international phone booths (pay when you leave), laundry, free pick-up from station or airport and an efficient travel centre. They also have a quieter guest house around the corner in Union Street with seven

ACCOMMODATION

extremely well-priced en-suite double/twin rooms with TVs and a communal kitchen. Lodge ❶, guest house ❷.

The Backpack

Map 4, B7. 74 New Church St, Tamboerskloof ⓣ021-423-4530,

ⓦwww.backpackers.co.za.

Excellent lodge that is one of the few in the same league as *Ashanti*, in three interleading houses on the cusp of the City Bowl suburbs and the city centre and easily walkable to both. Professionally run and service orientated, it's pleasantly furnished with bold colours and ethnic fabrics. Plenty of outdoor space, including a pool terrace in its own private garden among banana trees. Accommodation is in four dorms (sleeping six to ten) and eleven private rooms (several of which are en suite). Some rooms are suitable for families, although there's an unfenced pool. Dorms ❶, private rooms ❷.

Cloudbreak Backpackers' Lodge

Map 4, G8. 219 Upper Buitenkant St, Gardens ⓣ021-461-6892,

ⓦwww.cloudbreakbackpackers.co.za.

Friendly and fun place on a busy road close to the large Gardens shopping centre. Comprises eight doubles in a house with a garden, and three dorms sleeping six people in another house across the road. Surfing is a high priority, and daily trips are organized to good breaks and beaches. Free airport pick-up, and there's a travel and booking centre. ❶

Oak Lodge

Map 7, F1. 21 Breda St, Gardens ⓣ021-465-6182.

More an event than a lodge, this highly recommended hostel in an 1860s Victorian house has dramatic dungeons, dragon murals and a lively atmosphere. Spacious, well serviced and with an immaculate kitchen. There are four dorms and sixteen private rooms, one of which is en suite. ❶

Zebra Crossing

Map 4, B8. 82 New Church St
Ⓣ021-422-1265,
Ⓔzebracross@intekom.co.za.
Cape Town's only backpacker lodge that actually boasts about being quiet. On the northern edge of the City Bowl suburbs, it's an easy walk to the Kloof Street restaurants and pubs as well as those in the city centre. A café/bar serves full meals and decent coffee and there are two pleasant terraces under vines. Accommodation is in three spacious dorms (sleeping eight), eleven doubles and three singles. The best rooms are the three doubles in the annexe outside, with a balcony that has views of the mountain. Child friendly. ❶

SELF-CATERING, B&BS AND GUEST HOUSES

African Sun

Map 7, H1. 3 Florida Rd, Vredehoek ⓉO21-461-1601,
Ⓔafpress@iafrica.com.
Small, secluded, self-catering apartment, attached to a family house a little over 1km from the city centre. Furnished with ethnic decor, it's run by friendly, well-informed and interesting owners, one a novelist and children's author and the other a travel writer. Five percent discount if you produce this book. Great value. ❷

Ambleside Guesthouse

Map 7, F4. 11 Forest Rd, Oranjezicht ⓉO21-465-2503,
Ⓕ021-465-3814.
This guest house has been going for fifty years and comprises eight inexpensive and comfortable, though slightly stuffy, en-suite rooms, all with great views across the city to the harbour, and cable-car-watching from the back patio. A hot breakfast is served in the rooms and you can prepare your own meals in a communal kitchen. ❷

Belmont House

Map 7, F3. 10 Belmont Ave, Oranjezicht ⓉO21-461-5417,
Ⓦwww.capeguest.com.
Tastefully restored 1920s house with seven fresh rooms,

each with its own shower or bath. Either take the B&B option or self-cater in their communal kitchen. Discount of five percent if you produce this book. B&B ❸, self-catering ❷.

Blencathra

Map 7, B3. Corner De Hoop and Cambridge aves, Tamboerskloof ☎021-424-9571, ⓦwww.geocities.com /blencathra_ct.

Peaceful, spacious self-catering rooms, one of which is en suite, with stunning views in a large relaxed family house which attracts a young crowd that isn't part of the backpacker scene. On the slopes of Lion's Head, it's 2km from the city centre and 4km from the Atlantic Seaboard beaches. Garden with outdoor seating and a swimming pool. En-suite room ❷, non en-suite ❶.

Flower Street Villa Guest House

Map 7, G1. 3 Flower St, Oranjezicht ☎ & ⓕ021-465-7517.

Twenty spacious, budget rooms in a former nursing home. There's a small extra charge for breakfast, but guests have use of kitchen. En-suite rooms ❷, rooms sharing bathrooms ❶.

Leeuwenvoet House

Map 4, B8. 93 New Church St, Tamboerskloof ☎021-424-1133, ⓦwww.leeuwenvoet. co.za.

Tranquil restored Victorian guest house with eleven en-suite rooms kitted out with pine, wicker and all the hotel trimmings of TV, phone, fan and radio alarm. Situated on a major thoroughfare with secure parking, it's a fifteen-minute walk from the city centre with airport transfers also available. ❹

Lezard Bleu

Map 7, G3. 30 Upper Orange St, Oranjezicht ☎021-461-4601, ⓦwww.lezardbleu.co.za.

Seven luxurious en-suite rooms furnished with maple beds and cupboards in a spacious open-plan 1960s house. Sliding doors from each room open onto a garden. Located in a pleasant part of town, it's 1km from the centre and about half that distance to a nature reserve on the lower slopes of Table Mountain. There's also a standalone timber cottage nestling among trees in the garden with views across the city. Swimming pool and generous breakfasts. **6**

Saasveld Lodge

Map 4, B8. 73 Kloof St, Tamboerskloof ☎021-424-6169, ⓔsaasveld@icon.co.za. Clean but rather impersonal 1950s-style, four-storey lodge on a buzzing thoroughfare that's lined with good eateries, less than 1km from the centre. Rooms have TV and phone, and the rate excludes breakfast. Reasonable value with no frills. **2**

Underberg Guest House

Map 4, A8. 6 Tamboerskloof Rd, Tamboerskloof ☎021-426-2262, ⓦwww .underbergguesthouse.co.za. Located in the upmarket suburb of Tamboerskloof, this Victorian guest house offers possibly the best City Bowl value in its price band. Its high ceilings and compact size (there are only eleven rooms) create an atmosphere that is both intimate and airy. **4**

Welgelegen Guest House

Map 7, D2. 6 Stephen St, Gardens ☎021-426-2373, ⓦwww.welgelegen.co.za. Eight rooms in a Victorian guest house with mountain views furnished with considerable style – unsurprisingly since the owner is an interior decorator. Despite being down a quiet cul-de-sac, it's just minutes from the Kloof Street restaurant and nightlife strip and is easily walkable to the city-centre sights. **5**

HOTELS

Cape Milner Hotel

Map 4, A8. 2a Milner Rd, Tamboerskloof ☎021-426-1101, ⓦwww.capemilner.co.za. Reasonably priced smart hotel, partly incorporating an early eighteenth-century building, at the foot of Signal Hill about 1km from the centre. Under new ownership it was gutted and totally refurbished in 2001 as a boutique hotel with 59 airy rooms, all with views of Table Mountain. It's New York-style minimal decor gives rooms a light and pleasant atmosphere and you'll find a swimming pool, restaurant and bar on the premises. **5**

Mount Nelson Hotel

Map 4, D8. 76 Orange St, Gardens ℡ 021-423-1000, Ⓦ www.mountnelsonhotel.orient -express.com.

Cape Town's grande dame: a fine and famous high-colonial Victorian hotel, built in 1899 (and extended in the late 1990s in response to demand). Set in extensive established gardens, with arrival along a palm-lined colonnade, it takes itself terribly seriously and charges accordingly. Rate excludes breakfast. **9**

Villa Belmonte Hotel

Map 7, F3. 33 Belmont Ave, Oranjezicht ℡ 021-462-1576, Ⓦ www.villabelmontehotel.co .za.

The Western Cape's smallest five-star hotel, on the lower slopes of Table Mountain and 1km from the city centre, feels like an elegant Italian country villa. The fifteen rooms, some of which lead onto a lovely garden, are themed, and prices vary according to size. Their specialist seafood restaurant, open only to guests, serves fresh oysters and crayfish straight from the tank and their wine list is absolutely tops. Extremely good value given the level of comfort and style. **6–7**

MOUILLE POINT TO SEA POINT

Down the **Atlantic seaboard** lie the seaside suburbs of Mouille Point, Green Point, Three Anchor Bay and Sea Point. Historically Cape Town's hotel and high-rise land,

ACCOMMODATION

this is now packed with accommodation from backpacker lodges to swish hotels, making it a good alternative to the City Bowl if you want to be close to the city centre.

BACKPACKER LODGES

Carnaby the Backpacker

Map 6, H3. 219 Main Rd, Three Anchor Bay ⊕021-439-7410, Ⓦwww.carnabybackpackers.co.za. Sea Point bus.

Extraordinary and fun hostel, previously an old-fashioned three-star hotel, located about 100m from the sea (too rocky for swimming). The 1970s Spanish-style stucco decor has been retained for kitsch effect. A big attraction is that a number of its dorms (sleeping three to six) and double rooms are en suite and have phones which receive calls. There's even a honeymoon suite with its own TV. Shady outdoor pool terrace, bar, pool, pinball and travel centre. Dorms ❶, doubles ❷.

St John's Waterfront Lodge

Map 5, E5. 4–6 Braemar Rd, Green Point ⊕021-439-1404, Ⓦwww.stjohns.co.za. Sea Point bus.

The closest hostel to the V & A Waterfront, ten minutes away on foot, and well run by friendly and helpful staff. Accommodation is in four dorms (sleeping eight or nine) as well as some doubles, one of which is en suite. In addition to two swimming pools, a great garden and a bar, the restaurant serves reasonably priced light meals till midnight. They also have internet access, a coin-operated washing machine and a travel centre. ❶

Sunflower Stop

Map 5, C6. 179 Main Rd, Green Point ⊕021-434-6535, Ⓦwww.sunflowerstop.co.za. Sea Point bus.

Bright yellow lodge that claims to be the cleanest in Cape Town (it's serviced twice a day), in a two-storey 1940s house 1km from the Waterfront. Accommodation is

ACCOMMODATION

in two dorms (sleeping nine and twelve) and fourteen doubles. This child-friendly lodge has a bar, pool room, swimming pool, coin-operated washing machine, safe, travel centre and internet access. ❶

GUEST HOUSES AND B&BS

Altona Lodge

Map 5, C6. 19 Croxteth Rd, Green Point ⓣ 021-434-2572, ⓦ www.altona.co.za. Sea Point bus.

Quiet and friendly guest house in a Victorian house close to the city centre, with seventeen B&B rooms, five of which are en suite. Cheaper rooms share a bathroom, though each room has its own hand basin. Service is good, rates very reasonable, there's a small garden and the atmosphere is homely. ❷

Brenda's Guest House

Map 5, C6. 14 Pine Rd, Green Point ⓣ 021-434-0902 or 083-627-5583, ⓦ www.brendas.co.za. Sea Point bus.

Four rooms inside and another in the garden of a 1900s house, close to the Waterfront. There's poolside seating on a bricked terrace and rooms are brightly decorated with wicker furniture. ❹

Dungarvin House

Map 5, C6. 163 Main Rd, Green Point ⓣ 021-434-0677, ⓦ www.kom.co.za. Sea Point bus.

A grand Edwardian villa with moulded pediments on a busy road not far from the Sea Point restaurant action, with gracious, well-appointed rooms. ❹

Jambo Guest House

Map 5, C6. 1 Grove Rd, Green Point ⓣ 021-439-4219, ⓦ www.jambo.co.za. Sea Point bus.

Small atmospheric establishment with four double rooms in a quiet cul-de-sac off Main Road, just over 1km from the V & A Waterfront. Despite being in the inner-city suburbs, its lush leafy exterior and enclosed garden with pond

ACCOMMODATION

155

are delightfully relaxing and the service is excellent. A luxury suite has a large sitting area, jacuzzi and French doors opening onto the garden. **❹–❺**

Lion's Head Lodge

Map 6, F2. 319 Main Rd, Sea Point ⓣ 021-434-4163, ⓦ www.lions-head-lodge.co.za. Sea Point bus.

Plain but very comfortable en-suite hotel-style rooms that are clean and well maintained, despite the weather-worn exterior of the four-storey building. Some face the busy main road at the heart of Sea Point's restaurant strip, but there are quieter ones overlooking the courtyard. All have phones and TV and the lodge features a swimming pool, its own bar, beer terrace and an à la carte restaurant. Also offers fully equipped apartments that sleep two. Rooms and apartments. **❸**

Olaf's Guest House

Map 6, F2. 24 Wisbeach Rd, Sea Point ⓣ 021-439-8943, ⓦ www.olafs.co.za. Sea Point

bus.

Clean, comfortable and pleasantly decorated Victorian bungalow with a friendly owner, five minutes from the beachfront promenade and 3km from the city centre. Its eight en-suite rooms all have cable TV and telephones, and you can have breakfast on the patio beside the swimming pool. **❺**

Stonehurst Guest House

Map 6, G3. 3 Frere Rd, Sea Point ⓣ 021-434-9670, ⓔ stonehurstguesthouse@absafreemail.co.za. Sea Point bus.

Airy tin-roofed Victorian residence with original fittings, Cape furniture and a pleasant front garden. There's a kitchen and guest lounge. Some rooms have balconies, eleven are en suite and the remaining three cheaper ones share a bathroom. En-suite rooms **❸**, sharing bathroom **❷**.

Villa Rosa

Map 6, D4. 277 High Level Rd, Sea Point ⓣ 021-434-2768, ⓦ www.villa-rosa.com. Sea Point bus.

Friendly eight-room guest

house in a salmon-pink two-storey Victorian house on the lower slopes of Signal Hill, two blocks from the beachfront promenade. Decorated with simplicity and style, all rooms have TVs, phones and safes, but only some on the upper floor have sea views. ❹

SELF-CATERING

De Waterkant Village and De Waterkant House

Map 5, F6. 1 Loader St, De Waterkant ☎ 021-422-2721, ⓦ www.dewaterkant.co.za. Cape Town station and Sea Point buses.

Sixty-five attractively restored historic cottages in a villagey quarter of the eighteenth-century Waterkant district of Green Point, adjacent to the Bo-Kaap and less than 1km from the V & A Waterfront and city centre. The luxury cottages in Waterkant, Loader, Dixon and Napier streets, have from one to three bedrooms and provide varied facilities. Some come with garages, swimming pools

and roof gardens with harbour or mountain views. Also part of the district is De Waterkant House, which has nine rooms that share a pool and terrace with views over the V & A Waterfront. ❹

Don Suite Hotel

Map 6, E2. 249 Beach Rd, Sea Point ☎ 021-434-1083, ⓦ www.don.co.za. Sea Point bus.

Five-storey block of 27 self-catering apartments across the road from the beachfront promenade, 300m from the lively Main Road restaurant strip and 4km from the V & A Waterfront. All the flats, studios and one- and two-bedroom units are modern and well equipped. Rates depend on whether or not you get a view. ❹

Waterfront Suites

Map 5, D6. 153 Main Rd, Green Point ☎ 021-439-5020, ⓦ www.waterfront-suites.co.za. Sea Point bus.

Small four-storey block quite close to, but not actually at, the waterfront with 26 modern and extremely comfortable, but impersonal, apartments that offer brilliant value. Kitchens are well-equipped, rooms are serviced daily and you can have a continental breakfast in their cafeteria. ❷

HOTELS

Cape Town Ritz

Map 6, H2. Corner of Main and Camberwell roads, Three Anchor Bay ⓣ 021-439-6010, ⓦ www.gk-hotels.co.za. Sea Point bus.

Enormous 27-storey 1960s block with 222 rooms and no balconies, best known for the revolving restaurant on the twenty-second floor. Less than 2km from the V & A Waterfront, it's in the heart of the Sea Point wining and dining district. Good value if you don't mind high-rise accommodation. ❹

Winchester Mansions Hotel

Map 6, F1. 221 Beach Rd, Sea Point ⓣ 021-434-2351, ⓦ www.winchester.co.za. Sea Point bus.

Self-consciously colonial-style 1920s hotel, in a prime spot across the road from the seashore, with an ambience straight from the pages of Agatha Christie. Palm trees at the front of the three-storey Cape Dutch Revival building hint at the interior: rooms have ceiling fans, and a cool Italianate courtyard restaurant is overlooked by balconies draped in luxuriant creepers. ❻

SOUTHERN SUBURBS

The **southern suburbs** – the formerly whites-only areas closest to the mountain – are convenient for the Simon's Town train line, providing easy access to both the city centre and the False Bay seaboard. Closest to town, Observatory (see p.100), with its streets of tightly packed Victorian cottages, large student population, congenial cafés and live music joints, can rival the city centre. The more southerly suburbs of Rosebank, Claremont, Newlands and Rondebosch are leafier and quieter.

BACKPACKER LODGES

The Green Elephant
Map 3, H5. 57 Milton Rd, Observatory ⊤ 021-448-6359. Observatory station.
Five basic dorms and six doubles in a large, vibey house just off Main Road, with a jacuzzi, braai, solar-heated plunge pool and internet facilities. The owner leads outdoor expeditions up Table Mountain and Lion's Head. Camping is permitted in the garden. ❶

Riverview Lodge
Map 3, H5. 5 Anson/Station roads, Observatory ⊤ 021-447-9056, ⓔ info@riverview.co.za. Observatory station.
Huge, professionally run lodge with 43 single, double and dorm rooms in a converted two-storey former apartment block, two minutes' walk from Observatory station. It tends to attract large groups but has

several small, comfortable lounges, outdoor spaces and quiet nooks if you need some solitude. A massive plus is the large breakfast that's included in the price. ❶

B&BS AND SELF-CATERING

Carmichael House
Map 3, H6. 11 Wolmunster Rd, Rosebank ⊤ 021-689-8350, ⓦ www.carmichaelhouse.co.za. Rosebank station.
Turn-of-the-century two-storey house with six big rooms kitted out with phones, safes and hairdryers, with fax and email access. There's a peaceful garden, swimming pool and secure parking. It's a ten-minute walk to Rhodes Memorial and the Contour Path, while the Rondebosch shops are 1km away. ❹

Gloucester House Bed & Breakfast
Map 2, E3. 54 Weltevreden

Ave, Rondebosch ⓣ & ⓕ 021-689-3894. Rondebosch station. Private house with two bedrooms, and a lounge/dining room for self-catering. Guests may use the large garden, swimming pool and barbecue area, and there's the plus of being close to Rondebosch station. Price excludes breakfast. ❹

Ivydene

Map 2, E3. off Glebe Rd, Rondebosch ⓣ 021-685-1747, ⓔ ivydene@mweb.co.za. Rondebosch station.

Two small flats and three larger ones in a delightful old Cape farmhouse near the university, with an artistic and friendly atmosphere. Garden and swimming pool. If full the helpful owner will recommend other places in the vicinity. Discounts for stays over a week or more. ❹

Koornhoop Manor House

Map 3, H5. Corner of Wrensch and Nuttal roads, Observatory ⓣ 021-448-0595, ⓦ www.geocities.com/koornho

op. Observatory station.

Pleasant rooms in a spacious Victorian house with a tranquil, enclosed garden and small playground, close to the station, with secure parking and grounds. Besides B&B accommodation in seven double rooms, two of which are suitable for families, there's the option of a self-catering suite, which has three bedrooms and its own entrance. ❸

HOTELS

The Courtyard

Map 3, I6. Liesbeek Ave, Mowbray ⓣ 021-448-3929, ⓦ www.citylodge.co.za. Observatory/Mowbray stations.

Exceptional value considering the high level of luxury. A beautiful early nineteenth-century Cape Dutch homestead under thatch, with terracotta floors, brass chandeliers and large lawns in a semi-rural setting. There's a hotel minibus (chargeable). Breakfast is extra. ❺

The Vineyard Hotel

Map 2, E4. Corner of Colinton and Protea roads, Newlands ⓣ 021-683-3044, ⓦ www.vineyard.co.za. Claremont station.

An excellent classy hotel that gives its snootier competitors a good run for their money at half the price. In a restored country villa built for Lady Anne Barnard in 1799, it's decorated in elegant Cape Dutch style, and there's an outstanding panorama of Table Mountain from the extensive garden. For the level of luxury, it offers incredible value. Courtyard rooms ⑥, mountain-facing ⑦.

CONSTANTIA AND TOKAI

Lush **Constantia** is one of Cape Town's most salubrious suburbs, only twenty minutes' drive from either coast as well as the V & A Waterfront. Sharing the same valley is the adjoining suburb of **Tokai**, worth considering if you want to be well out of the centre; it's close to forest walks and ten minutes from the beach. Inexpensive accommodation is rare, but if money's no object and you're looking for somewhere exceptional and romantic, you might just find it in a Cape Dutch manor house.

A car is essential if you're staying in Constantia as there's no public transport. Rental companies are listed on p.251.

B&BS AND SELF-CATERING

Allandale Holiday Cottages

Map 2, D6. 72 Zwaanswyk Rd, Tokai ⓣ 021-715-3320, ⓦ www.allandale.co.za.

Sixteen one-, two- and three-bedroom self-catering brick cottages on a smallholding on the slopes of Constantiaberg, two minutes from the motorway and twenty from Cape Town. Each cottage has a garden area with a braai and outdoor seating, and also a key that opens the gate into adjoining Tokai Forest. There's also a pool and tennis courts. ❹

Elephant Eye Lodge
Map 2, D6. 9 Sunwood Drive, Tokai ⓣ 021-715-2432, ⓔ orsmond@iafrica.com.
Six reasonably priced rooms at a friendly B&B family home, in a converted Cape Dutch farmhouse, minutes' walk from Tokai Forest and with its own large grounds. Two rooms offer some basic self-catering facilities, and you can get evening meals delivered. A baby's cot is also available and the swimming pool is safely fenced. ❸

Houtkapperspoort
Map 2, C5. Hout Bay Rd ⓣ 021-794-5216, ⓦ www.houtkapperspoort.co.za.
Twenty-four rustic one- and two-bedroom stone and brick self-catering cottages set up against the Table Mountain Nature Reserve, close to Constantia Nek (around 5km from Hout Bay and 15km

from the city centre). You can take paths straight from the estate up the mountain slopes, play tennis or take a dip in the solar-heated pool. Highly recommended. ❹

Little Ruo
Map 2, D5. 11 Willow Rd, off Spaanschemat River Rd, Constantia ⓣ 021-794-2052, ⓦ www.littleruo.co.za.
Two pretty B&B rooms at the home of friendly architect owners, plus three self-catering units set in a huge landscaped garden with willows, a stream and a saltwater pool, with plenty of opportunity for serenely lazing about. ❹

The Stables
Map 2, D5. Chantercler Lane, Constantia
ⓣ & ⓕ 021-794-3653.
Five en-suite doubles, each with their own entrance and patio, in converted stables. They're known for the fabulous six-course breakfasts, and you can relax around the pool in a large garden. ❹

COUNTRY HOTELS

Constantia Uitsig Country Hotel

Map 2, D5. Spaanschemat River Rd, Constantia ⓣ 021-794-6500,
ⓦ www.constantiauitsig.co.za. Sixteen custom-built and luxurious Cape Dutch-style cottages, in a garden setting on Constantia Uitsig wine estate, next door to Steenberg. A fabulous restaurant, *La Colombe* (p.186), is on site. ❽

Steenberg

Map 2, D6. Corner Steenberg and Tokai roads ⓣ 021-713-2222, ⓕ 021-713-2221,
ⓦ www.steenberghotel.com. A luxurious place on South Africa's oldest wine estate at the foot of the Steenberg Mountain. Accommodation is in the original manor house and three other farm buildings (now National Monuments), which are perfect examples of Cape Dutch architecture, dating back to 1682. Arranged around a large formal garden, the buildings have whitewashed walls, thatched roofs, ornate gables and are furnished with seventeenth- and eighteenth-century Cape antiques. ❽

ATLANTIC SEABOARD

Moving south from Sea Point along Victoria Drive, the luxury mountainside suburb of **Camps Bay** has soaring views over the Atlantic, with the advantage of being close to the city centre, and with its own restaurants and shops. Nearby **Llandudno** has similar vistas, no shops or restaurants, but a supremely beautiful beach with clusters of granite boulders at either end. **Hout Bay** is the main urban concentration along the lower half of the peninsula, with a harbour, pleasant waterfront development and the only public transport beyond Camps Bay. South of Hout Bay is the semi-rural settlement of **Noordhoek**, close to the Cape of Good Hope Nature Reserve.

BACKPACKER LODGES AND CAMPING

Imhoff Caravan Park

Map 2, B8. 1 Wireless Rd, Kommetjie ☎ 021-783-1634, ⓕ 021-783-2871, ⓔ anderson@icon.co.za.
A hundred metres from spectacular Long Beach, this is the nicest campsite in the area. Two fully equipped self-catering chalets (sleeping four) are available, plus three on-site caravans (bring bedding). Camping ❶, chalets ❷.

B&BS AND SELF-CATERING

Beach House

Map 2, C5. Royal Ave, Hout Bay ☎ 021-790-4228, ⓦ www.wk.co.za/beachhouse.
Modern and friendly guest house with seven en-suite rooms, a five-minute walk from Mariner's Wharf and the beach. Features a patio with tables and chairs. ❹

Leeukop

Map 3, B6. 25 Sedgemoor Rd, Camps Bay ☎ 021-438-1361, ⓔ leeukopbb@hotmail.com.
Camps Bay bus.
Most reasonably priced B&B accommodation in Camps Bay, near the beach and cafés, in two stylishly arty and comfortable apartments adjoining the cheerful proprietor's home. The flats, the bigger one being pricier, are fully equipped, and you can either self-cater or stay on a B&B basis. Studio apartment ❹, larger apartment ❺.

Monkey Valley Resort

Map 2, C7. Mountain Rd, Noordhoek ☎ 021-789-1391, ⓦ www.monkeyvalleyresort.com.
Attractive group of mainly wooden and thatched two-storey chalets spread over several acres of Chapman's Peak, overlooking the seven-

ACCOMMODATION

kilometre Noordhoek beach, 40km south of the city centre. Surrounded by indigenous vegetation and with no other houses in sight, and there's an emphasis on natural products throughout. Either eat in the restaurant, self-cater or stay on a B&B basis. Cottages sleep six to eight people and work out reasonably cheaply for a group. Garden-facing ❺, sea-facing ❻.

HOTELS

Bay Hotel
Map 3, B6. Victoria Rd, Camps Bay ⓣ 021-438-4444, ⓦ www .thebay.co.za.
Luxurious, glitzy five-star hotel on the fashionable beachfront strip. Its late-1980s construction blends neo-Cape Dutch with Mediterranean styles and cane furniture, to conjure up a laidback colonial fantasy. Mountain-facing ❽, sea-facing and luxury suites ❾.

Chapman's Peak Hotel
Map 2, C6. Main Rd, Hout Bay ⓣ 021-790-1036, ⓕ 021-790-1089.
Impressive seaside setting overlooking Hout Bay beach, though not all of the rather ordinary rooms are sea-facing. The pubby restaurant does great calamari, though the other seafood is not particularly recommended. ❸

FALSE BAY SEABOARD

The Cape Town–Simon's Town Metrorail line runs through the southern suburbs to hit the coast at **Muizenberg**, the oldest of Cape Town's seaside suburbs. To its south are a series of settlements, including salubrious **St James**, **Kalk Bay**, with its working harbour and great cafés, and **Fish Hoek**, which is known for the best swimming beach along the False Bay seaboard. At the end of the line is the handsome and historic village of Simon's Town (see separate listing on pp.168-72).

BACKPACKER LODGES

Harbourside Backpackers

Map 2, D8. 136 Main Rd, Kalk Bay ☎ 021-788-2943, ⓕ 021-788-6452. Kalk Bay station.

A party atmosphere prevails in this popular hangout with views of the harbour. The hostel, two minutes' walk from the station, is on the same road as several cafés and very browsable antique shops, and a ten-minute walk to the lovely Dalebrook tidal pool. ❶

SELF-CATERING

Nautilus Lodge

Map 2, D8. 39 Simon's Town Rd, Fish Hoek ☎ 021-782-4168, ⓦ www.nautiluslodge.co.za. Sunny Cove station.

Three self-catering units next to Tudor House, on Jager's Walk leading to Fish Hoek Beach. Each unit has magnificent sea views and a patio with garden furniture. Two-bedroom unit R750, three-bedroom unit R850.

Tudor House by the Sea

Map 2, D8. 43 Simon's Town Rd, Fish Hoek ☎ 021-782-6238, ⓦ www.tudorhouse.co.za. Sunny Cove station.

Luxury self-catering apartments with slightly stuffy decor, but wide uninterrupted views of False Bay across the train tracks; each unit has its own balcony or garden. Sunny Cove Station is two minutes away on foot, providing transport to both the city centre (35km) and Simon's Town (5km). It's a five-minute walk along a coastal path to the wide, safe and sandy Fish Hoek swimming beach. Book as far ahead as possible. ❺

B&BS, GUEST HOUSES AND HOTELS

The Avenue Hotel

Map 2, D8. 7 First Ave, Fish Hoek ☎ 021-782-6026, ⓦ home.intekom.com/avenuehotel. Fish Hoek station.

Unglamorous two-storey hotel within walking distance of the beach and shops, but with no sea view. Well priced and perfectly adequate rooms make it popular with tour groups. Outside there's a pool with loungers and umbrellas, if it's too windy for the beach. ④

Chartfield Guest House

Map 2, D8. Corner of 30 Gatesville and Norman roads, Kalk Bay ☎ 021-788-3793, ⓦ www.chartfield.co.za. Kalk Bay station.

Unpretentious but newly refurbished accommodation, 100m from Kalk Bay station, in a well-kept rambling house halfway up the hill overlooking the harbour – there are terrific panoramas of the Hottentots Holland Mountains across False Bay. The best rooms are the one in the loft with its own balcony and the two semicircular corner ones with 180-degree views. It has its own bistro and is three minutes' walk to the Kalk Bay restaurant strip. Good value. ②–③

The Inn at Castle Hill

Map 2, D8. 37 Gatesville Rd, Kalk Bay ☎ 021-788-2554, ⓦ www.castlehill.co.za. Kalk Bay station.

Stylishly restored two-storey Edwardian guest house up a hill with grand views of the sun rising across False Bay and whale-watching in season. Five large bedrooms have high ceilings and timber floors. The best units are the Orca Whale and Humpback Whale rooms, which have French doors opening onto the upstairs verandah; avoid the disappointingly small and viewless back room. ④–⑤

Sunny Cove Manor

Map 2, D8. 72 Simon's Town Rd, Fish Hoek ☎ 021-782-2274, ⓔ sunnycovemanor@yahoo .com. Sunny Cove station.

Outstanding sea views (except for the back room) in this cheerful B&B, three minutes' walk to Sunny Cove station, with safe parking on the property. There are four suites, three of them with two bedrooms each, and if you cross the road and over the rail line, you're on Jager's Walk, which leads to Fish Hoek beach. ④

SIMON'S TOWN

Simon's Town (see p.130) is regarded by most Capetonians as a separate village, which it originally was, although it's now quite definitely part of the metropolis. During the day, all trains are met by Rikki's taxis, which will take you anywhere in the Simon's Town vicinity.

B&BS AND SELF-CATERING

Ark Studio

Map 2, E10. 4 Grant Ave, Boulders ☎ 021-786-2526 or 082-777-5562, ⓕ 021-786-3512. Simon's Town station. Two rather luxurious and fully equipped self-catering units sleeping two to four people, with unimpeded sweeping views across False Bay, a couple of minutes' walk from Boulders Beach. Guests have the use of the garden, a small heated plunge pool and off-street parking. Breakfast is available. ❹

Boulders Beach Guest House

Map 2, E10. 4 Boulders Place, Boulders Beach ☎ 021-786-1758, ⓕ 021-786-1825, ⓔ boulders@iafrica.com.

Simon's Town station. Thirteen B&B rooms and two self-catering flats above the Boulders Beach car park, two minutes from Boulders Coastal Park and the African penguin colony. The self-catering units sleeping two to six people have patios for outdoor breakfasts, and braai facilities. Meals available at the adjacent restaurant (Mon–Sun 8am–9pm). ❹

British Hotel Apartments

Map 2, D9. 90 St George's St ☎ 021-786-2214, ⓦ www.british-hotel.co.za. Simon's Town station. Three-bedroom self-catering apartments in a grand 1898 Victorian hotel, that once had Cecil Rhodes and the nineteenth-century-explorer Mary Kingsley as guests. Part of a highly picturesque main street, this is an experience

ACCOMMODATION

rather than just somewhere to stay, with Victorian colonial decor and enormous spaces with high ceilings and huge balconies overlooking the street and the docks, there are more modest doubles (with bath). The *Victorian Rose* restaurant does breakfast and teas (9am–noon) in the courtyard. ❹

Kijabe Lodge
Map 2, E10. 32 Disa Rd, Murdock Valley ⓣ & ⓕ 021-786-2433. Simon's Town station.
Two en-suite bedrooms in the modern mountainside home of friendly Belgian owners, five minutes by car from Simon's Town centre, and a ten-minute walk to Boulders Beach. The very reasonably priced rooms have good sea views, and there's a big pool with chairs and tables around it, plus braai facilities. One of the rooms can accommodate parents and a child. ❷

Oatlands Holiday Village
Map 2, E10. Froggy Pond ⓣ 021-786-1410,

ⓦ www.caraville.co.za/oatlands. htm. Simon's Town station.
Family resort across the road from the beach and near a golf course, 3km from Simon's Town and 1km from the Boulders Beach penguin colony. There are over twenty self-catering chalets of various sizes, sleeping two to six people. The cheapest of the lot are uncarpeted, without TV and have bunks, while the best have all you need for a family holiday. The grounds are large, with a pool, playground and trampoline, and there are a pub and restaurant on the premises. ❸

HOTELS

Lord Nelson Inn
Map 2, D9. 58 St George's St ⓣ 021-786-1386, ⓦ www.simonstown.com/hotels /lordnelson. Simon's Town station.
A comfortable and busy little inn, along the main road in the centre of town, whose name recalls the fact that Nelson once spent time convalescing in the harbour

ACCOMMODATION

village. The best of the hotel's compact rooms, all furnished in country style with pine,

have balconies and harbour views. Reasonable value. ❸

AFRICAN TOWNSHIP HOMESTAYS

One of the best ways of getting a taste of the African townships is spending a night there. The number of township residents offering B&B accommodation in their homes is still small, but growing. You'll have a chance to experience the warmth of *ubuntu*, traditional African hospitality, be part of a family with whom you'll generally eat breakfast and dinner and they'll also look after you while you're with them. They will usually take you around their area to shebeens, music venues or just to meet the neighbours. You'll need to phone ahead to arrange to get there. Many people are dropped off by tour operators, and some B&Bs will even meet you at the airport, which is nearby. But if you're self-driving they'll give you detailed directions or arrange to meet you at a convenient landmark, such as a garage or police station. For information about other B&Bs in the townships contact Sivuyile Tourism Centre in Guguletu (Mon–Fri 8am–5pm, Sat 8.30am–2pm, Sun 8.30am–1pm; ☎021-637-8449, ⓦwww.sivuyile.co.za) or Thuthuka Tours (☎021-439-2061 or 082-979-5831, ⓦwww.townshipcrawling.com), which aside from running township tours will also help with finding township accommodation.

Kopanong Khayelitsha (Map 2, I5; ☎021-361-2084 or 082-476-1278). One of the most dynamic B&B operations in the township, run by the tireless Thope Lekau, who has a mission to replace gawping tourists in their buses with guests who engage with township life. Her house has three rooms and this former NGO worker will treat you to a history of the township, introduce you to local music and dish up a traditional family breakfast. Dinner is also available on request, as is a guided tour. B&B rate ❸

Simon's Town Quayside Lodge

Map 2, D9. St George's St, off Jubilee Square ⓣ021-786-3838, ⓦwww.quayside.co.za. Simon's Town station.

Majoro's Khayelitsha (Map 2, I5; ⓣ021-361-3412 or 082-537-6882). Hosted by the charming and interesting Maria Maile in her family home, there are two rooms, which share a bath and toilet facilities. Dinner includes traditional food such as *mielie pap* (maize porridge), and you'll be treated to an English breakfast with a difference, which may include bacon and egg with fish cakes, sausage and homemade steamed bread. Half-board rate ❸

Malebo's Khayelitsha (Map 2, I5; ⓣ021-361-2391). Three rooms sharing bath and toilet facilities in the welcoming home of Lydea Masoleng and her husband. In the morning you'll be served a continental breakfast, while dinners, which combine familiar Western fare and traditional African food, are available on request. You're welcome to join them on outings to the shebeen or to church on Sunday. B&B rate ❸

Maneo Langa (Map 2, F2; ⓣ021-694-2504). B&B with two outside rooms and one inside the family house in Cape Town's oldest township and the closest to the city centre. The friendly hostess, Thandi Peter, takes guests to some of the township highlights including a local shebeen where you may see singing and dancing, and you can go to *Eziko Catering* for a bite. Since it's close to town, most visitors self-drive. B&B rate ❸

Vicky's Khayelitsha (Map 2, I5; ⓣ021-387-7104 or 082-225-2986). Under the proprietorship of Vicky Ntozini, this B&B, which has three rooms, is one of the pioneers of township homestays. You'll be taken on a walking tour to meet local people. Half-board rate ❸

A C C O M M O D A T I O N

Luxury hotel with 28 rooms, occupying a good part of the Simon's Town marina right in the centre of town, and with an annexe across the road above the post office. Views from the balconies of the sea-facing rooms take in the mountain-edged False Bay, the yacht basin and naval dock yard; the hotel is awash with nautical artefacts. Mountain- and sea-facing rooms ❺, sea-facing with balcony ❻.

Eating

ape Town has a large number of relaxed and convivial restaurants, generally serving imaginative and healthy food of a high quality. The range of styles is broad, with a full range of international cuisines available, and the devalued South African rand means that for many foreign visitors it's possible to eat in upmarket restaurants with outstanding chefs creating innovative food for the kind of money you'd spend on a pizza back home. This is the city to splash out on whatever takes your fancy, and you'll find the quality of meat and fish very high, with vegetarians also always getting a look in.

Cape cuisine – a spicy hybrid of the cooking styles brought to South Africa and adapted by slaves, principally from Asia and Madagascar – is not the thing to concentrate on when you're choosing somewhere to eat, though some elements of Cape and African cuisine find their way onto fusion-style menus at upmarket places, and, if you're curious, there are a couple of dedicated restaurants. Mild and semi-sweet curries with a strong Indonesian influence predominate, and include: *bredie* (stew), of which *water-blommetjiebredie*, made using water hyacinths, is a speciality; *bobotie*, a spicy mince dish served under a savoury custard; and *sosaties*, a local version of kebab using mincemeat. For dessert, dates stuffed with almonds make a light and delicious end to a meal, while *malva* pudding is a rich combination of milk, sugar, cream and apricot jam.

As far as **seafood** goes, you can be assured of fresh fish, done in all sorts of styles at every good restaurant. Cape Town itself offers cold-water fish such as kingklip, hake and snoek – every fish'n'chip shop in town offers fried snoek in season. The cold waters up the west coast yield quantities of crayfish and mussels while fresh fish, oysters and prawns are flown in from warmer waters.

As far as drinking is concerned, **Cape wines** are the obvious accompaniment to your meals, and where better to sample them than under the gaze of Table Mountain.

For the best delis and places to buy food and wine for picnics and self-catering, see p.210.
For top picnic spots see p.240.

BREAKFAST, SNACKS AND OUTDOOR EATING

Recently Cape Town's city centre has begun to enjoy a renaissance, and plenty of continental-style **cafés** are springing up. Service tends to be efficient and friendly, and most cafés stay open till around 11pm.

CITY CENTRE

Gallery Café
Map 4, D6. South African National Gallery, Government Avenue. Cape Town station. Tues–Sun 10am–5pm. Breakfast, lunch and tea with a small but good menu that includes pasta, salads and sandwiches in a pleasant space inside the gallery – the best place for refreshment if you're exploring the museums in the Gardens.

Long Street Café
Map 4, C5. 259 Long St. Cape Town station.

Mon–Sat 9.30am–midnight, Sun 6–11pm.

Cool bar/deli/restaurant in the city centre's most happening street, with tasteful open-plan decor and fresh continental-style food. Also good if you just want a drink.

Mr Pickwick's

Map 4, C5. 158 Long St. Cape Town station.

Mon & Tues 8am–2pm, Wed–Sat 8am–4pm.

Hearty and cheap meals served on tin plates, including a range of hot and cold "foot-long" sandwiches, which are quite a challenge.

Sunflower Health Café

Map 4, C4. 111 Long St. Cape Town station.

Mon–Fri 9.45am–5.30pm, Sat 9am–2pm.

Vegetarian restaurant attached to a health-food shop. Menu includes two hot meals each day, of the lentil bake or vegetable lasagne variety, as well as salads and tasty cold food.

Yellow Pepper

Map 4, C5. 138 Long St. Cape Town station.

Mon–Sat 8.30am–5pm, plus dinner Fri & Sat.

Good lunch spot near town centre, featuring big plate-glass windows to gawk at bustling Long Street, and pasta bakes that will set you up for an afternoon's sightseeing or shopping.

V & A WATERFRONT

Bayfront Blu

Map p.82, C6. Two Oceans Aquarium. Waterfront buses.

Daily 9am–11.30pm.

All-day breakfasts and fine coffee in an unbeatable location attached to the aquarium, with seating on a quayside deck that gives views of boats cutting across the water and clouds drifting over Table Mountain.

Caffe Balducci

Map p.82, F3. Quay 6, V & A Waterfront. Waterfront bus.

Daily 9am until midnight.

Upmarket coffee/shop restaurant open for breakfast, lunch and dinner, with interesting Californian/Italian food with South African overtones, and lovely views. Try their steak roll in peri-peri sauce.

Caffe San Marco

Map p.82, E4. Piazza level, Victoria Wharf, V & A Waterfront. Waterfront bus.

Daily 9am–midnight.

Coffee shop/bar with umbrellas on the piazza serving an all-day breakfast menu, good sandwiches on Italian breads, grilled vegetable salads, hot food and delicious calamari with garlic and chilli. They do eighteen flavours of gelato and sorbet.

Mugg & Bean

Map p.82, F3. Victoria Wharf. Waterfront buses.

Daily 9am–midnight.

Choose from a range of excellent coffees (if you need to tank up on caffeine try their bottomless cup of java). Light meals include toasted sandwiches and salads, but the location inside a shopping mall doesn't make the most of the Waterfront setting.

Zerban's

Map p.82, E3. Victoria Wharf. Waterfront buses.

Daily 8am–11pm.

The Waterfront incarnation of a Cape Town institution, previously known for its European-style cakes, bread and coffee but now successfully branching out into breakfasts as well as brunch and lunch.

CITY BOWL SUBURBS

Happy Wok

Map 7, D1. 62a Kloof St, Gardens. 1.5km from Cape Town station.

Daily 5.30pm–late, Mon–Fri noon–2.30pm.

Very informal and inexpensive café-style eatery serving a reliable range of dishes from China, Japan and Vietnam, plus self-service jasmine tea. Try their Singapore noodles and peppered stirfried beef.

EATING

There's no convenient public transport in the City Bowl suburbs, but most of the eateries listed here are walkable from the city centre and, if you're exploring the museums and Gardens, few will be more than ten to fifteen minutes away.

Melissa's

Map 7, D2. 94 Kloof St, Gardens. 3km from Cape Town station.

Weekdays 7.30am–9pm, weekends 8am–9pm.

In the food emporium you can buy freshly made Mediterranean fare, while the small café serves light meals and fine desserts.

Raith Gourmet

Map 4, G8. Gardens Centre, Mill St, Gardens. 2km from Cape Town station.

Mon–Fri 8.30am until 6pm, Sat until 1pm.

This meat-centred deli has an exceptional selection of foods. Enjoy the aromas while you eat one of their marvellous sandwiches at the tables dotted between enticing comestibles. German specialities include sauerkraut fried with strips of bacon.

SEA POINT AND GREEN POINT

Chariots Italian Coffee Bar

Map 5, D6. 107 Main Rd, Green Point. Sea Point bus.

Daily 9.30–11pm, Sundays until 5pm.

Stylish decor and great inexpensive food make this a fashionable haunt for Cape Town's yuppies. Come for foccacia and decent coffee.

Giovanni's Deliworld

Map 5, D5. 103 Main Rd, Green Point. Sea Point bus.

Daily 8am–9pm.

With some indoor as well as pavement seating, this friendly Italian deli/coffee shop is handy for coffee, excellent made-to-order sandwiches, pre-cooked hot meals and stocking up on Italian foodstuffs. They do a tempting

EATING

range of take-out salads and dips, if you're self-catering or picnicking in the vicinity.

Newport Market and Deli

Map 5, B5. 47 Beach Rd. Mouille Point. Sea Point Bus ⓣ021-439-1538.

Daily 7pm till late.

Light, airy deli with views onto Table Bay for coffee, excellent sandwiches, salads and some hot dishes.

New York Bagels

Map 6, C2. 51 Regent Rd, Sea Point. Sea Point bus.

Daily till late.

Fantastic supermarket of a deli with a sit-down section. Choose from a dizzying array of bagels and homemade fillings, from chopped liver to herring, plus stir-fry, pasta and pastries. Recommended.

SOUTHERN SUBURBS

Café Carte Blanche

Map 3, H5. 42a Trill Rd, Observatory. Observatory station.

Daily 7pm till late.

Former curio shop decorated with Eastern artefacts, where you can sip wine under a hanging Persian carpet or quaff beer on a Mongolian bedspread. Small, unique and exotic.

Gardener's Cottage

Map 2, E3. 31 Newlands Ave, Montebello Estate, Newlands.

Tues–Fri 8am–4.30pm, Sat & Sun 8.30am–4.30pm.

Set in a complex of old farm buildings under ancient pine trees, and serving hearty breakfasts and lunches as well as tea and coffee. Worthwhile if you want to browse through the neighbouring arts and crafts workshops.

Jonkershuis

Map 2, D5. Groot Constantia Wine Estate, off Ladies Mile Extension, Constantia.

Breakfast, tea & lunch daily, dinner Tues–Sat.

Rustic informal place, where you can enjoy traditional Cape dishes or tea, surrounded by vineyards and mountains. A children's playground adjacent to outdoor seating makes this

EATING

congenial and easygoing for a family outing.

Obz Café

Map 3, H5. 115 Lower Main Rd, Observatory. Observatory station.
Daily all day till late.
Trendy deli/café/bar, where you can get tasty meals, bacon-and-egg breakfasts and Danish pastries, or nurse a drink all evening.

ATLANTIC SEABOARD

Fish on the Rocks
Map 2, B6. Beyond Mariner's Wharf, Hout Bay, drive through the dock and factory. Hout Bay bus.
Daily 9am–7pm.
Delicious fresh fish'n'chips, served under red umbrellas or eaten on the rocks overlooking the bay. A fabulous place, during the season, to watch whales.

La Cuccina Food Store
Map 2, B5. Victoria Mall, Victoria Rd, Hout Bay.
Daily 8am–7pm.

Open for breakfast and lunch buffets with tea and cake in between. High-quality deli food in pleasant surroundings, though no views.

Mariners Wharf Bistro
Map 2, B5. The Harbour, Hout Bay. Hout Bay bus.
Daily 10am–6pm.
Relaxed, well-run place with terrace seating overlooking the harbour. Good for seafood to eat in or take away.

Red Herring
Map 2, B7. Beach Rd/Pine Rd, Noordhoek.
Tues–Sun lunch & dinner.
Snacks and drinks on the upstairs deck, which offers marvellous sea and mountain views, attached to a country restaurant that does fish dishes, grilled meats and vegetarian options.

FALSE BAY SEABOARD

Artvaark Gallery and Café
Map 2, D8. Main Rd, Kalk Bay. Kalk Bay station.

Daily 9am–5pm.
Relaxed café with upstairs seating dominated by an old palm tree. Small menu and sea views.

The Meeting Place
Map 2, D9. 98 St George's Street. Simon's Town station.
Sun–Wed 9am–5pm & Thurs–Sat 9am–9pm.
Chill out on the upstairs balcony on Simon's Town's main drag, with views of the harbour and enjoy funky Mediterranean café food.

The Olympia Café & Deli
Map 2, D8. Main Rd, Kalk Bay. Kalk Bay station.
Tues–Sat 7am–7pm, Sun 7am–3pm.
One of the few places that will draw parochially territorial uptown Capetonians down the False Bay seaboard. Always buzzing, *Olympia* with its views of Kalk Bay harbour, is a regular village meeting spot for residents of Kalk Bay and St James. Great coffee or freshly squeezed orange juice can be accompanied by Danish pastries, filled croissants or delicious homemade biscuits for breakfast, while imaginative gourmet lunch menus are chalked up on a board.

VegiTable
Map 2, D8. 138 Main Rd, Kalk Bay. Kalk Bay Station.
Daily 8am–6pm. Thurs, Fri & Sat until 9pm.
Spacious, friendly vegetarian café looking onto the harbour with a section of fresh veggies and odd groceries. There's live music some weekend evenings.

RESTAURANTS

The greatest concentration of **restaurants** is in the city centre and the surrounding areas, with Sea Point, Green Point and the Waterfront having well-established reputations for good food.

As far as **prices** go, expect to pay under R40 for a main course at an inexpensive restaurant, up to R60 at a moderately priced one and over R70 at an expensive place.

CITY CENTRE AND V & A WATERFRONT

Africa Café

Map 4, B4. 108 Shortmarket St, Heritage Square ☎021-422-0221. Cape Town station.

Dinner Mon–Sat. Inexpensive–moderate.

Probably the best restaurant in Cape Town for African cuisine, with a fantastic selection from around the continent. Given that you're served a communal feast of sixteen dishes and can have as many refills as you like, its R105 per head price tag is pretty reasonable. Booking essential.

Anatoli

Map 5, G5. 24 Napier St ☎021-419-2501. Cape Town station.

Tues–Sun until 11pm. Moderate.

Turkish restaurant in a turn-of-the-century warehouse that buzzes with atmosphere. Excellent *meze* include exceptionally delicious dolmades, and superb desserts include pressed dates topped with cream.

Bayfront Blu

Map p.82, C6. Two Oceans Aquarium, Waterfront ☎021-419-9068. Waterfront buses.

Daily lunch & dinner. Moderate–expensive.

Traditional African food as well as Californian dishes, a good vegetarian selection and some exciting seafood options such as Swahili prawn curry. Best of all is its situation on the edge of the marina, with outdoor seating that offers a stunning view of Table Mountain.

Biesmiellah

Map 5, G7. Upper Wale St/Pentz St ☎021-423-0850. Cape Town station.

Daily, except Sun noon–3pm & 6–11pm. Moderate.

One of the oldest and best-known restaurants for traditional Cape cuisine. Try their spicy stews and round things off with a wickedly rich *malva* pudding made with apricot jam and cream. No alcohol.

Bukhara

Map 4, C4. 33 Church St
☏021-424-0000. Cape Town
Station.

Mon–Sat lunch & dinner, Sun
dinner. Moderate–expensive.
Popular upmarket North
Indian place, with green
marble floors and a show
kitchen where you can watch
chefs at work. The food is
superlative but not cheap.
You'll need to book to get
into one of the two sittings in
the evening.

Caravan Cafe

Map 4, C5. 167 Long St ☏021-
426-4671. Cape Town station.
Lunch & dinner Mon–Sat.
Moderate.
Small, inexpensive portions of
starters followed by huge
dishes of couscous and main
courses such as fish in ginger
and orange sauce and lamb
tagine. While you don't
lounge on the floor here, there
is a hookah to puff away on.

Col'Cacchio

Map 4, B1. Seeff House, 42
Hans Strijdom Ave. Cape Town
station.
Lunch Mon–Fri, dinner daily.

Inexpensive.
Offbeat pizza restaurant,
which also serves pasta and
salads, and often spills onto
the pavement outside. Has
over forty different and
original pizza toppings, such
as smoked salmon, sour cream
and caviar, and bills itself as
low fat and heart friendly. No
bookings.

Emily's Bistro

Map p.82, F6. Shop 202, Clock
Tower Centre, V & A Waterfront
☏021-421-1133.
Lunch daily, dinner Mon–Sat.
Moderate–expensive.
Flamboyant and chic South
African creations, modernizing
some traditional Afrikaans
dishes and generally offering a
cuisine firmly grounded in
Africa. A cooking school is
also based here, and the
restaurant rates as one of the
Western Cape's tops. Every
table has a view of the water.

Five Flies

Map 4, C5. 14-16 Keerom St
☏021-424-4442. Cape Town
station.
Mon–Fri lunch and dinner, Sat &
Sun dinner.

Moderate–expensive. Wonderfully imaginative food, with a sophisticated blend of global styles which really works. The presentation delights, the ambience is elegant, but not formal. Not cheap, but you won't find better in Cape Town.

Floris Smit Huijs

Map 4, C4. 55 Church St Ⓣ021-423-3414. Cape Town station.

Daily until 10.30pm, closed Sun all day, & Mon lunch. Moderate. The beautiful decor in this eighteenth-century town house is as big an attraction as the eclectic international cuisine, which features some local specialities such as Malay chicken salad and kudu venison served with a delicious apple sauce.

Jewel Tavern

Map 3, G3. Off Vanguard Rd, Duncan Dock Ⓣ021-448-1977. Daily mid-morning till 10pm. Moderate. Unpretentious Taiwanese sailors' eating house, which has been "discovered" by Cape Town's *bon viveurs*. Located in the middle of the docks, it serves superb food, including great hot and sour soup and spring rolls made while you watch.

Long Life Noodle Bar

Map 4, C6. 192 Long St Ⓣ021-426-5805. Cape Town station. Dinner Mon–Sat. Inexpensive–moderate. Canteen-style eatery with long benches that does a vast variety of tasty noodle dishes, from Thai-style broth to Japanese miso.

Mama Africa

Map 4, C5. 178 Long St Ⓣ021-424-8634. Cape Town station. Dinner Mon–Sat. Moderate. Food from around the continent, including local Cape specialities and succulent Karoo lamb, served in a relaxed atmosphere. The highlight is a twelve-metre bar in the form of a sinuous green mamba.

EATING

Mexican Kitchen Café
Map 4, C6. 13 Bloem St ⓣ021-423-1541. Cape Town station.
Daily until midnight.
Inexpensive.
Excellent, casual restaurant serving up good-value burritos, enchiladas, nachos and calamari fajitas, with some fine vegetarian options. They also do deli-style takeaways.

Tasca de Belem
Map p.82, E4. Shop 154, Piazza Level, Victoria Wharf, Waterfront ⓣ021-419-3009. Waterfront buses.
Daily 12.30–2.30pm & 6.30–10.30pm. Moderate.
Portuguese specialities with funky outdoor seating in summer, while winters are cosy inside. The flame-grilled chicken is good, as are the peri-peri chicken livers.

Vasco da Gama Tavern
Map 4, A2. 3 Alfred St ⓣ021-425-2157. Cape Town station.
Daily 10.45am–7.30pm.
Inexpensive.
Known locally as the "Portuguese embassy", this unpretentious restaurant with a blaring TV is a genuine working man's pub. Grilled tongue with bread, accompanied by wine mixed with Coke – a Portuguese "speciality" called *catemba* – are standard. It's also a great seafood restaurant at half the usual price, and better than many of the upmarket joints.

Willoughby & Co.
Map p.82, F2. Lower Level, Victoria Wharf ⓣ021-418-6115. Waterfront Bus.
Daily lunch & dinner, Sushi bar closed 3pm–6pm. Moderate.
Excellent sushi with some master sushi makers on hand. Buy fresh seafood in the deli section if you're cooking for yourself or go for their Namibian oysters, crayfish or seafood platters.

CITY BOWL SUBURBS

Amigos Mediterranean Restaurant
Map 7, D3.158 Kloof St, Gardens ⓣ021-423-6805.
2.5km from Cape Town station.
Lunch & dinner daily until midnight. Moderate.

A tasty mixture of Greek *meze* combined with Italian and Spanish food. Lively joint with some tables outside and a loyal clientele.

The Blue Plate Restaurant and Bar

Map 4, C7. 35 Kloof St, Gardens ☎ 021-424-1515. 1.5km from Cape Town station. Dinner daily till late, lunch Fri only. Moderate.

Spacious restaurant in an elegant Victorian home offering global cuisine. Friendly and well-informed waiters and some outdoor seating along the sidewalk.

Buccaneer Steakhouse

Map 4, C7. 64 Orange St, Gardens ☎ 021-424-4966. 1.5km from Cape Town station. Dinner daily, lunch Mon–Fri. Inexpensive.

Swiss-owned eatery that does good steaks and great sauces. The atmosphere borders on dowdy, but it makes for a relaxed and low-cost evening.

Café Paradiso

Map 7, D3. 110 Kloof St, Gardens ☎ 021-423-8653. Daily lunch & dinner. Moderate.

Good Greek and Mediterranean dishes, including a weigh-your-plate *meze* bar and outside terrace with views up to the mountain and down over the city and docks.

Chef Pon's Asian Kitchen

Map 4, F8. 12 Mill St, Gardens, next to the Holiday Inn ☎ 021-465-5846. 2km from Cape Town station. Lunch & dinner daily, except Sun. Moderate.

Very popular, noisy neighbourhood restaurant serving Thai, Vietnamese, Japanese and Chinese food.

Ocean Basket Southern Africa

Map 4, C9. 75 Kloof St, Gardens ☎ 021-422-0322. 2.5km from Cape Town station. Lunch Mon–Sat & dinner every evening. Moderate.

Long queues and delicious aromas speak eloquently of the outstanding dishes – from fish'n'chips to prawns and calamari – at this slick quick-in, quick-out seafood chain.

EATING

Yindees

Map 7, D1. 22 Camp St, Tamboerskloof ℡021-422-1012. 3km from Cape Town station. Lunch Mon–Sat, dinner Mon–Sat. Moderate.

Deservedly popular Thai restaurant offering good food. Try their brilliant spicy prawn soup served by dour waiters.

SOUTHERN SUBURBS

Buitenverwachting

Map 2, D5. Buitenverwachting Estate, Klein Constantia Rd ℡021-794-3522. Tues–Fri lunch & dinner, Sat lunch. Expensive.

One of South Africa's top restaurants, wonderfully located on the Buiten-verwachting wine estate with views of the vineyards and mountains from the terrace. The food is imaginative, fusing international and Cape flavours, but can be uneven.

Enrica Rocca

Map 2, E4. 19 Wolfe St, Wynberg ℡021-762-3855. Wynberg station. Mon–Sat lunch & dinner.

Moderate–expensive.

A real authentic Italian, with a vast antipasto spread followed by a limited range of interesting pasta dishes. Fixed-price set-menu options are a good deal if you want to have the works: antipasta, pasta, main dish and dessert.

La Colombe

Map 2, D5. Constantia Uitsig Wine Estate, Spaanschemat River Rd, Constantia ℡021-794-2390. Lunch & dinner, closed Sun dinner & all day Tues. Expensive.

Airy restaurant, rated one of South Africa's best, overlooking a pool and beautiful gardens. An imaginative Provençale menu dreamed up by the French chef varies from day to day, depending on what's in season. Book way in advance.

Pancho's Mexican Kitchen

Map 3, H5. 127 Lower Main Rd, Observatory ℡021-447-4854. Observatory station. Daily–late. Inexpensive.

Highly popular and

inexpensive cantina-style restaurant serving Mexican dishes.

SEA POINT AND GREEN POINT

Aris Souvlaki
Map 6, B2. 83a Regent Rd, Sea Point ⓣ 021-439-6683. Sea Point bus.
Daily until 11pm. Inexpensive. Reliable terrace restaurant with Greek shwarma and souvlaki. You can also get takeaways.

Nando's Chickenland
Map 6, F2. 128 Main Rd, Sea Point ⓣ 021-439-7999. Sea Point bus.
Daily until 10pm. Inexpensive. South Africa's answer to KFC. Surprisingly good grilled Portuguese-style peri-peri poultry with a choice of seasoning.

Pizzeria Napoletana
Map 6, D3. 178 Main Rd, Sea Point. Sea Point bus.
Closed Mon. Moderate. A family business since 1956, the best pizza joint in Cape Town offers good value and tasty cuisine. Try the veal parmigiano, or their crayfish – the best value you'll find on the peninsula.

San Marco
Map 6, G2. 92 Main Rd, Sea Point ⓣ 021-439-2758. Sea Point bus.
Lunch Sun, dinner Wed–Mon. Moderate–expensive. Stunning Italian seafood as well as pasta. The grilled calamari tossed in chilli and garlic is wonderful, and their antipasto trolley is especially good for vegetarians. Finish with their wonderful ice cream.

Theo's Grill Butcher and Seafood.
Map 5, B5. Beach Rd, Mouille Point ⓣ 021-439-3494. Sea Point bus.
Lunch Mon–Fri, dinner Mon–Sat. Moderate. Upmarket atmospheric place right on the beachfront, offering superb Greek-style steaks and seafood.

EATING

Wang Thai

Map 5, D6. 105 Main Rd, Green Point ☎ 021-439-6164. Sea Point bus.

Lunch Sun–Fri, dinner daily. Moderate.

Cape Town's best Thai restaurant. Try their hot and spicy prawn soup, Hanoi beef salad, steamed fish with lemon juice and chilli, or their special of thinly sliced, seared sirloin.

Zeroninethreetwo

Map 5, D5. 79 Main Rd, Exhibition Building, Green Point ☎ 021-439-6306. Sea Point bus.

Daily 11am till late. Moderate.

Belgian cuisine and beer, with mussels, excellent *frites*, prawns and salads in funky minimalist surroundings.

ATLANTIC SEABOARD
- - - - - - - - - - - - - - - - - - - -

Primi Piatti

Map 3, B6. 9 Victoria Rd, Camps Bay ☎ 021-438-3120. Hout Bay bus.

Daily lunch and dinner. Moderate.

Pizza, pasta and salads in a noisy, busy restaurant on the bay.

Red Herring

Map 2, C7. Beach Rd/Pine St, Noordhoek ☎ 021-789-1783.

Lunch & dinner Tues–Sun. Moderate.

Beautiful sea and mountain views at this relaxed out-of-town restaurant. Choices include springbok and kudu, plus a good choice of vegetarian options and fresh fish.

Theo's Grill Butcher and Seafood

Map 3, B6. Promenade Building, Victoria Rd, Camps Bay ☎ 021-438-3120. Hout Bay bus.

Daily lunch & dinner. Moderate.

Brilliant steaks (the meat is sold by weight), seafood and a buzzy ambience, with some outdoor seating.

Vilamoura

Map 3, B6. 9 The Broadway, Victoria Rd, Camps Bay ☎ 021-438-1850. Hout Bay bus.

Daily noon until after midnight.

EATING

Expensive.

Cape Town's best seafood restaurant doesn't come cheap, but makes a fine choice for a special occasion. Slick and modern it has fantastic views, superb service and includes traditional Portuguese dishes like salt cod soup and Lourenço Marques chicken on the menu.

FALSE BAY SEABOARD

- -

Black Marlin
Map 2, E11. Main Rd, Miller's Point ⓣ 021-786-1621.
Lunch & dinner daily, closed Sun evening.
Good choice for seafood if you're heading out to Simon's Town or beyond. Their crayfish or fish kebabs are recommended.

Brass Bell
Map 2, D8. Main Rd, Kalk Bay ⓣ 021-788-5456. Kalk Bay station.
Daily until late. Moderate.
Primarily a drinking spot with arguably the best location on the peninsula, this unpretentious Cape Town institution is located in the station building and has False Bay's waves breaking against the wall of its outdoor terrace. Unbeatable views of both the peninsula mountains and the Hottentots Holland peaks, but the seafood meals don't always match the magnificent setting.

Gaylords Indian Cuisine
Map 2, E7. 65 Main Rd, Muizenberg ⓣ 021-788-5470. Muizenberg station.
Dinner & lunch Wed–Sun, dinner only Mon.
Inexpensive–moderate.
The tacky interior belies an imaginative menu that adapts great North Indian cooking and local ingredients to create something unique – and reasonably priced. Expect to wait for your food though.

Harbour House Restaurant
Map 2, D8. Kalk Bay Harbour ⓣ 021-788-4133. Kalk Bay station.
Lunch & dinner daily.
Moderate–expensive.
Seafood and Mediterranean fare, at a venue situated

EATING

spectacularly on the breakwater of Kalk Bay Harbour. Freshly caught fish from the local boats is a speciality. Winter specials are great value and there's a fire inside. Book a table with bay views.

Kalky's
Map 2, D8. Kalk Bay Harbour. Kalk Bay station.

Daily. Inexpensive.

The best traditional fish 'n' chips on the peninsula where fish is hauled off the boats and straight into the frying pan at a totally unpretentious harbourside eatery that has been serving the fishing community for years. Sit down at benches covered in plastic or take away. Also great-value seafood platters.

Clubs, bars and live music

Cape Town's **nightlife** has traditionally been a little sleepy compared with Johannesburg's, but this is changing. Things have become much more open and cosmopolitan in recent years, spiced up by thousands of African and European visitors and immigrants. A general loosening up of the city's staid personality has made it a diverse and exciting place to go out in.

Cape Town is well populated with **bars**, ranging from the hip to the eccentric to the seedy. Most liquor licences stipulate that the last round is served at 2am, but this is far from strictly followed. Expect a cover charge if live music is featured. Traditional pubs are not a big feature: where they do exist they're generally either cod-Irish franchises or depressing empty dives.

Music is a passion for Capetonians, and while mainstream house is very popular, there are also strong followings for drum'n'bass, trance, hip hop, dub and Latin grooves, as well as **kwaito**, the dance style of young black Jo'burg. Much more laid-back than European club sounds, *kwaito* can be described as slowed-down, bass-heavy house fused with township pop. Sexy and jubilant, it makes for a positive and uproarious party. Though *kwaito* is still predominately a black scene, coloured and white youth are gradually getting into it.

Many dance **clubs** have a short lifespan – and many of the best regular parties hop from venue to venue. Some of the more enduring clubs are listed below, but watch the press for up-to-the-minute information. The daily news papers, the *Cape Argus* and the *Cape Times*, run weekly club columns on Thursdays and Fridays respectively, and the monthly listings magazine *Cape Review* is also useful. Backpacker hostels are often the best sources of party infor-mation. Cover charges vary from R20 to over R100 for big events with international DJs. It's worth being aware that all

POP MUSIC AND CAPE JAZZ

Cape Town's greatest musical treasure is Cape jazz, a sub-genre of South African township jazz whose greatest expo-nent is the internationally acclaimed Abdullah Ibrahim (known as Dollar Brand before his conversion to Islam). Born and raised in District Six, Ibrahim is a supremely gifted pianist and composer, who for decades has produced a hypnotic fusion of African, American and Cape Muslim idioms. In his greatest recordings, *Mannenberg* and *African Marketplace*, the fluttering rhythms of *goema* – traditional Cape carnival music – are combined with the cascading call-and-answer structure of African gospel. This is emotional jazz, full of sim-ple, euphoric melody and enchanting brass lines.

Other Cape Town jazz legends are the late Basil Coetzee, a phenomenal tenor saxophonist who played on *Mannenberg*; Robbie Jansen, another saxman with a raunchy, fiery style who worked with Afro-pop greats Juluka; and alto saxman Winston "Ngozi" Mankunku, an old-school hepcat whose gigs are an exercise in good vibes. Both

drugs are illegal in South Africa, and aggressive police raids on clubs are by no means unknown.

Gay clubs are listed from p.228.

CITY CENTRE AND CITY BOWL SUBURBS

The highest concentration of places is on and around **Long Street** and Waterkant Street in the **Lower City Centre**. Nearby, Somerset Road in Green Point, with its string of mostly, though not exclusively, gay bars, is generally very lively.

Jansen and Mankunku can occasionally be heard live in the city – watch the press. Other veteran stars to look out for are guitarist Errol Dyers, pianist Hotep Galeta and bassist Spencer Mbadu.

Two young stars stand out as talented heirs to the Cape jazz tradition: astronomically cool guitarist Jimmy Dludlu and subtle, mellow pianist Paul Hanmer. Catch them live if you can. Also watch out for the powerful singer Judith Sephuma, and Jo'burg-based maestros Moses Molelekwa, McCoy Mrubata and Sipho Gumede. Check the press for upcoming performances and venues.

Cape Town is also well stocked with charismatic rock, reggae and pop bands. Notable exports include township bubblegum star Brenda Fassie, radical hip hop crew Prophets of Da City and R'n'B crooner Jonathan Butler. The best live acts are the Springbok Nude Girls, cheesy funk merchants The Honeymoon Suites, funk-reggae crew Firing Squad and the innovative live trance outfit Colorfields.

There's no public transport in Cape Town after mid-evening and walking around the city centre alone and at night is a bad idea. If you're out clubbing or partying arrange reliable transport beforehand, or call one of the metered taxis listed on p.254.

Chilli'n'Lime

Map 5, F5. 23 Somerset Rd, Green Point ☎ 021-426-4469.
Tues–Sat 8pm–4am.

A stylish split-level club which hosts pulsing house and hip-hop parties on weekend and Wednesday nights. Frequented by a left-field student crowd, around the 20-28 age group.

Club Georgia

Map 4, B7. 30 Georgia St, off Buitensingel ☎ 021-422-0261.
Tues–Sat 9.30pm–late.

Lively over-25s club that celebrates music from across Africa, including *kwassa-kwassa*, *kwaito*, *ndombolo*, *rai*, *kizamba* and *makossa*.

Club More

Map 4, B4. 74 Loop St ☎ 021-422-0544.
Wed, Fri and Sat 10pm till late.
Entry R40.

Fresh and funky house music in a New York-style club.

Drum Café

Map 4, F6. 32 Glynn St, Gardens ☎ 021-461-1305.
Mon, Wed, Fri & Sat 8pm–late.
Entrance R30, drums R20.

Have a drink and hire a drum for a communal drumming session. Every Monday and Wednesday at 9pm there's a drum circle led by a South African or West African drum teacher, suitable for all levels of experience, though the Monday groups are smaller and preferable if you're a complete novice. Saturday afternoons at 3pm are for families. If you prefer to leave things to the professionals, there are often parties at the weekends. Ring for the current schedule. Light meals available. Fully licensed.

The Jam

Map 3, E4. 43 De Villiers St, District Six ℡ 021-465-2106. Quality live music and underground hip-hop parties at a minimalist venue with space to move in. No rigid schedule, but there's an event on most nights – watch the press for details.

Jo'burg

Map 4, C6. 218 Long St, City Centre ℡ 021-422-0142. Daily 5pm–4am. Great decor, and a good place to schmooze to a funky soundtrack. Frequented by a hip art-school and media crowd. Live music on Sunday nights.

Kennedy's Restaurant and Cigar Lounge

Map 4, C3. 251 Long St, City Centre ℡ 021-424-1212. Mon–Fri noon till late, Sat 7pm till late. Swanky cigar bar offering cigars from all over the world, with brilliant martinis and margueritas, good food, an older crowd and live jazz every evening.

The Lounge

Map 4, C6. 194 Long St, City Centre ℡ 021-424-7636. Mon–Sat 8pm–2am. R20 when there's live music. Unabashedly trendy long-serving refuge for Cape Town's smart and glamorous. Once upstairs, make for the superb balcony and grab a table overlooking vibrant Long Street. House and jungle dominate the turntables.

Mama Africa

Map 4, C6. 178 Long St, City Centre ℡ 021-424-8634. Mon–Sat 8.30pm–late. A relaxed and spacious restaurant-bar in the heart of Long Street clubland, *Mama Africa* boasts a twelve-metre bar in the form of a green mamba. Traditional percussion groups perform regularly. Popular with European and North American visitors.

On Broadway

Map 5, F5. 21 Somerset Rd, Green Point ℡ 021-418-8338. Daily 7pm–late. Cabaret restaurant-bar with

Mediterranean-style food and live performances every night. See p.229 for more information.

The Purple Turtle

Map 4, C4. Corner Shortmarket and Long streets, City Centre.

Daily 11am–late.

A cavernous, vaguely seedy bar frequented by Goths, metalheads and other nocturnal creatures. Catch live music on Saturday nights, but don't expect easy listening.

Rhodes House

Map 4, C6. 60 Queen Victoria St ☏ 021-424-8844.

Wed–Sat 10pm till late.

Rather smart, though

relaxed, fashion-conscious place with progressive, French and Deep House sounds and lounge suites to fall into. Themed parties with dress codes also happen – ring before turning up.

The Shack

Map 3, E4. 45b De Villiers St, District Six ☏ 021-465-2106, ⓦ www.theshack.co.za.

Mon–Sat 1pm–late, Sun 6pm–late.

Walk-through venue with a restaurant, bar and pool hall. Music at *The Shack* ranges from the 1960s to 1980s. The adjoining *Blue Lizard* plays acidy jazz house music and trip hop.

V & A WATERFRONT

The **V & A Waterfront** offers a lot if you want to eat well and your budget is fairly generous. You'll also find a reasonable amount of mainstream after-dark nightlife in safe surroundings: the area has an emphatically clean-cut atmosphere.

Den Anker Restaurant and Bar

Map p.82, F5. Victoria and Alfred Pierhead ☏ 021-419-0251.

Daily 11am–midnight.

A smart busy pub and

continental bistro style restaurant populated by tourists and well-heeled locals. *Den Anker* specializes in imported Belgian beers, both on tap and in a bottle. One of

CLUBS, BARS AND LIVE MUSIC

the more spirited places to visit at the Waterfront.

Green Dolphin
Map p.82, E5. Victoria and Alfred Pierhead ☎ 021-421-7471.
Daily noon–midnight (music from 8.30pm). R20.
Top notch, though a tad chilly, jazz venue, serving excellent seafood and hosting quality jazz bands nightly at 8.15pm. Dinner is served from 6pm.

SOUTHERN SUBURBS

If you're on foot, **Observatory** is a good destination, with the area around Lower Main Road compact and safe. The buildings are old and characterful, the vibe is warm, mellow and multi-ethnic, and there's a gaggle of bohemian restaurants and bars. Of the neighbouring suburbs, **Woodstock** is in the same vein, while upmarket **Newlands** has more sedate offerings, as does **Constantia**, Cape Town's leafiest and richest suburb.

Bar 89 Woodstock
Map 3, G5. 89 Roodebloem Rd, Woodstock.
Tues–Sun 6pm–2am.
A friendly and intimate bar filled with elegant decor. Once an artisan's cottage, *89* offers a welcoming hearthfire in winter and – for the rest of the year – a great space to chill out in. Gay-friendly.

Boer and Brit Pub
Map 2, D4. *Alphen Hotel,* Alphen Drive, off the M41, Constantia.
Daily 10am–11pm.
Tables and umbrellas under oaks at a historic Cape Dutch hotel, with bar meals and a fire indoors on cold nights in a cosy English-style pub. Gracious yet relaxed.

Café Ganesh
Map 3, H5. 66 Lower Main Rd/Trill Rd, Observatory ☎ 021-448-3435.
Daily 6pm–late. Closed Mon & during July.
Café Ganesh is the cosmopolitan heart of

Observatory, and the place to meet artists, writers, performers and students. Spontaneous *kwaito* parties sometimes break out.

Don Pedros

Map 3, G5. 113 Roodebloem Rd, Woodstock
℡021-447-4493.
Daily 9am–late.
Since the 1980s, when it was a chosen haunt of struggling activists, *Don Pedros* has been a place for good cheap food and scruffy Capetonian ambience. Linger all evening over a beer or a coffee without feeling hassled. Gay-friendly place where people tend to hang out after shows, with a great atmosphere and smoking as well as non-smoking rooms.

Foresters' Arms

Map 2, E3. 52 Newlands Ave, Newlands.
Mon–Sat 10am–11pm, Sun 9am–4pm.
Preppie students and professionals gather to quaff draught beer at "Forries", in the heart of leafy Newlands. A big wood-panelled pub in the Anglo-Celtic tradition, it boasts a beautiful hedged-in courtyard. Grab a bench for a drowsy afternoon pint in the great outdoors. Very popular and busy place.

Independent Armchair Theatre

Map 3, H5. 135 Lower Main Rd, Observatory
℡021-447-1514.
A spacious club with several lounge suites, the *Independent Armchair Theatre* is a stylish, innovative venue with a small art gallery attached. Cult and art-house films are screened on week nights, and a steady stream of notable bands plays here.

Pedlars on the Bend

Map 2, D5. Spaanschemat River Rd, Constantia
℡021-794-7747.
Daily 11am–11pm.
Upmarket bar at one of the posher restaurants in this ritzy suburb, with a delightful outdoor area shaded by oaks. A good place to drop in while touring the Constantia winelands.

FALSE BAY AND ATLANTIC SEABOARDS

Sea Point is still a good place for a night out; otherwise head for the places listed here, further south along the Atlantic coast in Camps Bay and Clifton. On the **False Bay** side, the string of seaside villages has just a couple of bars worth making for.

Brass Bell

Map 2, D8. Kalk Bay station.

Daily 11am–late.

A pub and restaurant tucked neatly between the sea and the rail line that's a superb place to be on a summer afternoon. Eat chips and seafood, nurse a pint of draught Guinness, admire the mountains across the bay and take a splash in the tidal pool.

Dizzy Jazz Café

Map 3, B6. 41 Camps Bay Drive, Camps Bay

℡ 021-438-2686.

Daily noon–4am (music from 8.30pm).

R20 cover charge.

Crowded and lively nightspot with a big verandah, draught beer and sea views. Live music of varying persuasions nightly. Dinner before the show offers quality seafood.

La Med Bar and Restaurant

Map 3, B5. Glen Country Club, Victoria Rd, Clifton

℡ 021-438-5600.

Daily noon till late.

Overlooking the rocks at Clifton beach, this spot draws a sporty, mainstream crowd; it's a favourite place for hang-gliders from Lion's Head to drop into after landing in the adjacent field. Great sundowner venue with live music Wednesday, Friday and Saturday.

Red Herring

Map 2, C7. Corner of Pine and Beach roads, Noordhoek.

Tues–Sun 11am–midnight.

A pub above a smart restaurant with an outdoor deck overlooking the panoramic Noordhoek valley: ideal for a refreshing break while you're driving down

CLUBS, BARS AND LIVE MUSIC

the peninsula. Busy on warm weekend afternoons when a clean-cut twenty-something crowd gathers.

CAPE FLATS

The **townships** are blessed with countless backyard bars and shebeens, but there are few established and formal clubs. The best nightlife option is to join a township jazz tour (see p.29).

Club Vibe

Map 2, F4. Rigel Rd/Castor Rd, Lansdowne ☎ 021-762-8962. Fri & Sat 9pm–late.

A vast nightclub catering mainly to a well-dressed coloured crowd. Features two dance floors (mainstream and uplifting house), a hundred television screens and a groundbreaking sound technology feature known as "The Earthquake". Security is strong, the door policy is smart–casual and strictly no under-18s are allowed.

West End & Club Galaxy

Map 2, F3. College Rd, Rylands ☎ 021-637-9132. Thurs, Fri & Sat 8pm–late.

Definitely the most happening place on the Flats, with some good international musicians appearing from time to time. Two nightclubs in one building – you can circulate between them in the course of an evening. *West End* is a top jazz venue with a wine, dine and dance ambience. The last Sunday of every month sees several acts sharing the bill (call the club for details). Dress up, and book a good table if you want to be seated and see the stage. *Club Galaxy* is a straight-up dance club playing R'n'B and mainstream house to a young and smart crowd. The club is not in a particularly dodgy area, and there are a number of security guards about.

Shopping

The V & A Waterfront is the city's most popular shopping venue, with good reason: it has a vast range of shops, the setting on the harbour is lovely and there's a huge choice of places to eat and drink when you want to rest your feet – but expect to pay over the odds for everything. The city centre also offers variety and, for some people's taste, a grittier and more interesting venue for browsing, especially if you're looking for collectibles, antiques and secondhand books. Cape Town's suburbanites tend to do their shopping closer to home at the upmarket Cavendish Square Mall in Claremont or one of the other shopping centres that include the monstrously outsized Tygerberg Mall and the pastiche-Venice Canal Walk in the northern suburbs. If you're staying in the inner-city suburbs of Green Point or Sea Point, adjacent to the V & A Waterfront, you'll find supermarkets and other functional shops along Main Road, and the City Bowl suburbs are served by the Gardens Shopping Centre. There are other smaller shopping areas dotted about the other suburbs.

Shopping hours are generally Monday to Friday 8.30am–5pm, and Saturday till 1pm, but lots of supermarkets, bookshops and other specialist outlets now stay open beyond 5pm and also open on Sunday.

MALLS AND SHOPPING CENTRES

South African shopping tends to follow an American rather than a European model, with huge **malls** where you can browse in a bookshop as well as bank, buy clothes and groceries and go to the movies. They always have several coffee shops and restaurants.

Blue Route Mall
Map 2, D6. Tokai Rd, Tokai.
Mon–Fri 9am–5.30pm, Sat & Sun 9am–5pm.
Pretty functional single-storey centre that's handy if you're staying in Constantia or along False Bay. Has branches of Pick'n'Pay and Woolworths.

Cavendish Square
Map 2, E3. Vineyard Rd, Claremont. Claremont station.
Mon–Thurs 9am–6pm, Fri 9am–9pm, Sat 9am–6pm, Sun 10am–4pm.
Huge upmarket multi-storey complex that is the major shopping focus for the southern suburbs. With 200 shops, fifteen restaurants, sixteen cinemas and parking for 1800 cars, this is the best place in Cape Town to shop, but its scale can be a bit overwhelming.

Gardens Shopping Centre
Map 4, F8. Mill St, Gardens. 2km from Cape Town station.
Mon–Fri 9am–6pm, Sat 9am–3pm; selected shops Sun 10am–2pm.
Small shopping mall in the City Bowl, very close to the Company's Gardens and city centre, with a large supermarket, excellent deli and most of the shops you'll need.

Golden Acre
Map 4, D3. Adderley St. Cape Town station.
Mall 6am–midnight; most shops 8.30am–5pm.
Dark and not entirely pleasant complex linked by walkway to the station. Handy if you're about to catch a train, but otherwise best avoided.

V & A Waterfront
Map p.82, also Map 5, E2–E4.
Waterfront buses.
Mon–Sat 9am–9pm, Sun
10am–9pm.
It would be possible to visit
Cape Town and never leave
the Waterfront complex,
which has a vast range of
upmarket shops packed into
the Victoria Wharf Shopping
Centre, including outlets of
all the major South African
chains, selling books, clothes,
food and crafts.

ARTS AND CRAFTS

Cape Town is not known for its indigenous **arts and crafts** in the way that Durban is, and much of the stuff you'll buy here is from elsewhere in Africa: goods from Zimbabwe and Zambia are particularly well represented. There are several places in the city centre and the V & A Waterfront, but you'll often pick up the same arts and crafts for a lot less money at the sidewalk **markets** scattered around town. Don't expect exotic West African-style market-places however; Cape Town's venues are more like European or North American flea markets.

For some of the best arts, crafts, collectors' china and Africana antiques and books, make for Main Road at Kalk Bay (see p.128), which has a strip of trendy outlets and cafés clustered around the station.

SHOPS
- - - - - - - - - - - - - - - - - - -

Africa Nova
Map 2, C5. Main Rd, Hout Bay
☎ 021-790-4454. Hout Bay bus.
Mon–Fri 9am–5pm, Sat & Sun
10am–2pm.
A better than average selection of ethnic crafts and curios as well as contemporary African textiles and artwork, with an emphasis on the individual and handmade.

African Image

Map 4, C4. Church St/Burg St ☎021-423-8385. Cape Town station.

Mon–Fri 9am–5pm, Sat 9am–1.30pm.

Map p.82, F3. Shop 6228, Victoria Wharf, V & A Waterfront ☎021-419-0382. Waterfront buses.

Daily 9am–9pm.

One of the best places for authentic traditional and contemporary African arts and crafts, from fabrics and antique sculpture to beadwork, but a little overpriced.

Ethno Bongo

Map 2, C5. Mainsteam Shopping Centre, Main Rd, Hout Bay ☎021-790-0802. Hout Bay bus.

Mon–Fri 9.30am–6pm, Sat 9.30am–4pm, Sun 10am–4pm.

Charming shop in the main shopping centre in Hout Bay, selling wonderful and well-priced crafts, jewellery and accessories made from recycled metal and wood. Also quirky kaftans and ethnic clothing. Highly recommended for genuinely unique gifts and souvenirs.

Kalk Bay Gallery

Map 2, D8. 62 Main Rd, Kalk Bay ☎021-788-1674. Kalk Bay station.

Mon–Fri 9am–5pm, Sat & Sun 9.30am–5pm.

Graphics and engravings as well as African art and artefacts – good value, with the chance of picking up something very collectable.

Out of Africa

Map p.82, E3. Shop 125, Victoria Wharf, V & A Waterfront ☎021-418-5505. Waterfront buses.

Daily 9am–9pm.

Expensive baskets, beads and African arts and antiques, in the pleasant spending fields of the Waterfront.

Rose Korber Art Consultancy

Map 3, B6. 48 Sedgemoor Rd, Camps Bay ☎021-438-9152. Hout Bay bus.

Mon–Fri 9am–5pm.

The first stop for the serious collector, with an exceptional selection of contemporary art and crafts, including ceramics and beadwork from around the continent.

SHOPPING

Yellow Door

Map 4, G8. Upper Floor, Gardens Centre, Gardens ☎ 021-465-4702. 2km from Cape Town station.

Mon–Fri 9am–6pm, Sat 9am–4pm, Sun 10am–2pm.

One of the largest and best selections of local crafts and design, including ceramics, fabrics, jewellery, basketry, metalwork and interior decor.

MARKETS

Cape Town Station

Map 4, D2. Forecourt, Adderley St. Cape Town station.

Mon–Fri 8am–5pm, Sat 8am–2pm.

Thronging ranks of market traders selling radios, leather goods and African crafts. Not principally aimed at tourists, so it's pretty authentic.

Constantia Craft Market

Map 2, D5. Alphen Common, corner of Spaanschemat River and Ladies Mile roads, Constantia.

First and last Sat and first Sun of the month.

Sizeable outdoor flea market where you can pick up good local crafts and items from around the continent, ride a camel or a pony and have a cup of tea.

Greenmarket Square

Map 4, C4. Burg St. Cape Town station.

Mon–Fri 8am–5pm, Sat 8am–2pm.

Open-air market that's the best place in town for colourful handmade Cape Town beachwear, from T-shirts to shorts and sandals, as well as being a place to pick up knick-knacks.

The Pan African Market

Map 4, C4. 76 Long St. Cape Town station.

Mon–Fri 9am–5pm, Sat 9am–3pm.

Multicultural hothouse of township and contemporary art, artefacts, curios and crafts. There's music, a café specializing in African cuisine, a bookshop, a Cameroonian hairbraider and a West African tailor.

SHOPPING

The Red Shed Craft Workshop

Map p.82, D3–4. Victoria Wharf, V & A Waterfront. Waterfront buses.
Mon–Sat 9am–9pm, Sun 10am–9pm.
Market where some two dozen craft-workers make and sell ceramics, textiles, candles and jewellery and you can see glass blowers at work.

Sivuyile Craft Centre

Map 2, G3. Corner NY1 and NY4, Guguletu, Cape Flats.
Mon–Fri 8am–5pm, Sat 8am–2pm, Sun 9am–1pm.
Township market attached to an information centre close to the N2 freeway, where bead-workers, wire-workers and other artists make traditional and modern crafts.

Victoria Road Market

Map 2, C3. 1km south of Bakoven along the coast road. Daily.
Carvings, beads, fabrics and baskets sold from a spectacularly sited market – on a clifftop viewpoint overlooking the Atlantic.

BOOKS AND MUSIC

South Africa produces a lot of **books** given the size of its reading population: you'll find scores of good, locally produced novels and endless volumes on history, politics and natural history. For new books there are some pleasant places in the suburbs or at the Waterfront to browse for half an hour, while Upper Long Street has over half a dozen secondhand book and specialist comic shops in close proximity, interspersed with congenial cafés.

Most **music** is sold on CD, and the ubiquitous chains such as CNA and Musica tend to stock pretty unadventurous selections of mainly British and American sounds. For South African bands and music from the rest of the continent, the outlets listed on p.208 are by far the best.

Recommended books on South Africa are listed on p.344.

Clarke's Bookshop

Map 4, C6. 211 Long St ⓣ 021-423-5739. Cape Town station. Mon–Fri 8.45am–5pm, Sat 9am–1pm.

The best place in Cape Town for South African books, with a huge selection of locally published titles covering literature, history, politics, natural history and the arts, plus very well-informed staff. They also deal in collectors' editions of South African books.

Exclusive Books

Map p.82, E3. Victoria Wharf, V & A Waterfront ⓣ 021-419-0905. Waterfront buses. Mon–Fri 9am–10.30pm, Sat 9am–11pm, Sun 10am–9pm. **Map 2, E3.** Lower Mall, Cavendish Square, Claremont ⓣ 021-674-3030. Claremont station. Mon–Thurs 9am–9pm, Fri & Sat 9am–10.30pm, Sun 9.30am–9pm. **Map 2, D5.** Constantia Village Shopping Centre, Spaanschemat River Rd, Constantia ⓣ 021-794-7800. Mon–Sat 9am–8pm, Sun 9am–5pm.

Friendly bookshop, ideal for browsing. Well-stocked shelves include magazines and a wide choice of coffee-table books on Cape Town and South African topics.

Kirstenbosch Shop

Map 2, D4. Kirstenbosch National Botanical Garden ⓣ 021-762-2510. Shuttle bus from Cape Town Tourism. Daily 9am–7pm.

Excellent and well-chosen selection of natural history books, field guides and travel guides covering Southern Africa, as well as a range of titles for kids.

The Travellers Bookshop

Map p.82, E3. King's Warehouse, Victoria Wharf, V & A Waterfront ⓣ 021-425-6880. Waterfront buses. Daily 9am–9pm.

Cape Town's only specialist travel bookshop stocks a good range of titles, mainly about South Africa and especially the Cape, covering history, politics, natural history and the arts as well as travel guides.

SHOPPING

●

MUSIC

African Music Store
Map 4, 4C. 90a Long St ☏ 021-426-0867. Cape Town station. Mon–Fri 9am–5pm, Sat 9am–2pm.
Small very central specialist shop that, true to its name, specializes in African music.

Look & Listen
Map 2, E3. Shop F14, Upper Level, Cavendish Square, Claremont ☏ 021-683-1810. Claremont station. Daily 9am–10.30pm.
Africa's first music megastore, with late-night opening seven days a week and a vast selection of all kinds of music, including good local jazz and a respectable selection from all over the continent.

Sessions Music
Map p.82, E3. Lower Level, Victoria Wharf, V & A Waterfront ☏ 021-419-7892. Waterfront buses. Mon–Thurs & Sun 9am–9pm, Fri & Sat 9am–10pm.
One of the best places in Cape Town to buy music, with an extensive selection of South African and African sounds and helpful staff.

FOOD AND PROVISIONS

Self-catering is the cheapest way to eat in Cape Town, and can also be good fun. Apart from **braais**, which happen anywhere with any excuse, there are countless places on beaches, in the forests or up Table Mountain where you can enjoy a terrific **picnic**, or you may just want to buy stuff to cook at your accommodation. Lots of delis can be found down Kloof Street and in Green Point and Sea Point. By far the most atmospheric places to buy seafood are the Hout Bay and Kalk Bay harbours (see p.121 & p.129 respectively).

SHOPPING

SUPERMARKETS

The easiest places to shop for food are at the big **supermarket** chains. The larger branches of the better supermarkets also have fishmonger counters where you can buy fresh fish.

Woolworths

Map 4, D3. Adderley St. Cape Town station.
Mon–Fri 8.30am–5.30pm, Sat 8am–2pm.

Map p.82, E3. V & A Waterfront. Waterfront buses.
Daily 9am–9pm.

Map 2, E3. Cavendish Square Mall, Claremont. Claremont station.
Mon–Thurs 9am–6pm, Fri 8.30am–8pm, Sat 8am–6pm, Sun 9am–5pm.

Map 2, D6. Blue Route Mall, Tokai.
Mon–Thurs 9am–5.30pm, Fri 8.30am–7pm, Sat 8.30am–5pm, Sun 9am–2pm.

The South African equivalent of Britain's Marks & Spencer stores is excellent for quality fast-cook meals, fresh produce and cold foods, such as olives, hummus and various Mediterranean dips, but can be pricey.

Pick'n'Pay

Map p.82, E3. V & A Waterfront. Waterfront buses.
Daily 9am–8pm.

Map 4, F8. Gardens Shopping Centre, Mill St, Gardens. 2km from Cape Town station.
Mon–Thurs 8am–7pm, Fri 8am–9pm, Sat 8am–5pm, Sun 9am–2pm.

Map 3, B6. Main Rd, Camps Bay. Hout Bay bus.
Daily 9am–7pm.

Map 3, H5. Main Rd, Observatory. Observatory station.
Mon–Thurs 7am–8.30pm, Fri 7am–10pm, Sat 7am–10pm, Sun 8am–2pm.

Map 2, E3. Corner Main Rd and Campground Rd, Claremont. Newlands station.
Mon–Thurs 8am–6pm, Fri 8am–7pm, Sat 8am–4pm, Sun 9am–2pm.

Map 2, D6. Blue Route Mall, Tokai.
Mon–Thurs 8.30am–6pm, Fri 8.30am–7pm, Sat 8am–2pm, Sun 9am–2pm.

In a similar vein to Woolworths but considerably

larger and cheaper with a good deli counter and a choice of prepared meals, among which you'll find their excellent-value ready-grilled whole chickens. Also one of the best places for dry goods and a range of groceries.

DELICATESSENS AND FARM STALLS

Thanks to the city's cosmopolitan population there are some excellent (if pricey) **delicatessens**, several of which are strung along Main Road, Green Point and Sea Point. You'll also find delicious food and some unusual fruit and vegetables at the more sophisticated farm stalls.

The Barnyard Farm Stall
Map 2, D6. Steenberg Rd, adjacent to the well-signposted Steenberg Wine Estate, Tokai ⊤021-712-6934.
Daily 8.30am–5.30pm.
One of Cape Town's nicest farm stalls, with a selection of high-class cheeses, breads, home-baked cakes, wines, patés, coffee beans and many

other delights. Also has the major attraction of a very good outdoor café with a children's playground attached.

Giovanni's
Map 5, D5. 103 Main Rd, Green Point ⊤021-434-6893. Sea Point bus.
Mon–Sun 8.30am–9pm.
Excellent breads and delicious Italian foods to take away and – if temptation overcomes you – there's always the option of sitting down for a coffee and a snack.

Melissa's
Map 7, D2. 94 Kloof St, Gardens ⊤021-424-5540. 2.5km from Cape Town station.
Mon–Fri 7.30am–9pm, Sat & Sun 8am–9pm.
Expensive imported and local specialities, which you can either eat in or take away.

New York Bagel Deli
Map 6, C2. 51 Regent Rd, Sea Point ⊤021-439-7523. Sea Point bus.
Daily 7am–9pm.
Sea Point has the best bagels in town, a great selection of Eastern European Jewish

fillings – salt beef, gherkins, chopped liver and pickled herring – and an array of delicious pastries.

Old Cape Farm Stall
Map 2, D5. Turnoff to Groot Constantia, on Constantia Nek Rd ☎021-794-7062.
Daily 8.15am–6pm.
A good place to pick up a picnic, where you can choose from their delicious selection of dips and ready-made foods such as olive bread, couscous and other salads, as well as fresh fruit and vegetables.

FRESH FISH
- - - - - - - - - - - - - - - - - - - -

Fish Market
Map 2, C5. Mariner's Wharf, Hout Bay Harbour. Hout Bay bus.
Mon–Fri 9am–5.30pm, Sat &

Sun 9am–6pm.
Fresh seafood from South Africa's original waterfront emporium, but slicker and less atmospheric than Kalk Bay harbour.

Kalk Bay Harbour
Map 2, D8. Harbourside, Kalk Bay. Kalk Bay station.
Buy fresh fish directly from the fishermen and have it gutted and scaled on the spot. Availability is subject to weather.

WINE
- - - - - - - - - - - - - - - - - - - -

Supermarkets tend to have decent **wine** at competitive prices, but for more interesting labels and well-informed staff, there are some first-rate specialist wine merchants in town.

- -
The best – and cheapest – places to buy wines are at the estates that produce them. Coverage of the Constantia wineries begins on p.106, and the estates outside Cape Town on p.280.
- -

Enoteca
Map 4, B3. Corner 125c Buitengracht and Bloem streets. Cape Town station.

Mon–Fri 9am–8pm, Sat 9am–6pm.
Map 2, E3. Castle Building, corner of Kildare Lane and

Mains Rd, Newlands. 1.5km from Newlands station.

Mon–Fri 10am–9pm, Sat 9am–7pm.

Excellent broad selection of South African and foreign wines from a knowledgeable and helpful outfit.

Vaughan Johnson's

Map p.82, C4. Dock Rd, V & A Waterfront ⊤021-419-2121. Waterfront buses.

Mon–Fri 9am–6pm, Sat 9am–5pm, Sun 10am–5pm.

One of Cape Town's best-known wine shops, which has a huge range of labels from all over the country, but can be a bit pricey.

Woolworths

For branches and opening hours see under "Supermarkets", p.209.

The own-label wines of South Africa's upmarket supermarket chain have come a long way since the days when you'd sneakily decant them so no one would know their source. Cognoscenti now happily flaunt these competitively priced wines, which consistently represent good quality and value.

HOLISM

Cape Town is South Africa's alternative-culture and **holism** capital. To find out what's on, the best **publications** are *Link-Up,* a free listings magazine, and the glossier *Odyssey* (R15), which is also the place to track down sources of Southern African crystals, gemstones and essential oils – disappointingly though, there are few oils from Cape plants except for geraniums. Both publications are available from health-food shops and alternative health venues.

Fields Health Store

Map 7, D1. 84 Kloof St, Gardens ⊤021-423-9587. 2.5km from Cape Town station.

Mon–Fri 8am–7pm, Sat 8.30am–4pm.

Sells health and beauty products, with a juice bar

serving a daily vegetarian lunch buffet and cakes. Upstairs you can get massage, shiatsu, acupuncture and the like, but appointments are essential.

Natural Remedies

Map 2, E3. Pearce St, Claremont ☎ 021-674-1692. Claremont station.

Mon–Fri 9am–5.15pm, Sat 8.30am–1pm.

The best place in the southern suburbs for homeopathic and herbal remedies, aromatherapy oils, beauty products and a range of health foods.

Sunflower Health Café

Map 4, C4. 111 Long St. Cape Town station.

Mon–Fri 9.45am–5.30pm, Sat 9am–2pm.

Health-food shop and vegetarian restaurant that sells a good selection of natural remedies, organic and whole foods.

Waldorf School Shop

Map 2, D5. Spaanschemat River Rd, 400m west of Ladies Mile, Constantia ☎ 021-794-4997.

Mon–Fri 8.30am–3.30pm, Sat 8.30am–2pm.

Excellent organic vegetables, rye bread, cheeses, homeopathic and other health products, as well as a small range of handmade toys at the school's shop, next to the car park. The outdoor café, which serves teas and healthy snacks, may tempt you to dally a while.

White's Chemist

Map 4, E4. 77 Plein Park, Plein St ☎ 021-465-3332. Cape Town station.

Mon–Fri 7.30am–5pm, Sat 8am–12.30pm.

A long-established manufacturer and supplier of homeopathic remedies, powders, tinctures and books. They also sell homeopathic first-aid kits and herbal products.

Theatre and cinema

Despite scarce resources (state funds have been redirected to more pressing areas), theatre and live performance in South Africa is making a valiant attempt to lift itself out of its post-democracy doldrums. Protest theatre, a fertile genre in the oppressive 1970s and 1980s, is now obsolete and it's no longer regarded as self-indulgent for plays to deal with personal rather than political issues. A steady trickle of new plays is being written and performed in Cape Town, some of them innovative and hard-hitting. As yet there is no real successor to Athol Fugard, the world-renowned playwright, several of whose works were first staged here, but writers and directors to look out for include Brett Bailey, Marthinus Basson, Reza de Wet, Fiona Coyne, Roy Sargeant and the duo of Heinrich Rosehofer and Oscar Petersen.

On the **musical** front, David Kramer and Taliep Petersen have produced several hit shows that celebrate the history and culture of Cape Town. Their most recent, *Kat and the Kings*, took Broadway and London's West End by storm, bagging the 1999 Olivier Award for the best new musical. **Comedy**, too, is starting to shape up well with the annual Smirnoff International Comedy Festival, at the Baxter Theatre around October, showcasing global and local talent. South Africa's best-known stage satirist, Pieter Dirk Uys, has been relentlessly roasting South African society since apartheid days with his character Evita Bezuidenhout, South Africa's answer to Dame Edna Everidge, while new homegrown comedians include Marc Lottering, a coloured Capetonian, who derives his material from his own community, and David Kau, an African, who is as caustic about Jo'burg township dwellers as he is about white South Africans.

Despite the fact that Cape Town is booming as a film-production centre, local feature **films** are scarce. Mainstream Hollywood releases are shown at several commercial cinemas, all of which advertise daily in the *Cape Times* and *Cape Argus*, while a couple of independent cinemas include arthouse films in their programmes. A handful of small film theatres posing as arthouse cinemas – the Ster-Kinekor Cinemas Nouveau and the two Labias – show the odd subtitled movie and slightly less mainstream fare, but don't expect anything too exotic.

Most events in Cape Town, including theatre, cinema, concerts and sport, can be booked by phone through Computicket (☎ 083-915-800, ⓦ www.computicket.com) or through Ticketweb (ⓦ www.ticketweb.co.za).

THEATRES

Artscape
Map 5, I4. DF Malan St ☎ 021-421-5470.
Once the Camelot of state-funded white performing arts, Artscape has reinvented itself as a more popular, less elitist theatre. High-quality ballet and opera continues to be produced, while adventurous new dramas appear periodically. Don't be intimidated by the monumental 1970s architecture.

Baxter Theatre Centre

Map 3, H7. Main Rd, Rondebosch ☎ 021-685-780. A mammoth face-brick theatre complex whose design was inspired by Soviet Moscow's central railway station. Mounts an eclectic programme of shows, ranging from innovative plays to comedy festivals, jazz concerts and kids' theatre.

Evita se Perron Theatre/Café

Map 1, B1. Darling Station, Darling ☎ 022-492-2831. 55min north of Cape Town by train or car.
Evita Bezuidenhout (aka Pieter Dirk Uys) is South Africa's Dame Edna Everidge, a socialite, diplomat and sharp commentator on current affairs. Catch her and Uys' other alter egos at *Evita se Perron* ("Evita's Platform"), a theatre-café in Darling railway station, north of the city. Enjoy traditional South African food (vegetarian meals available), drink at *Bambi's Berlin Bar*, or shop at the Bapetikosweti Duty-Free Shop. There's also a good

craft shop next door focusing on West Coast crafters and South African artists. Shows are Friday to Sunday, or seven days a week during the festive season. Darling has several guest houses, making it practical for an overnight stay if you're arriving and leaving by train. Contact Metrorail (☎ 0800-656-463) for information on services.

Little Theatre

Map 3, H7. University of Cape Town, Orange St ☎ 021-480-7129.
Showcase for innovative work from the University of Cape Town drama school. Productions can be self-indulgent and/or breathtaking. The drama school has a long tradition of producing fine actors, and counts Richard E. Grant among its graduates.

Maynardville Open Air Theatre

Map 2, E4. Church St/Wolfe St, Wynberg. Book through Artscape ☎ 021-421-5470. Every year in January and February, a Shakespeare comedy is staged under the summer stars in Maynardville Park. The setting is pure romance and the plays are presented with great imagination by the cream of Cape Town's actors and designers.

Theatre On The Bay
Map 3, B6. Link St, Camps Bay ☎021-438-3300.
Upmarket theatre catering to a mature establishment audience. Productions include contemporary mainstream plays, farces, musical tributes and revues. Rather predictable fare, but generally good-quality performances.

The Warehouse
Map 5, F6. 6 Dixon Rd, Green Point ☎ 021-421-0777.
A 280-seat venue that provides a minimalist space for modern drama. One of the few genuinely adventurous, youth-orientated theatres in town.

CINEMAS

The **mainstream cinemas** most convenient for visitors are: the Nu-Metro (☎021-419-9700) and Ster-Kinekor Cinema Nouveau at the V & A Waterfront (☎021-425-8222); the Ster-Kinekor Cavendish Commercial (☎0860-300-222) at Cavendish Square Shopping Centre, Claremont; and, at the same shopping centre, the Ster-Kinekor Cinema Nouveau (☎021-683-4063). The Ster-Kinekor complex at the Blue Route Mall in Tokai (☎021-713-1280) is convenient if you're staying along the False Bay seaboard.

Independent cinemas are listed below. Tickets cost around R26 and many cinemas have discounted tickets one day a week, which you'll find advertised in the press.

The Labia & Labia on Kloof
Map 4, C8. 69 Orange St, Gardens, and round the corner at Lifestyles on Kloof St; ☎ 021-424-5927.
Formerly the flea-ridden temple of alternative cinema

in Cape Town, the Labia has been spruced up in recent times and now screens an intelligent mix of art films, cult classics and new releases. Three screens, at the Orange Street Labia and two at the new Labia on Kloof, both with tasty snacks for sale. Screenings are advertised in the daily papers and programmes are distributed at various outlets.

Independent Armchair Theatre

Map 3, H5. 135 Lower Main Rd, Observatory ☎ 021-447-1514. An adventurous club/cinema which screens cult and art movies with a video projector. Sprawl in one of an extended family of comfy couches, have a drink and enjoy the show. Screenings are on Monday to Friday evenings – contact the venue for details, or pick up a programme when you're in the area.

For megascreen movies, Cape Town's Imax cinema on the V & A Waterfront is covered on p.83.

THEATRE AND CINEMA

Sports and outdoor activities

One of Cape Town's most remarkable features is the fact that it melds with the Cape Peninsula National Park, a patchwork of mountains, forests and coastline – all literally on the city's doorstep. There are few, if any, cities in the world where outdoor pursuits are so easily and affordably available. If you've ever thought of trying sea kayaking, abseiling, rock climbing, scuba diving or you name it, here's your chance – and for little more than the price of a night out back home. Alternatively, just let everyone else get on with it while you sink a few beers and watch the cricket, rugby or soccer.

Tickets for all the sports events listed here can be booked through Computicket (☎ 083-915-8000), ⓦ www.computicket .com) or Ticketweb (ⓦ www.ticketweb.co.za).

CRICKET

Cricket is keenly followed by a wide range of Capetonians. The city's **cricketing** heart beats at

Newlands Cricket Ground, 61 Campground Rd, Newlands (℡021-674-4146, ⊛www.cricket.org). One of the most beautiful grounds in the world, Newlands nestles beneath venerable oaks and the elegant profile of Devil's Peak. Provincial, test and one-day international matches are played here. **Tickets** range from R25–45 for provincial matches to R60–175 for internationals.

RUGBY

The Western Cape is one of the world's **rugby** heartlands, and the game enjoys religious support. Provincial, international and Super 12 contests are fought on the hallowed turf of Newlands Rugby Stadium, Boundary Road, Newlands (℡021-689-4921). Find out whether either Western Province or the Stormers (the Western Cape regional team) are on a winning run – and then get a ticket. The stadium will be packed and the atmosphere exhilarating. Expect to pay R40–60 for stand **tickets** for lower profile events and up to R75 for crowd-pullers like the Super 12.

SOCCER

Though never as well attended as cricket or rugby, Cape Town **soccer** is burgeoning with talent. The dusty streets of the Cape Flats have produced superb young footballers such as Benni McCarthy (Ajax Amsterdam, Celta Vigo) and Quinton Fortune (Atletico Madrid, Manchester United). The most ambitious and professional club in the city is Ajax – pronounced "I-axe" – Cape Town (℡021-930-6001, ⊛www.ajaxct.org), jointly owned by its Amsterdam namesake. The most exciting games to attend are those between a local outfit and either of the Soweto glamour teams, Orlando Pirates and Kaizer Chiefs: they draw a buzzing crowd wherever they play. Matches are at Green Point

Stadium, off Beach Road; Athlone Stadium, off Klipfontein Road, Athlone; and Newlands Rugby Stadium (see above). Tickets for league matches are cheap at around R20.

PARTICIPATION SPORTS

ABSEILING AND KLOOFING

You can **abseil** off Table Mountain with Abseil Africa (℡021-424-1580) for around R200 for a half-day trip. They also do full-day trips twice a week to Kamikaze Canyon, that include *kloofing* (following a mountain river by boulder hopping and swimming from its source through rapids and waterfalls), hiking and abseiling for R395.

BIRD-WATCHING

The peninsula's varied habitats attract nearly 400 different species of **birds**. Fertile ground for the activity is on Lion's Head, in Kirstenbosch Gardens and the Cape of Good Hope section of the National Park, as well as at Kommetjie and Hout Bay; you can find out about guided outings with knowledgeable guides through the Cape Bird Club (℡021-559-0726). For a more institutionalized experience, there's World of Birds, Valley Road, Hout Bay (℡021-790-2730; see p.121 for more).

CYCLING AND MOUNTAIN-BIKING

Cycling is popular all over the peninsula, and is a great way to take in the scenery. For information about the *Cape Argus* Pick'n'Pay Cycle Tour (see p.246), the largest individually timed **bike race** in the world, contact Pedal Power Associates (℡021-689-8420), who also organize fun rides from September to May.

Downhill Adventures (☎082-459-2422), corner of Kloof and Orange streets in the city centre, take organized **mountain-biking** trips down Table Mountain, around Cape Point and through the Winelands (from R350 for a full day; R250 for a half day). Day Trippers (☎021-531-3274, ⓦwww.daytrippers.co.za) do similar half-day trips that include a popular one going from Scarborough to Cape Point.

GOLF

The Milnerton **golf** course, Bridge Rd, Milnerton (☎021-552-1047), is tucked in between a lagoon and Table Bay and boasts classic views of Table Mountain. Other popular local courses are at Rondebosch Golf Club, Klipfontein Rd, Rondebosch (☎021-689-4176), and Royal Cape Golf Club, 174 Ottery Rd, Wynberg (☎021-761-6551). Prices are around

R160/R260 for 9/18 holes; clubs can be rented for R80; and caddy fees are R70. Booking is essential.

GYMS

Virgin Active clubs are upmarket but well-appointed **gyms** dotted around the peninsula. Contact their call centre (☎0860-200-911, ⓦwww.virginactive.co.za) to find out where the nearest one is to you and the cost of day rates.

HORSE-RIDING

Horse Trail Safaris, Indicator Lodge, Skaapskraal Rd, Ottery (☎082-575-5669) offers **riding** through the dunes to Strandfontein and Muizenberg beaches; Sleepy Hollow Horse Riding, Sleepy Hollow Lane, Noordhoek (☎021-789-2341) covers the spectacular Noordhoek Beach. Both cost around R130 for 1hr 30min; two-hour sunset rides cost R160.

ROLLER-BLADING

Especially popular along the long smooth promenade that runs from Mouille Point to Sea Point, **roller-blading** (also known as inline skating) is a growing activity. You can rent blades from Rent 'n' Ride, 1 Park Rd, Mouille Point (℡021-434-1122; around R40 for 2hr).

KITE-FLYING

The Kite Shop (℡021-421-6231), Shop 110, Ground Floor, Main Shopping Complex, V & A Waterfront, sells **kites** of all shapes, colours and sizes.

PARAGLIDING

Fun 2 Fly (℡021-557-9735) offers one-day, one-and-a-half day and full-licence **paragliding** courses, from R350 to R2500.

ROCK CLIMBING

You can learn how to rock climb up Table Mountain's famous facade with the Cape Town School of Mountaineering (℡021-685-6972), which charges R600 for a two-day **rock-climbing** course, usually over weekends. They also guide experienced climbers.

SEA KAYAKING

The Cape Peninsula is extensive and very varied and one of the nicest ways to experience it is from the water. Real Cape Adventures (℡021-790-5611 or 082-556-2520, ⓦwww.seakayak.co.za) offers a range of half- or full-day packages that include trips around Cape Point, to the penguin colony at Boulders Beach and around Hout Bay. They also do trips of several days around the peninsula, where you spend nights at guest houses, and longer safaris all over South Africa and even further north. Half-days start at R180 per person.

SCUBA DIVING

Cape waters are cold but can be clear and are good for seeing wrecks, reefs and magnificent kelp forests. Because it's invariably warmer than the Atlantic seaboard, False Bay is preferred in winter. **Dives** cost from R180 for a short dive from the shore to around R220 from a boat; prices include dive gear. An internationally recognized PADI open-water diving qualification can be completed for around R1700. For information and arranging scuba-diving courses and equipment rental, contact: Ian's Scuba School, Master Mariners Sports Club, Stephan Way, Mouille Point (☎021-439-9322); Orca Industries, Herschel Rd/Bowwood Rd, Claremont (☎021-671-9673); and Time Out Adventures, Avalon Building, 8 Mill St, Gardens (☎021-461-2709).

SURFING

Top **surfing** spots include Big Bay at Bloubergstrand, where competitions are held every summer, Llandudno, Muizenberg, Kalk Bay and Long Beach at Kommetjie and Noordhoek. For further information, contact Surfing South Africa (☎021-674-2972); or surf the excellent ⓦwww .wavescape.co.za, the best place on the web for everything you could want to know about surfing in SA.

SWIMMING

There are livesaver patrols on duty at Milnerton, Camps Bay, Llandudno, Muizenberg and Fish Hoek beaches. For **pools**, try Long Street Swimming Pool, Long Street (☎021-400-3302), Cape Town's only heated indoor pool; or Newlands Swimming Pool, corner of Main and San Souci roads, Newlands (☎021-467-4197), an

Olympic-sized chlorinated pool. Sea Point Swimming Pool, Beach Rd, Sea Point (☎021-434-3341), is an enormous and wonderful sea-water pool.

WALKING

The best places for gentle **strolls** are Newlands Forest, up from the Rhodes Memorial, or the beaches. For longer **walks**, head for anywhere on Table Mountain (see p.94), Tokai Forest, Silvermine Nature Reserve or Cape Point Nature Reserve.

WINDSURFING AND KITESURFING

In summer, most Capetonians moan about the howling southeaster – handy, though, if you're into **windsurfing**. Langebaan, 75 minutes' drive north of town, is one of the best spots; for further help contact Cape Sport Centre, Langebaan (☎022-772-1114, ⓦwww.capesport.co.za), who also do **kitesurfing**. Prices for windsurfing are quoted in US dollars and start at $31 for two hours for rigs; windsurfing instruction for beginners starts at R195 and kitesurfing lessons at R220 inclusive of gear and teacher. Otherwise, the place to go in Cape Town is Bloubergstrand. The Blouberg Windsurf and Leisure (☎021-554-1663 or 082-420-2990, ⓔblouwind@mweb.co.za) rents equipment and cars with racks and has long-term accommodation at Bloubergstrand, as well as being able to offer general advice to its clients, for example on which airlines offer free carriage of windsurfing equipment.

Gay Cape Town

ape Town is South Africa's – and indeed, the African continent's – gay capital. The city has always had a strident and vibrant gay culture, and is on its way to becoming an African Sydney, attracting gay travellers from across the country and the globe. Cape Town Tourism (the official tourism organization) has recently woken up to the potential of pink spending power and is actively wooing gay travellers – an effort that is evidently paying off with the *Spartacus* gay guide ranking Cape Town among the world's top gay destinations.

The city has a growing number of **gay-friendly businesses**: Cape Town's **gay quarter**, with B&Bs, guest houses, pubs, clubs, cruise bars, video shows, restaurants with cabaret, strip shows and steam baths, is concentrated along the entertainment strips of Somerset Road and Main Road in the interconnected inner-city suburbs of Green Point, Sea Point and De Waterkant, adjacent to the centre, where a number of establishments flaunt their pink credentials by flying the distinctive multi-coloured gay flag.

INFORMATION

Cape Town Tourism's visitors' centre in downtown Cape Town has good **information** on gay-friendly establishments in the city and their website (Ⓦ www.cape-town.org) has a substantial gay section. For information on **what's on** check out the gay section of the Western Cape listings magazine *Cape Review* or the gay supplement published on the last Thursday of the month in the *Cape Argus*, Cape Town's daily afternoon newspaper, both widely available at newsagents. There are a number of dedicated gay print **publications** among them *Exit* newspaper (Ⓦ www.exit.co.za) and *Rush* magazine (Ⓦ www.q.co.za/rush) both of which are available at newsagents. The *Cape Gay Guide* (Ⓦ www.capegayguide.co.za) is a free booklet covering accommodation, clubs, restaurants and a "naughty" section; it's given away at most gay venues. Another excellent resource is **The Pink Map**, published by A&C Maps (Ⓣ 021-685-4260, Ⓦ www.capeinfo.com), which lists gay-friendly and gay-owned places and is distributed at the Cape Town Tourism visitors' centres in town and the one in the Clock Tower Precinct at the V & A Waterfront, as well as the airport and hotels; they'll also send a copy free anywhere in the world on request. For books and other paraphernalia try Rainbow Trade **bookshop** (daily 4pm–late; Ⓣ 082-359-4343) at 29a Somerset Road, which, in addition to books, sells stickers, caps, flags and leather accessories.

For online information there are numerous South African gay **websites**, but among the most useful are Gaynet (Ⓦ www.gaynetcapetown.co.za), a gay tourist resource with weather reports, currency converter, events calendar, male and female personal boards, clubs, eateries and accommodation; and Gay South Africa (Ⓦ www.GaySouthAfrica.org.za), a huge directory with a vast number of links.

While in town, tune into Bush Radio's (89.5FM) gay programme, called In the Pink, every Thursday 8–10pm.

SPORT AND EVENTS

If you're up for some **sport** in the company of gay and gay-friendly Capetonians and visitors, contact COGS (Cape Organization Of Gay Sport, ☎021-788-9310, ℮cogs@africamail.com), which co-ordinates hikes around the peninsula and various sporting and social outings, with travellers warmly welcomed.

In a different vein, the popular and comprehensive **Gay and Lesbian Film Festival** (☎021-424-1532, ⓦwww.oia.co.za), is an annual highlight showcasing gay and lesbian films, features and documentaries from across the globe. It happens simultaneously in Cape Town, Pretoria and Johannesburg; dates and venues vary from year to year.

Cape Town also hosts an annual **gay party**, organized by Mother City Queer Projects (ⓦwww.mcqp.co.za), a hugely popular event held in December. People dress as outrageously as possible according to a theme (past ones have included "on safari", "underwater" and "farm fresh") and the event seeks to rival Sydney's Mardi Gras. There's also an annual **gay pride festival** (ⓦwww.sapride.org) around the same time.

CLUBS AND PUBS

Bar Code
Map 5, F6. 16 Hudson St, Green Point ☎ 021-421-5305.
Daily 9pm till late.
Leather uniform and jeans bar that attracts an older crowd. It has monthly underwear and fetish parties. The atmosphere is industrial hardcore with cruising areas, a darkroom, video, pool table and outdoor garden.

Bar 89 Woodstock
Map 3, G5. 89 Roodebloem Rd, Woodstock ☎ 021-447-0982.
Tues–Sun 6pm–2am.
Elegant, beautifully fitted out

gay-friendly pub in a Victorian house. Nestled in increasingly trendy upper Woodstock, it strikes a refreshing chord, halfway between an intimate local and a sleekly cosmopolitan meeting place.

The Bronx, Angels, Sky

Map 5, F6. 35 Somerset Rd, Green Point ☏ 021-419-9216.
Daily till late.

A complex of clubs that share a courtyard and a reputation as the heartbeat of Cape Town's gay nightlife. *Angels* and *Sky* are two cavernous dance venues, while *The Bronx* is a hugely popular and energetic bar. The crowd here is mixed, unpretentious and committed to having a good time.

Café Manhattan

Map 5, G6. 74 Waterkant St, Green Point ☏ 021-421-6666.
1km from Cape Town station.
Daily noon–late.

A cultured, relaxed restaurant-bar which serves good affordable food (even Sunday roasts) and hosts live music every Thursday night

(no cover charge). Decor changes regularly as new exhibitions are mounted. Also features an outside terrace beneath oak trees. Straight-friendly.

Club 55

Map 5, F5. 22 Somerset Rd, Green Point ☏ 021-425-2739.
Daily 10am till late.

A young and sassy theatre/club/bistro attracting a cosmopolitan crowd. The decor is "warehouse chic", and regular live entertainment includes drag shows (Wed) and revues (Thurs) – cover charge R35. It takes on its club persona on Fridays and Saturdays.

On Broadway

Map 5, G6. 21 Somerset Rd, Green Point ☏ 021-418-8338.
1km from Cape Town station.
Daily 7pm till late.

Great cabaret restaurant-bar with Mediterranean-style food and live performances every night of the week. One of the few venues committed to the city's small but sassy cabaret scene. Top comic and satirist Pieter Dirk Uys

GAY CAPE TOWN

●

performs every Monday night, there are feature shows Wednesdays to Sundays, and drag shows on Sunday and Tuesday. All shows start at 9pm and cost R45. You can go earlier for dinner, but booking is essential. Mixed crowd, and definitely straight-friendly.

Robert's Café and Cigar Bar

Map 5, F6. 74 Waterkant St, De Waterkant ☎021-425-2478. Daily noon–very late.
Relaxed and convivial place in De Waterkant gay village, where you can have good food and socialize at the bar. Nice place to eat out with sexy, bluesey atmosphere.

Rosie's

Map 5, F6. 125a Waterkant St, De Waterkant, opposite *Manhattan* ☎072-250-7621. Tues–Sat 4pm–late, Sat & Sun 2pm–late.
Small intimate pool bar attracting a bear crowd and leather boys with a restaurant that's a popular after-work drinking spot with angels and demons.

STEAMBATHS

The Hothouse Steam and Leisure

Map 5, F6. 18 Jarvis St, Green Point ☎021-418-3888, ⒺInfo@hothouse.co.za. 1km from Cape Town station. Mon–Fri noon–2am, Sat & Sun 24hr.
Luxurious pleasure complex featuring Jacuzzis, sauna, a sundeck with a superb view, a full bar with a limited food menu, video room, fireplace and satellite TV. Luxury cabins R50. Entrance R35-50 depending on days and times.

Steamers

Map 4, G7. Corner Wembley and Solan roads, Gardens ☎021-461 6210, Ⓔinfo@steamers.co.za. 1km from Cape Town station. Feb–Nov daily noon–3am; Dec & Jan Mon–Fri noon–8am, Sat & Sun 24hr.

The ultimate cruise venue featuring a swimming pool, steam room, sauna, jacuzzi, glory holes, leather room, cabins, voyeurs' room, sunbed and more.

BEACHES

Clifton Third Beach
Map 3, A5.
Cape Town's most fashionable beach, where you can watch the best built boys in town flexing their pecs and working on their tans.

Graaff's Pool
Map 6, 1E.
Popular nudist sunbathing and cruising area just off the Sea Point Promenade. Best visited during the day, as it takes on a rather unsavoury character after dark.

Sandy Bay
Map 2, B5.
Gay-friendly nudist beach that can only be reached via a twenty-minute walk from Llandudno. Gay cruising on the rocks, bushes and far side of the beach. To get there, take the path from the south end of the Llandudno car park, through vegetation and across some rocks to the beach. It's a fairly easy walk, but watch out for broken glass – and bring your own picnic, as there are no facilities of any kind.

Kids' Cape Town

C ape Town is an excellent place to travel with children. The city enjoys fine weather, and activities in its many nature reserves, gardens and historic estates let under-10s work off some energy in a safe environment. Much of what there is to do for kids is either free or inexpensive, though renting a car is pretty well essential given the poor public transport.

Where the prices in this chapter refer to children, they mean under-16s, unless specified.

The V & A Waterfront is a good place to go with kids –
several of its attractions are listed below – and it also has the
added appeal of ships and seals in the harbour, boat rides
and umpteen child-friendly fast-food outlets.

Museums and sights

Cable Car
Map 3, C6. Lower Cable Station, Tafelberg Rd;

ⓦ www.tablemountain.co.za.
Shuttle bus from Cape Town Tourism.
Cable-car return fares; May to Oct R68, children R35, under-4s free; Nov to April R85,

children R45.

A ride in the cable car can't fail to thrill, and once on the tabletop there are views, pathways to explore and outdoor and indoor refreshments, albeit expensive. The furry little dassies (see box on p.93) always provide some amusement, but don't feed them as they may bite.

Groot Constantia

Map 2, D5. Groot Constantia Wine Estate, off Ladies Mile Extension, Constantia ⓣ 021-794-5128, Ⓦ www.museums.org.za/grootcon.

Museum daily 10am–5pm; R8. Cellar tours and wine tasting (booking essential ⓣ 021-794-5128): April–Sept 11am & 3pm; Oct–March daily every hour 10am–4pm; R20. Wine tasting only: May–Nov daily 10am–4.30pm; Dec–April daily 9am–6pm; R14. Grounds free. Beautiful seventeenth-century Cape Dutch manor house with large grounds that are ideal for a wander. The most child-friendly of the Constantia wine estates, its congenial outdoor

Jonkershuis restaurant has a playground.

SA Museum and Planetarium

Map 4, C–D7. 25 Queen Victoria St ⓣ 021-424-3330, Ⓦ www.museums.org.za/sam. Cape Town central station. Daily 10am–5pm; adults: museum R8, planetarium R10, combined R15; kids: museum free, planetarium R5. Cape Town station.

The museum is great for rainy days, especially for 5- to 12-year-olds, who'll enjoy the four-storey whale well and African animal dioramas, as well as the dinosaur displays. The Museum's Discovery Room (weekdays 10am–3pm, Sat & Sun 11am–4.30pm) features live ants, massive spiders and a crocodile display. For exceedingly cheap internet access (R8 for 30min), there are ten computers with natural history websites bookmarked and interactive CD-ROMs. The Planetarium has special children's shows over weekends and in school holidays, while the adjoining

Gardens are full of friendly squirrels.

Telkom Exploratorium

Map p.82, E4–5. Union Castle Building, V & A Waterfront. ⓦwww.exploratorium.co.za. Waterfront buses.
Daily 9am–9pm; R15, under-18s R9.

Interactive science museum where kids over 4 are invited to let their itchy fingers loose on knobs, buttons and dials. Activities include stomach-turning rotation inside a gyroscope, simulated speeding at 315kph in a Ferrari and virtual-reality rides as well as fairground favourites such as distorting mirrors.

Two Oceans Aquarium

Map p.82, C6. V & A Waterfront ⓣ021-418-3823, ⓦwww.aquarium.co.za. Waterfront buses.
Daily 9.30am–6pm; R45, kids R20.

One of Cape Town's most rewarding museums (see also p.85) has loads for kids to do, apart from the excitement of just looking at the weird and wonderful sea creatures. The touch pool provides the chance to handle a few species – sometimes this includes a small shark or sea urchins – while the Alpha Activity Centre usually has puppet shows or face painting as well as computer terminals where older kids can learn about marine ecology.

AMUSEMENT AND THEME PARKS

Ratanga Junction

Map 2, F1. N1 to Bellville, take exit 10 (Sable St exit) ⓣ0861-200-300, ⓦwww.ratanga.co.za. Rides: Wed–Fri 10am–5pm, Sat 10am–6pm, Sun 10am–5pm; unlimited rides R75, unlimited rides for people under 1.3m R39;

non-riders and under-2s free. Spectacular multimillion-rand theme park that recreates a mythological late nineteenth-century mining town, with loads of activities and eateries. The real attractions are the 24 rides, which include family rides, thrill rides, steam trains and boats. The biggie is the Cobra, a towering spine-like roller coaster which speeds you along at 100kph and delivers four-times gravity traction around the bends. A rider ticket entitles you to sample all the rides as many times as you wish. Certain rides are restricted to people over 1.3m tall.

Scratch Patch and Mineral World

Map 2, D9. Dido Valley Rd, off Main Rd, Simon's Town ⊤021-786-2020.
Map p.82, C5. V & A Waterfront ⊤021-419-9429. Waterfront buses.
Mon–Fri 9am–4.45pm, Sat & Sun 9am–5.15pm; R10–32, depending on size of container. Over-3s will enjoy taking a bag and filling it with the reject polished gemstones which literally cover the floor. From the Simon's Town Scratch Patch, you can cross the catwalk to see one of the world's biggest gemstone tumbling plants in operation (Mon–Fri).

Spier

Map 1, E3. 50km from Cape Town, along the R310 ⊤021-809-1100, ⓦwww.spier.co.za. Daily 9am–5pm, free.
A brilliant family outing that dovetails nicely with a tour of the Winelands. Spier is a historic manor house in vast grounds with a large lake – a good setting for picnics. There's a kids' playground and space to run about, as well as guided pony rides (Sat & Sun 11am–4pm; R10 for ten minutes). Another highlight is the cheetah park, part of a breeding programme, where you can enter the enclosure to pet a purring big cat (viewing free; cheetah encounter R40, kids R20). You're not allowed to consume your own food on the estate, but their farmstall and coffee shop has a deli that bakes delicious fresh bread and pastries and sells cheeses, cold meats and dips, from which you can compile your own picnic basket. There's also a choice of five eateries: the *Jonkershuis Restaurant*, *Spier Café*, the *Taphuis Grill*, the *Riverside Pub* and *Figaro's* at the on-site hotel.

World of Birds

Map 2, C5. Valley Rd, Hout Bay
℡ 021-790-2730.
Daily 9am–5pm, R30, kids R20,
under-3s free.

Allow at least two hours to see the more than 3000 birds and small animals housed in surprisingly pleasant and peaceful walk-through aviaries. You can watch penguins being fed at 11.30am and 3.30pm, pelicans at 12.30pm and birds of prey at 4.10pm Tues–Thurs, Sat & Sun. A large walk-in aviary open 11.30am–1pm & 2–3.30pm includes cute squirrel monkeys, which you can handle and play with, among its inhabitants. There's a café and restaurant serving light lunches, or you can picnic at the Flamingo Terrace.

BEACHES

Cape Town is literally surrounded by **beaches** – a classic and easy summer weekend family outing. This selection is particularly suitable for toddlers and smaller kids and generally also offers something for parents. Most beaches are pretty undeveloped, so it's best to take what you need in the way of food and drinks with you. Sea water and swimming pool temperatures are published each day in the *Cape Times* in the weather section.

Get to the beach as early as possible so you can leave by
10–11am before the sun gets too strong, and to avoid the
wind which often gusts up in the late morning.

FALSE BAY SEABOARD

The warmer **False Bay seaboard** has the advantage of being accessible by Metrorail train from central Cape Town. By car, take the M3 in the direction of Muizenberg; it'll take about 40 minutes from central Cape Town to Fish Hoek by car, a little longer on the train.

Boulders Beach

Map 2, E10. Entry R10, kids R5. 39km south of central Cape Town. Simon's Town station, then Rikki's taxi.

One of the few places to go when the southeaster is blowing, Boulders has safe, flat water, making it ideal for kids – and its resident penguin breeding colony. The granite boulders create a beautiful, protected setting, and there's some shade in the morning. It's an extremely popular beach, and fills up fast during the December school holidays, so go as early in the day as you can. There's a pleasant café with views across False Bay at the car park.

Fish Hoek

Map 2, D8. 30km south of central Cape Town. Fish Hoek station.

One of the best peninsula beaches, with gentle waves that are warm in summer and a long stretch of sand. There's

a playground, and a reasonable café on the beach, and with a pushchair you can stroll along Jager's Walk, a paved pathway following the rocky coast which has beautiful views of the Hottentots Holland mountains. When it's windy, you'll find the small grassy area next to the showers the most protected area for sunbathing.

St James

Map 2, D8. 38km south of central Cape Town. St James station.

A safe tidal pool with a small sandy beach next to the photogenic bathing boxes. With a pushchair, you can walk to Muizenberg along a concreted coastal pathway, with views of the distant mountains across the water. St James can be overcrowded at weekends, and parking can be inadequate, so get here early. There are no tea shops on site, but there are tea and scones at the Labia Museum on Main Road, between St James and Muizenberg, and an Italian restaurant across the road from St James Station.

KIDS' CAPE TOWN

237

ATLANTIC SEABOARD

The **Atlantic seaboard** is too cold for serious swimming, but does have some lovely stretches of sand, boulders and rock pools – and astonishing scenery. Beaches are excellent for picnics, and on calm summer evenings idyllic for sundowners and sunsets. In the summer they are less windy than the False Bay beaches, but tend to absolutely bake in the afternoons. South of Hout Bay, there's no public transport.

Camps Bay

Map 3, B6. 8km southwest of central Cape Town. Hout Bay or Cape Town Explorer bus.
Sandy beach with some grass and shade-giving palm trees, lying below the impressive Twelve Apostles rampart. There's a tidal pool and small rock pools to explore, and it's easily reachable from the centre by car or bus. The road opposite the beach is lined with pavement cafés restaurants and bars.

Noordhoek and Kommetjie

Map 2, B7–8. 41km southwest of central Cape Town.
The eight-kilometre stretch of white sand from Noordhoek to Kommetjie provides fine walking, kite-flying and horse-riding, with stupendous views of Chapman's Peak. Some good restaurants and farmstalls in the rural and wooded Noordhoek area make for a pleasant outing, and if you're going to Kommetjie, there's camel riding (see p.240). Kommetjie itself has some nice groves of milkwood trees, and rocks and pathways to explore. You'll need your own transport to get out here.

Sea Point Promenade

Map 6. 4km west of central Cape Town. Sea Point bus.
Stretching 3km from the Lighthouse in Mouille Point to Sea Point Pavilion, the paved promenade, bordered by lawns, hotels and apartment blocks hugs the rocky coastline. It's the closest stretch of coast to the centre, with several parking spots

along the promenade, and is ideal for pram pushing or roller-blading. There's also the draw of playgrounds and ice-cream sellers. While there are two little beaches strewn with slimy kelp, they are not safe for swimming, although you could take a bucket and spade to them. For swimming, head for the pool at the Sea Point Pavilion.

SWIMMING POOLS

Long Street Baths
Map 4, C6–7. Corner Long St and Buitensingel ☎021-400-3302. Cape Town station. Mon–Fri 7am–8pm, Sat 7am–7pm, Sun 8am–6pm; R7, kids R4.
Conveniently central, Cape Town's only heated indoor pool is great when the weather is poor.

Newlands Pool
Map 2, E3. Corner Main and Sans Souci roads, Newlands ☎021-674-4197. Newlands station.
Daily: April–Sept 9am–5pm; Oct–March 7am–6.30pm; R7, kids R4.

Olympic-sized unheated pool surrounded by lawns and mountain views. Its summer high temperature of 24°C drops to an unappealing 15°C in winter.

Sea Point Pool
Map 6, C2. Sea Point Pavilion, Beach Rd. 5km west of central Cape Town ☎021-434-3341. Sea Point bus.
Daily: April–Sept 9am–5pm; Oct–March 7am–6.45pm; R7, kids R4.
Marvellous Olympic-sized chlorinated seawater pool on the sea edge, with two paddling pools for children, and seagulls flapping overhead.

OUTDOOR AND PICNIC SPOTS

The Barnyard Farmstall

Map 2, D6. Steenberg Rd (M42), next to Steenberg Estate, between Tokai Rd and the Ou Kaapse Weg.

Excellent place for an outdoor snack or cup of coffee at a small farmyard with ducks and chickens wandering around, and an unusually good kids' playground. The farmstall itself has delectable breads, dips, baked goods and deli fare and is a good stop if you're doing the Constantia winelands.

Imhoff Farm

Map 2, B8. Kommetjie Rd, opposite Ocean View turnoff ☏021-783-4545 or 083-735-5227.

Camel rides are laid on daily between noon and 4pm at Imhoff Farm, where a ride costs R50 for thirty minutes. Walks lead into the surrounding woods and sandy areas, but not on the beach itself. Toddlers can ride with a parent in the same saddle, and 4-year-olds and upwards can do it alone.

Kirstenbosch National Botanical Garden

Map 2, D4. Rhodes Drive ☏021-799-8999. Shuttle bus from Cape Town Tourism. Daily April–Aug 8am–6pm, Sept–March 8am–7pm; R15, kids R5.

Without doubt top of the list for a family outing: the extensive lawns here offer miles of space for running about, there are trees to climb, rocks to jump off and streams to paddle in. There's no litter or dogs and it's extremely safe. Great for picnics or to have tea outdoors at the café. For older kids there are short waymarked walks, the Stinkwood and Yellowwood trails (1.2km and 2.5km), or you can scale the mountain up Skeleton Gorge (see p.98). Their summer sunset concerts on Sundays can also make a nice picnic outing (see p.248).

Newlands Forest

Map 2, D3. 9km south of the centre, off the M3 to Muizenberg.

Dawn to dusk; free.

Gentle walks in and around pine forests and streams on the wooded southern slopes of Table Mountain, with a flattish pathway suitable for pushchairs. It's good for picnics if you want to get out of the city and don't have time to go further afield. The small risk of crime means it's safest at weekends and in the afternoons when the joggers and dog walkers are out. Use the access point off the M3 signposted "Forestry Office", where there's ample parking.

Noordhoek Farm Village

Map 2, C7. Noordhoek Main Rd, just before the road climbs up to Chapman's Peak ☏ 021-789-1317.

Daily 8.30am–5.30pm.

Very much geared to the tour buses en route to Cape Point via Chapman's Peak, but nevertheless a delightfully tranquil place under oak trees, where you can buy fresh produce, clothes, souvenirs and Zimbabwean sculpture. Best of all is the shady playground next to the café with outdoor seating, which can be a life-saver if you're doing Chapman's Peak with restless children in the car.

Silvermine Nature Reserve

Map 2, D7. Ou Kaapse Weg (M64).

Dawn to dusk; R10, kids R5.

Beautiful nature reserve on the mountains above Muizenberg and Kalk Bay, about 25km from the centre, accessed from a signposted entry gate at the top of Ou Kaapse Weg (M64). It's a good place to see fynbos vegetation, stroll around the pine-fringed lake and picnic with small children. It is exposed though, and not recommended in heavy winds or mist. With older children there are some mountain-top walks with relatively gentle gradients, which give spectacular views over both sides of the peninsula. Friends of Silvermine (☏ 021-782-5079 or 021-785-1477) offer free walks with members at various times of the week.

Tokai Forest Arboretum

Map 2, C–D6. Tokai Rd; take the Tokai exit from the M3 towards Muizenberg, then head to the mountains at the end of Tokai Rd, or access it from the signpost on the M42.
Dawn to dusk; R2.
Peaceful forest with trees from all over the world, established in 1885 on the slopes of Constantiaberg. A wonderful place to escape to when the southeast wind blows, it offers walks and mountain biking, as well as a thatched tea shop with outdoor seating. A great place for young children to explore, with logs to jump off and a gentle walk to a stream.

SHOPS

If you're looking for something local to take home, your best bet is to check out some of the bright cotton printed **clothes** that have a uniquely Cape Town ethnic look. While there are many labels about, the ones listed tend to be superior (and more expensive). Locally made toys and other goods are generally inferior in quality to what you'd find in Europe or North America.

Baby City

Map 5, F6. 53 Somerset Rd, Green Point ☎021-419-6040. Warehouse-style shop that offers rather indifferent service, but stocks a wide range of baby gear such as toys, pushchairs and cots. Amongst the cheapest places in Cape Town for disposable nappies and babywipes.

Mad Dogs

Map p.82, E3. Upper Level, Victoria Mall, V & A Waterfront ☎021-421-7426. Waterfront buses.
Map 2, E3. Cavendish Shopping Centre, Claremont ☎021-671-8477. Claremont station.
Zany kids' clothes which are durable and well made.

Naartjie and Naartjie factory shop

Map p.82, E3. Upper Level, Victoria Mall, V & A Waterfront ☏021-418-0733. Waterfront buses.

Map 2, E3. Cavendish Shopping Centre, Claremont ☏021-683-7184. Claremont station.

Map 2, B5. Naartjie factory shop, above the Spar Supermarket, Victoria Ave, Hout Bay ☏021-790-3093. Hout Bay bus.

Funky kids' clothing of a similar quality to Mad Dogs. Cheaper seconds are available from their factory shop in Hout Bay, near the harbour.

Peggity's Toys

Map p.82, E3. Lower Level, Victoria Wharf, V & A Waterfront ☏021-419-873. Waterfront buses.

Conveniently central but slightly pricey shop, stuffed to the brim with good-quality toys for all ages, including beach goods, books and tapes.

Reggies

Map 4, D3. Golden Acre Shopping Centre, Adderley St ☏021-419-2955. Cape Town central station.

Map 2, E3. Cavendish Shopping Centre, Claremont ☏021-683-2312. Claremont station.

Map 2, D6. Blue Route Shopping Centre, Tokai ☏021-712-0120.

Reliable, countrywide chain of shops that sells baby goods and toys for all ages, with a couple of branches in the southern suburbs.

Festivals and events

Many of Cape Town's events take place outdoors in summer, and make full use of the city's wonderful setting. They include the Coon Carnival (the name it's widely known by despite the pejorative connotations), a unique event rooted in the city's coloured community, while the Kirstenbosch Summer Sunset Concerts, which run from December to March, are a must. Winter tends to be quiet, but it does herald the arrival of calving whales, and in their wake the Hermanus Whale Festival in September, which packs out this small southern Cape settlement.

JANUARY

The Coon Carnival
Jan 2, and following three Saturdays.
South Africa's longest and most raucous annual party, the **Coon Carnival** (aka the Cape Minstrel Carnival), brings over ten thousand spectators to Green Point stadium (Map 5, C5). It starts on January 2 for the *Tweedenuwejaar* or

"Second New Year" cele-
brations – an extension of
New Year's Day unique to
the Western Cape. Central
to the festivities are the
brightly decked-out
coloured minstrel troupes
that vie in singing and
dancing contests.

One good reason to
come is to hear the locally
evolved style of singing
known as *ghommaliedjies*
(drum songs), accompanied
by banjos, which began as
slave songs performed at
New Year and evolved in
the twentieth century into a
part of working-class
coloured culture. The style
of minstrelsy that character-
izes the carnival dates back
to the 1880s, when minstrel
entertainers from visiting
US ocean liners joined in

the city's New Year revelry.
Up to the 1970s, an important part of the carnival was
a parade from District Six
through the streets of Cape
Town; sadly this died out
when District Six was
razed, and with it some of
the spontaneity and vigour
of the event. Many
coloureds were moved out
to the Cape Flats, and now
have to be bussed to stadiums.

Tickets (R20–50) to
watch the event at Green
Point Stadium on January 2
and the following three
Saturdays can be reserved
through Computicket
(℡083-915-8000,
ⓦwww.computicket.com);
you won't get such a good
view if you buy tickets at
the gate on the day (R20).

FEBRUARY

Cape to Rio Yacht Race

Held in Feb in even years.
Cape Town's largest sea-
faring event is the biennial
Cape to Rio Yacht Race,
a 3640-nautical-mile run

sailing from Cape Town's
docks. Good free vantage
points are the breakwater at
the V & A Waterfront and
Signal Hill.

MARCH

Cape Argus Pick'n'Pay Cycle Tour

Early March.

The 105-kilometre **Cape Argus Pick'n'Pay Cycle Tour** is the largest individually timed bike race in the world with 35,000 participants. You can pick up entry forms from Pick'n'Pay supermarkets, cycle shops or enter online at Ⓦwww.cycletour.co.za. Book early as it is heavily subscribed and numbers are now limited.

North Sea Jazz Festival Cape Town

End of March/beginning of April.

Initiated as a two-day event in 2000, the Cape Town counterpart of the world-famous **North Sea Jazz Festival** combines international jazz with African sounds. Notable performers at the launch event included Courtney Pine, Herbie Hancock, Jimmy Dludlu, Moses Molelekwa and Hugh Masakela. Day/weekend passes (R235/360) can be bought through Computicket (Ⓣ083-915-8000, Ⓦwww.computicket.com); the programme and latest information as well as travel packages can be checked out at Ⓦwww.atp.nl/capetown/eng.

APRIL

Two Oceans Marathon

Second half of April.

The **Two Oceans Marathon**, another of the Cape's big sports events, is in fact a marathon and a half (56km), and takes place every April. Information and entry forms can be obtained from Old Mutual Two Oceans Marathon, PO Box 2276, Clareinch 7740 Ⓣ021-671-9407 (Mon–Fri 8.30am–4.30pm), Ⓦwww.TwoOceansMarathon.org.za.

JULY

Whale migrations

There's obviously no fixed schedule for the annual migration of calving **southern right whales**, but they usually start appearing any time from July, and remain along the Cape Town and Western Cape coast as late as December. For details about whale-watching off the Cape Peninsula see p.126, and off the Whale Coast p.264.

SEPTEMBER/OCTOBER

Hermanus Whale Festival
End of Sept/beginning of Oct.

To coincide with peak whale-watching season, the Western Cape town of Hermanus (see p.260) stages the week-long annual **Whale Festival** of arts and the environment. Held in September/October, its activities include plays, a craft market, a children's festival and live music (further information ⊤028-313-0928, ⓦwww.whale-festival.co.za).

DECEMBER

Mother City Queer Project
Early Dec.

Mother City Queer Project is a hugely popular party, usually held in early December, for which a vast venue is chartered (thus far, Observatory's River Club and the Artscape Centre). Thousands of gay revellers form teams and converge in outrageous fancy dress following a pre-advertised theme – past ones have been "The Secret Garden",

"The Twinkly Sea", "The Shopping Trolley" and "Heavenly Bodies". Many partygoers spend frenetic months conceiving and preparing their costumes for an MCQP party. Outlandish get-ups, fabulous decor, multiple dance floors and a mood of sustained delirium make this event a real draw (further information ☎021-426-5709, ⓦwww.mcqp.co.za).

Kirstenbosch Summer Sunset Concerts
Late Dec to early March. Amongst the musical highlights of the Cape Town calendar are the popular

Kirstenbosch Summer Sunset Concerts, held on Sunday evenings from December to March on the magnificent lawns of the botanical gardens at the foot of Table Mountain. Performances begin at 5.30pm and cover a range of genres, from local jazz to classical music. Come early to find a parking place, bring a picnic and some Cape fizz – and enjoy. Tickets, available at the gate, cost R25 for adults and R10 for kids. Contact ☎021-799-8999, ⓦwww.nbi.ac.za/whatson/s unsetconcerts.htm for further information, or see the press.

Directory

Accommodation agencies
Cape Town Tourism
(ⓦ www.cape-town.org) runs a Hotel and Accommodation Booking Desk from its two information bureaux: the city Visitors' Centre (March–Nov: Mon–Fri 8am–6pm, Sat 8.30am–1pm & Sun 9am–1pm; Dec–Feb: Mon–Fri 8am–7pm, Sat 8.30am–1pm & Sun 9am–1pm; ⓣ 021-426-4260, ⓕ 021-426-4266), at the corner of Burg and Castle streets, a five-minute walk two blocks northwest of the station; and the Clock tower Precinct Visitors' Centre (daily 9am–9pm; ⓣ 021-405-4500) at the V & A Waterfront next to the Nelson Mandela Gateway. Bed'n'Breakfast, PO Box 2739, Clareinch 7740, Claremont (ⓣ 021-683-3505,

ⓔ holtz@intekom.co.za) has places from R160–200 per person per night, while for self-catering accommodation during December and January, A–Z Holiday Accommodation, 15 Winton Crescent, Woodbridge Island 7441 (ⓣ 021-551-2785, ⓦ www.a-zholidayhomes.co.za) can provide accommodation from R500 a day for a two-person apartment to R8000 for a superluxury house. Roger and Kay's Travel Selection (ⓣ 021-715-7130, ⓦ www.travelselection.co.za) produces a South African accommodation guide, which lists a fair number of properties in Cape Town with rooms for R100–200 per person per night – choose your place and book directly with the host. The booklet is available free from

South African Tourism offices worldwide, can be posted (small charge for airmail, surface mail free), or you can visit their website.

Airlines British Airways ⓣ 021-936-9000, ⓦ www.britishairways.com/regional/sa; KLM Royal Dutch Airlines ⓣ 0860-247-747, ⓦ www.klm.com; Kulula ⓣ 0861-585-852, ⓦ www.kulula.com; Lufthansa ⓣ 021-934-8534, ⓦ www.lufthansa.com; Nationwide ⓣ 021-936-2050, ⓦ www.nationwideair.co.za; Olympic Airways ⓣ 021-423-0260, ⓦ www.olympic-airways.co.uk; Qantas ⓣ 011-441-8550, wwww.qantas.com.au; SA Airlink ⓣ 021-936–1111, ⓦ www.saairlink.co.za; South African Airways ⓣ 021-936-1111, ⓦ www.flysaa.com; Virgin Atlantic ⓣ 011-340-3400, ⓦ www.virgin-atlantic.com.

Airport information ⓣ 021-934-0407.

Airport tax is included in the price of domestic and international fares.

American Express Thibault House, Thibault Square, city centre ⓣ 021-421-5586. Offers full Amex facilities, including help with lost cards.

Banks Main branches are easy to find in the shopping areas of the city centre, the middle-class suburbs and at the Waterfront (Mon–Fri 8.30am–3.30pm, Sat 8–11am). Wherever you find banks, you'll also find cash points/ATMs that take cards on the Cirrus and Maestro networks.

Bike rental Mountain bikes are available from Rent 'n' Ride, (ⓣ 021-434-1122) for R75 a day including helmet and lock (R1000 credit-card deposit required). Downhill Adventures (ⓣ 021-422-0388, ⓦ www.downhilladventures.co.za) offer similar rentals for R95 a day or R570 a week.

Bureaux de change For foreign exchange transactions outside normal banking hours, try one of the following: American Express, Shop 11a, Alfred Mall, Waterfront (Mon–Fri 9am–7pm, Sat & Sun 9am–5pm; ⓣ 021-419-3917); Rennies Foreign Exchange, Victoria Wharf, V & A Waterfront (Mon–Sat 9am–9pm, Sun 10am–9pm; ⓣ 021-418-3744); Rennies Travel, Riebeeck

Street, City Centre (Mon–Thurs 8.30am–5pm, Fri 9–11.30am, Sat 9am–noon; ⓣ 021-425-2370); Absa Bank, Cape Town International Airport (Mon 7am–8pm, Tues 6am–8pm, Wed 7am–9pm, Thurs 7am–8m, Fri 7am–9pm, Sat 7am–8pm, Sun 6am–9pm; ⓣ 021-934-0223).

Car parks These are dotted all over the place in this car-friendly city. At pay-and-display car parks at street level all around the centre, hustlers will offer to look after your car and clean it for a tip, especially on the Grand Parade and Loop and Church streets. If you want to park in peace, head for one of the multi-storey parking garages; there's one attached to the Golden Acre complex, and another at the north end of Lower Burg Street. Most hotels and a large number of B&Bs and guest houses offer secure parking.

Car rental One of the cheapest is Discount Drive Car Hire (ⓣ 021-511-6802), which rents out vehicles for as little as R160 a day (including 200km a day free) on the basis of a one-week rental, while Berea Car and Bakkie Hire (ⓣ 021-386-4054) offers a rate of R260 a day for three to six days with 250km free a day. For one-way rental (to drive down the Garden Route and fly back from Port Elizabeth, for example), you'll have to rely on one of the bigger companies, such as Avis ⓣ 0861-021-111, ⓦ www.avis.co.za; Budget ⓣ 0861-016-622, ⓦ www.budget.co.za; Europcar ⓣ 0800-011-344, ⓦ www.europcar.co.za; Hertz ⓣ 0861-600-136, ⓦ www.hertz.co.za; Imperial ⓣ 0800-131-000, ⓦ www.imperial.ih.co.za; Tempest ⓣ 0800-031-666, ⓦ www.tempestcarhire.co.za. Although pricier, they have nationwide offices. You'll need a credit card to arrange car rental.

Credit cards For lost credit cards call freefone to be put through to their global service centres: Mastercard ⓣ 0800/990 418; Visa ⓣ 0800/990 475. You'll be asked to give the card number in order to block it.

Dental care Dentists are listed in the Yellow Pages telephone directory and are well up to

British and North American standards, and generally no more expensive.

Disabled travellers A growing number of tourist attractions in Cape Town are being designed to accommodate disabled visitors. For example, the Kirstenbosch National Botanical Gardens have Braille and wheelchair trails, and the V & A Waterfront has been designed as a wheelchair-friendly venue. More details about specific sites can be found on the excellent "Enabled Traveller" website Ⓦ www.enabled.24.com, hosted by Cheshire Homes, who can help with all aspects of travel for disabled tourists.

Educational tours For arranging specialist educational exchanges, cultural visits or fact-finding missions, there are few better operators in Cape Town than Ida Cooper Associates (☏ 021-683-4648, Ⓔ idaca@iafrica.com), who facilitate contacts with a wide range of South Africans, including leading academics, artists, writers and government ministers.

Electricity Electricity runs on 220/230V, 50Hz AC, and sockets take unique round-pinned plugs. Most hotel rooms have sockets that will take 110V electric razors, but for other appliances US visitors will need a transformer.

Embassies and consulates Canada, 60 St George's Mall ☏ 021-423-5240; UK, Southern Life Centre, 8 Riebeeck St ☏ 021-405-2400; US, 4th Floor, Broadway Centre, Heerengracht ☏ 021-421-4280. The main embassies for most countries are in Pretoria, South Africa's executive capital.

Emergencies Ambulance ☏ 10177; Police (Flying Squad) ☏ 10111; Rape Crisis ☏ 021-447-9762.

Hospitals and doctors Doctors are listed in the telephone directory under "Medical" and hospitals under "Hospitals and Associated Institutions". The largest state hospital is Groote Schuur, Hospital Drive, Observatory (☏ 021-404-9111), just off the M3. Somerset Hospital, Beach Road, Mouille Point (☏ 021-402-6911), nearer the centre, has outpatient and emergency departments and is convenient for the City Bowl and Atlantic seaboard, although it's generally overcrowded, understaffed and seemingly under-equipped. If you have medical insurance you might prefer to be treated at one of the well-staffed and well-equipped private hospitals listed in the phone directory. The two largest hospital groups are the Netcare (emergency response 082-911) and Medi-clinic chains, with hospitals all over the Cape Peninsula. Most central is Netcare's Chris Barnard Hospital (formerly the City Park) on Loop Street (☎480 6111).

Inoculations No inoculations are compulsory, and you need take no special precautions unless you're venturing into remote areas of other provinces or neighbouring countries.

Internet Cape Town is well wired and you should have no problem finding somewhere to send or receive your email or do a bit of surfing. Among the numerous places offering the service you'll find a conveniently central cybercafé at Cape Town Tourism, at the corner of Burg and Castle streets, while the cheapest surfing in town is at the South African Museum in the Gardens (even taking into account the R10 entrance fee for adults), which costs R7 per half-hour.

Laundries Most backpacker hostels have coin-operated washing machines, while guest houses, hotels and B&Bs will usually offer a laundry service for a charge. There are also laundries in the city centre and most suburban areas that will do a service wash for you.

Left luggage backpacker hostel provides luggage storage facilities and most other accommodation will be happy to take care of your luggage for a day or two. The left-luggage facility next to platform 24 at the train station (Mon–Fri 7am–4pm) is inexpensive and convenient if you're arriving by intercity bus or train, or catching an airport shuttle into the city centre.

Malaria Malaria is absent from the Western Cape, but is a real risk in the eastern or northern parts of South Africa as well as neighbouring countries, and malaria prophylactics may be necessary.

Mobile phone rental Available from Cellucity, Shop 6193, V & A Waterfront (☏ 021-418-1306) for around R13 per day for the handset, with calls charged at a little under R2.50 per minute. For security reasons you'll need a credit card.

Pharmacies Chemists with extended opening hours include: Hypermed Pharmacy, corner York and Main roads, Green Point (Mon–Sat 8.30am–9pm, Sun 9am–9pm; ☏ 021-434-1414); Sunset Pharmacy, Sea Point Medical Centre, Kloof Road, Sea Point (daily 8.30am–9pm; ☏ 021-434-3333); Tamboerskloof Pharmacy, 16 Kloof Nek Rd, Tamboerskloof (daily 9.30am–6pm; ☏ 021-424-4450).

Police Head office: Caledon Square, Buitenkant Street (☏ 021-467-8000).

Post office The main branch, on Parliament Street, City Centre (Mon–Tues, Thurs–Fri 8am–4.30pm, Wed 8.30am–4.30pm, Sat 8am–noon; ☏ 021-464-1700), has a poste restante and enquiry desk.

Taxis There are a number of reliable companies, including Marine Taxi Hire (☏ 021-434-0434), Sea Point Radio Taxis (☏ 021-434-4444), Unicab (☏ 021-448-1720) and Rikki's (☏ 021-423-4892).

Telephones There are phone booths all over Cape Town taking phone cards and coins. For cash calls, it's easiest to use the phones found at the Main Post Office, Parliament Street (Mon–Sat 8am–9.45pm, Sun & public holidays 9.30am–8.30pm).

Television Cape Town receives broadcasts from SABC 1, 2 and 3 as well as the free-to-air independent channel, e.tv. SABC 3 and e.tv broadcast exclusively in English, while the others mix English-language broadcasts with output in the ten other official languages. Many hotels and guest houses also get the M-Net satellite service, which has channels offering wall-to-wall sport, movies, news and specialist topics in English.

Ticket agency Computicket (☏ 083-915-8000, ⓦwww.computicket.com) and Ticketweb (ⓦwww.ticketweb.co.za) book most theatre, cinema and sporting events, as well as airline and bus tickets.

Time In common with the rest of South Africa, Cape Town is two hours ahead of Greenwich Mean Time throughout the year; seven hours ahead of North American Eastern Standard Time; and eight hours behind Australian Eastern Standard Time. If you're flying from anywhere in Europe, you shouldn't experience any jet lag as you'll be travelling virtually due south.

Travel Agents The largest travel franchise in the country is Sure Travel, which has about two dozen centres across Cape Town; call ☎ 0800-221-656 for the nearest office. Try also STA, 31 Riebeeck Street ☎ 021-418-6570.

Weights and measures South Africa is fully metric, and kilometres, grams, kilograms, litres and degrees Celsius are the norm. Shoe sizes follow the British system.

DAY-TRIPS

DAY-TRIPS

The Whale Coast

Until recently, South Africans have been pretty blasé about the fact that hundreds of southern right whales spend the second half of every year close to the Cape's shores. However, it's the Whale Coast, the couple of hundred kilometres east of Cape Town, which offers the best shore-based whale-watching in the world, and the place most closely associated with their annual migration is Hermanus, the largest town along the shores of Walker Bay, whose warm, shallow waters attract the aquatic mammals. While the town is a viable day-trip from Cape Town, the coastal scenic route there is so spectacular that it's worth savouring. With whales, fine beaches, some of the best wineries in the Cape and a wonderful cliff-top setting, Hermanus makes a good weekend away, but with a couple more days in hand, you can get a taste of the sparsely populated Overberg ("over the mountain") region that was a wild hinterland to the early white settlers.

East down the coast, the first of the Overberg towns is **De Kelders**, which outshines smarter Hermanus as a whale-watching spot, while, further down the bay, you hit the fishing town of **Gansbaai** (Afrikaans for Goose Bay), which these days is far better known for its sharks than its waterfowl. Curving back to Hermanus, **Danger Point**, at the southern extent of Walker Bay, marks the spot where *HMS Birkenhead* went down in 1852.

An easy excursion from Hermanus takes you through dry sheeplands and undulating wheatfields to Bredasdorp, a junction town on the R316 that gives you the choice of branching out to Africa's southern tip at **Cape Agulhas**, the well-preserved Moravian mission town of **Elim** or the fishing village of **Arniston**. And, if you enjoy solitude, then **De Hoop Nature Reserve**, to the east of Arniston, is the best Whale Coast destination, an exciting wilderness of bleached dunes and craggy coast that sometimes sees whales by the score.

HERMANUS

On the edge of rocky cliffs and backed by mountains, **Hermanus**, 112km east of Cape Town, sits at the north-ernmost end of Walker Bay. The town trumpets itself as the whale capital of South Africa and, to prove it, has an official whale crier who struts around armed with a mobile phone and a dried kelp horn through which he yells the latest sightings. There is still the barest trace of a once-quiet fishing village around the historic harbour and in some understated seaside cottages, but for the most part Hermanus has gorged itself on its whale-generated income that has produced modern shopping malls, supermarkets and craft shops.

Walker Bay does provide some of the finest **shore-based whale-watching** in the world; from about July until November/December, southern right whales start appear-ing in the warmer sheltered bays of the Western Cape. Whales aside, Hermanus has good swimming and beaches, some excellent wineries, and makes a good base for explor-ing the coast to either side.

HERMANUS

ACCOMMODATION

Auberge Burgundy	12
Eastbury Cottages	9
Forty Five Marine Drive	6
Hermanus Backpackers	4
Hermanus Guest House	7
Kenjockity	2
Livesey Lodge	11
Marine Hotel	13
Nelshof Blue Beach House	3
Robin's Nest	1
Whale Cottage Guest House	10
Windsor Hotel	5

To Hemel-en-Aarde
Valley & Walker
Bay wineries

To New Harbour

Hermanus
Accommodation
Centre

Museum

Old
Harbour

To Langbaai,
Voëlklip, Kammabaai,
Grotto beaches &
Fernkloof Nature Reserve

0   250m

Arrival and information

Scant public transport passes through Hermanus, the exception being the **Splash bus** (℡082-658-5375, Ⓔsplash@hermanus.co.za), which runs at least once daily between Cape Town central train station and Hermanus, where it will drop you off anywhere. The Baz **backpacker bus** (℡021-439-2323, Ⓦwww.bazbus.com), an extremely useful hop-on/hop-off service aimed at backpackers and budget travellers, runs daily up and down the coast in both directions between Cape Town and Port Elizabeth. It drops people off at Bot River, 28km to the north on the N2, from where you can arrange to be collected by a shuttle operated by Hermanus Backpackers (see below) – booking is recommended, but the Baz carries a mobile phone and can call ahead while you're en route. The return fare to Bot River is around R100. Most people come to Hermanus by **car**, which takes about ninety minutes from Cape Town along the N2, or two hours via Gordon's Bay. Travelling along the N2 and striking south onto the R43 at Bot River is the more direct of the two main routes, but the winding road that hugs the coast from Strand, leaving the N2 just before Sir Lowrie's Pass, is the more scenic.

Hermanus has a helpful **tourist information** bureau (Mon–Sat 9am–5pm; ℡028-312-2629, Ⓕ028-313-0305, Ⓦwww.hermanus.co.za/info) at the old station building in Mitchell Street, with maps, useful brochures about the area and an internet café as well.

For the lowdown on whales and their behaviour, and for the best spots to sight them, see the box on p.264.

The town and beaches

Main Road, the continuation of the R43, meanders through Hermanus, briefly becoming Seventh Street. **Market Square**, just above the old harbour and to the south of Main Street, is the closest thing to a centre, and here you'll find the highest concentration of restaurants, craft shops and flea markets – the principal forms of entertainment in town when the whales are taking time out.

Just below Market Square is the **Old Harbour Museum** (Mon–Sat 9am–1pm & 2–5pm, Sun noon–4pm; R2), whose only real attraction is its live transmission of **whale calls** from a hydrophone anchored in the bay (replaced by recordings out of season). An almost continuous five-kilometre **cliff path** through coastal fynbos hugs the rocky coastline from the old harbour to Grotto Beach in the eastern suburbs. For one short stretch the path heads away from the coast and follows Main Street before returning to the shore. East of the Old Harbour, just below the *Marine Hotel*, a beautiful **tidal pool** offers the only sea swimming around the town centre's craggy coast.

For **beaches**, head out east across the Mossel River to the suburbs, where you'll find a decent choice, starting with secluded **Langbaai**, closest to town, a cove beneath cliffs at the bottom of Sixth Avenue. **Voëlklip**, at the bottom of Eighth Avenue, has grassed terraces and is great for picnics. Adjacent is **Kammabaai**, with the best surfing break around Hermanus and, 1km further east, **Grotto Beach** marks the start of a twelve-kilometre curve of dazzlingly white sand that stretches all the way to De Kelders.

Also on the east side of town, the **Fernkloof Nature Reserve** (dawn to dusk; free), encompasses fifteen square kilometres of mountainous terrain and offers sweeping views of Walker Bay. This highly recommended wilderness area is more than just another nature reserve on the edge of

HERMANUS

WHALE-SPOTTING

The Southern Cape, including Cape Town, provides some of the easiest and best places in the world for whale-watching. You don't need to rent a boat or take a pricey tour to get out to sea; if you come at the right time of year, whales are often visible from the shore, although a good pair of binoculars will always come in useful.

All nine of the great whale species of the southern hemisphere pass by South Africa's shores, but the most commonly seen off the Cape coast are southern right whales (their name derives from being the "right" ones to kill because of their high oil and bone yields and because, conveniently, they float when dead). Southern right whales are black and easily recognized from their pale, brownish callosities (rock gardens). These are patches of raised, roughened skin on their snouts and heads, which form a distinct pattern on each individual and can help scientists keep track of them. What gives away the presence of a whale is the blow or spout, a tall smoky plume which disperses after a few seconds and is actually the whale breathing out before it surfaces. If luck is on your side, you may see whales breaching – the movement when they thrust high out of the water and fall back with a great splash.

Female whales come inshore for calving in sheltered bays, and stay to nurse their young for up to three months. The period from August to October is the best time to see them,

town and has some forty kilometres of **waymarked footpaths** for strolls or longer walks, including a 4.5km circular nature trail. This is an excellent way to get close to the astonishing variety of delicate montane coastal fynbos (over a thousand species have been identified in the reserve), much of it flowering species that attract scores of birds, including brightly coloured sunbirds and sugarbirds that are endemic to the area.

HERMANUS

although they can start appearing in June and some stay around until December. When the calves are big enough, the whales head off south again, to colder stormy waters where they feed on enormous quantities of plankton, making up for the nursing months when the females don't eat at all. Though you're most likely to see females and young, you may see males early in the season, boisterously flopping about the females: they neither help rear the calves nor form lasting bonds with females.

In Hermanus, the best vantage points to spot whales are from the concreted cliff paths, which ring the rocky shore from New Harbour to Grotto Beach. There are interpretation boards at three of the popular lookouts (Gearing's Point, Die Gang and Bientang's Cave).

Hermanus is the most congested venue during the whale season and there are equally good – if not better – spots elsewhere along the Walker Bay coast. De Kelders (see p.272), 39km east of Hermanus, is a good possibility, while De Hoop Nature Reserve (see p.278), east of Arniston, is reckoned to be the ultimate place along the entire southern African coast for whale-watching, with far greater numbers of southern rights breaching here than anywhere else.

During the season, the Whale Information Hotline (☎ 083-212-1074) can tell you where the latest sightings have been.

A couple of kilometres west of town along Westcliff, the **New Harbour** is a working fishing harbour, dramatically surrounded by steep cliffs, and projects a gutsy counterpoint to the more manicured central area. The whales sometimes enter the harbour and if they do, there is nowhere better to watch them than from the *Harbour Rock* or (see "Eating and drinking", p.268).

HERMANUS

ACCOMMODATION

- - - - - - - - - - - - - - - - - - - -

Auberge Burgundy
16 Harbour Rd ⓣ028-313-1201, ⓦwww.auberge.co.za.
Imitation-Provençal country house in the town centre projecting a stylish Mediterranean feel. ⑤

Eastbury Cottages
36 Luyt St; contact Jenny Bowes Meyer ⓣ082-658-4945.
Two very reasonably priced, fully equipped self-catering cottages on the same site close to the Marine Hotel. ①

Forty Five Marine Drive
45 Marine Drive ⓣ028-312-3610, ⓦwww.windsor-hotel.com.
Luxury cliffside self-catering apartments next to the *Windsor Hotel*, with two bedrooms, two bathrooms, a kitchen and terrific views across the bay. R600 per apartment.

Hermanus Backpackers
26 Flower St ⓣ028-312-4293 or 082-890-1485, ⓔmoobag@mweb.co.za.
Professionally run, clean and brightly decorated two-storey house two blocks back from the shore, with dorms and doubles. They run a shuttle to Bot River to meet the Baz bus (booking recommended). ①

Hermanus Guest House
8 Mountain Drive ⓣ028-313-0212, ⓕ028-313-0224.
Self-catering unit that sleeps four, as well as two comfortable and very reasonably priced B&B rooms in a suburban bungalow some way back from the shore. ②

Kenjockity
15 Church St ⓣ & ⓕ028-312-1772.
Centrally located and friendly B&B, where you can't see the sea but you can hear the whales at night in season. ①–③

Livesey Lodge
13 Main Rd ⓣ028-313-0026, ⓦwww.liveseylodge.co.za.
Welcoming and simply furnished B&B with a variety of en-suite rooms mostly arranged around a lovely courtyard garden with a large swimming pool. ③

HERMANUS

Marine Hotel

Marine Drive ⊤ 028-313-1000,
ⓦ www.marine-hermanus.co.za.
Grand seafront hotel with a
rather formal ambience, but
unquestionably Hermanus's
best and easily up to the
standard of the top
establishments in the country.
Mountain-facing ❼, sea-
facing ❾.

Nelshof Blue Beach House

37 Tenth St ⊤ 028-314-0201.
Situated right on Voëlklip
Beach in a renovated
Victorian house, this is the
only B&B in Hermanus
where you have a choice of
lying in bed or lounging in
the jacuzzi to watch whales.
Rear rooms ❹, sea-facing
rooms ❺.

Robin's Nest

Meadow Ave; contact Trixie
Krum ⊤ 082-893-9911,
ⓔ robinsnest@hermanus.co.za.
Three fully equipped, self-
catering studio flats in the
gardens of what was once the
farm Rheezicht, 4km from
town. ❷

Whale Cottage Guest House

20 Main Rd ⊤ 028-313-0929,
ⓦ www.whalecot.co.za.
Simple, pleasantly furnished
guest house offering five
rooms (some larger)
decorated with marine
themes. The only drawback is
it's away from the sea. ❹

Windsor Hotel

Marine Drive ⊤ 028/312 3727,
ⓦ www.windsor-hotel.com.
The town's second hotel has
the best location in town –
right on the edge of the cliffs
– but otherwise isn't a patch
on the *Marine*. Booking is
essential. Sea-facing ❺, non-
sea-facing ❹

Zoete Inval

23 Main Rd ⊤ 028-312-1242,
ⓦ www.zoeteinval.co.za.
Excellent-value and friendly
establishment with a variety
of accommodation: B&B
rooms with or without their
own bathrooms as well as
backpacker dorms and
doubles. ❶–❷

HERMANUS

EATING AND DRINKING

B'S Steakhouse

Hemel-en-Aarde Village ⓣ 028-316-3625.

A friendly and fun steakhouse – the real thing, not part of a chain – that serves brilliantly prepared, mid-priced slabs of real beef (they hasten to tell punters that they don't do burgers), has a formidable wine list and is child-friendly. Dinner Tues–Sun, lunch Fri & Sun.

The Burgundy

Marine Drive ⓣ 028-312-2800.
Fairly expensive Mediterranean-influenced restaurant above the Old Harbour, offering a seafood-dominated menu in one of the town's oldest buildings. There's indoor as well as shady outdoor seating. Teas, lunch and dinner daily.

Fisherman's Cottage

Lemms Corner
ⓣ 028-312-3642.
Excellent spot for drinks – but not that hot an eatery – in an old cottage off Market Square, with verandah seating. Tues–Sat 11am–11pm, Sun lunch only.

The Greek's Coffee Shop & Restaurant

Royal St ⓣ 028-312-3707.
Tiny fisherman's cottage where you can eat genuine Greek taverna fare cooked up by owner Yannie Dzerefos including dolmades, calamari and spit-roast lamb, finishing off with homemade yoghurt and honey. Breakfast and lunch daily, dinner Sat.

Harbour Rock Seagrill & Bar

New Harbour ⓣ 028-312-2920.
Great, easygoing place for sundowners or reasonably priced fish 'n' chips or other seafood dishes, with an outdoor deck that offers stunning views from the cliffs. Daily for breakfast, lunch and dinner.

Marimba Cafe

108d Main Rd ⓣ 028-312-2148.
Lively evening joint with a constantly changing mid-priced menu from across

HERMANUS

Africa. Past dishes have included Ethiopian roast lamb seasoned with cardamom and ginger, and *yassa* – Senegalese-style chicken. Booking essential. Dinner daily.

Milkwood Restaurant

Atlantic Drive, Onrus ⓣ 028-316-1516.

Nice outdoor family venue, especially recommended for its deck in an unsurpassed setting on a seaside lagoon. A 15min drive west of Hermanus, it does medium-priced steaks and great freshly caught fish.

Mogg's Country Cookhouse

Hemel-en-Aarde Valley, 12km from Hermanus along the R320 to Caledon ⓣ 028-312-4321.

A most unlikely location for one of Hermanus's most successful restaurants – on a working farm in the back country. An intimate, mid-priced place that's always full and unfailingly excellent, it dishes up whatever country-cooking surprises take the fancy of chefs Jenny Mogg and her daughter Julia, but there's always a choice of three starters, main courses and desserts – all topped off with superb views across the valley. Booking essential. Open Wed–Sun lunch and Fri & Sat evening.

Rossi's Italian Restaurant

10 High St ⓣ 028-312-2848.

Cheap child-friendly joint that serves reliable pastas and furnace-baked pizzas seven nights a week.

HEMEL-EN-AARDE WINERIES

Some of South Africa's top wines come from the **Hemel-en-Aarde Valley**, about fifteen minutes' drive west of Hermanus. Vineyards in the area date back to the early nineteenth century, when the Klein Hemel-en-Aarde Vineyard was part of a Moravian mission station, but wine-making has only been established here since the early-1980s. Several small wineries are dotted along a few gravel kilometres of the R320 to Caledon, which branches off the main road to Cape Town 2km west of Hermanus, and are worth a visit for their intimate tasting rooms and first-class wines, and to see the stark scrubby mountains just inland.

Bouchard Finlayson

6km along the R320 after the Caledon turnoff ☎ 028-312-3515.
Tasting & sales Mon–Fri 9am–5pm, Sat 10.30am–12.30pm; free.
Adjacent to Hamilton Russell, towards Caledon, lies Bouchard Finlayson, another establishment with a formidable reputation for its Pinot Noir and Chardonnay.

Cape Bay

Just under 7km from the Hemel-en-Aarde turnoff and about half a kilometre after the tar ends ☎ 028-312-3862, ⓔ capebay@netactive.co.za.
Tasting & sales Mon–Fri 9am–4pm & summer only Sun 9am–noon; free.
They produce a notable Cabernet Sauvignon, Pinotage, Chardonnay and Sauvignon Blanc under their heavyweight Newton Johnson label as well as some decent quaffers under their Cape Bay and Sandown Bay labels.

Hamilton Russell

5km along the R320 after the Caledon turnoff ☎ 028-312-3595, ⓔ hrv@hermanus.co.za.
Tasting & sales Mon–Fri 9am–5pm, Sat 9am–1pm; free.
Further on from WhaleHaven you'll come to the longest established of the Walker Bay wineries, which is noted for its exceptionally good Chardonnay. They also bottle a range of wines under the very collectable Southern Right label, which are available at the town liquor stores, and are popular as souvenirs.

WhaleHaven

200m along the R320 after the Caledon turnoff ☎ 028-312-1585, ⓔ whwines@itec.co.za.
Tasting & sales Mon–Fri 9.30am–5pm, Sat 10.30am–1pm; free.
The first winery you'll reach is WhaleHaven, which released its first vintage in 1995 and whose reputation has been growing ever since.

STANFORD

East of Hermanus the R43 takes a detour inland around the Klein River Lagoon, past the pretty riverside hamlet of **Stanford**, which was established in 1857. Despite its proximity to hyped-up Hermanus, the historic village has become something of a refuge for arty types seeking a tranquil escape from the urban rat race. To keep visitors racing around their town they've created an **arts and crafts route** that takes in over a dozen artists' studios. But apart from the town's excellent micro-brewery, Stanford's principal attraction is its publicity-brochure streetscape of simple Victorian architecture that includes an Anglican church, limewashed houses and sandstone cottages with thatched roofs which glow under the late afternoon sun. Although the **Birkenhead Brewery** (tasting daily 11am–5pm, pub lunches daily 11am–3pm, free tours Mon–Fri 11am & hourly 1–4pm) just across the R43 from the village, bills itself as a "craft brewery", the gleaming stainless steel pipes and equipment inside soon dispel any images of bloodshot hillbillies knocking up a bit of moonshine on the quiet. This is a very slick operation and a great place to go for a lunch with mountain views or to sample and buy their excellent beers that put SAB, South Africa's big brewing near-monopoly, in its place.

ACCOMMODATION

B's Cottage

Morton St ☎028-341-0430, ✉milkwood@hermanus.co.za. The nicest of the self-catering places is a very reasonably priced small open-plan thatched house in an English country garden that sleeps two adults. ❷

Stanford House

Corner of Queen Victoria and Church streets ☎028-341-0300. Stanford's top stay, with twenty en-suite double rooms in Victorian cottages. ❺

STANFORD

EATING

Marianne's Bistro and Home Deli

Du Toit St ☎ 028-341-0272.
Fri–Sun 9am–4pm.
Good enough to draw Cape Town gourmands out for the day, this restaurant is recommended for its cream teas, homemade fare and delicious lunches.

Paprika

Shortmarket St ☎ 028-341-0662.
Excellent eatery which does Mediterranean-style dinners from Tuesday to Saturday and Sunday lunches in a cottage with a convivial atmosphere.

DE KELDERS

De Kelders, a haphazard and treeless hamlet stares from bleak cliffs across Walker Bay to Hermanus, fifty-three meandering kilometres to its north along the R43. These cliffs offer the best vantage point along the bay for **whale-watching** – find a spot and relax with your binoculars. Despite surpassing fashionable Hermanus as a whale-watching venue and having a marvellous long sandy beach, De Kelders has somehow escaped the hype, and this small cluster of holiday homes remains a backwater devoid of facilities, with only a couple of places renting out rooms.

Liesje van Voorkom the owner of Liseje's Lodge (see below) takes guests whale-watching and can advise you about the shark-cage diving operations at nearby Gansbaai

---

ACCOMMODATION

Liesje's Lodge

77 Main Rd ☎028-384-1277 or 072-222-0885.
Self-catering units which can also be taken as B&B rooms, some with sea views. ❶–❷

GANSBAAI

Gansbaai is a workaday place, economically dependent on its fishing industry and the seafood canning factory at the harbour. This all serves to give it a more gutsy feel than the surrounding holidaylands, but there's little reason to spend time here unless you want to engage in **great white shark safaris**, Gansbaai's other major industry. Boats set out from here to Dyer Island, east of Danger Point, where great white sharks come to feed on the resident colony of seals.

Shark **diving packages**, including breakfast, lunch, diving gear and a shark T-shirt start at around R1500 (contact Gansbaai Tourism Bureau ☎ & ℻028-384-1439). Bait is thrown into the water to lure the sharks near the boat, but sightings are certainly not guaranteed, especially over December and January when the abundance of seal pups keeps the sharks well fed and less inclined to show up for tourists. Even if a shark does come along it may not hang around long enough for all the people on the boat to get into the cage for a viewing (only two can fit in at a time).

DANGER POINT

True to its name, **Danger Point** lured the ill-fated *HMS Birkenhead* – bound for Algoa Bay with 600 reinforcements for British regiments fighting the Xhosa in the Eighth Frontier War – onto its hidden rocks on February 26, 1852. As was the custom, the captain of the troopship gave the order: "Every man for himself." Displaying true British pluck though, the soldiers are said to have lined up in their ranks on deck where they stood stock-still, knowing that if one man broke rank it could lead to a rush that might overwhelm the two lifeboats which would carry the seven women and thirteen children to safety. The precedent of "women and children first", which became known as the **Birkenhead Drill**, was thus established, but 445 lives were lost in the disaster, the twenty civilians all surviving.

CAPE AGULHAS

Along the east flank of the Danger Point promontory, the rocky and shallow coastline with heavy swells and strong currents makes this one of South Africa's most treacherous stretches of coast – one that has taken over 250 wrecks and around 2500 lives. Its rocky terrain also accounts for the lack of a coastal road from Gansbaai and Danger Point to **Cape Agulhas** – the southernmost tip of Africa.

The plain around the southern tip has been declared the **Agulhas National Park** to conserve its estimated 2000 species of indigenous plants and marine and intertidal life as well as a cultural heritage, which includes shipwrecks, archeological sites – stone hearths, pottery and shell middens have been discovered. There are no facilities apart from a basic **tea shop** inside the terrific **Agulhas Lighthouse** (Tues–Sat 9.30am–4.45pm, Sun 10am–3.30pm; R2), which was commissioned in 1849 and is a local highlight. Apart from the thrill of climbing the precipitous winding stairway to the top, from which you get vertiginous views, there are also some interesting exhibits about lighthouses around South Africa and the world.

Three-hour tours that take in the flora, history and archeology of Agulhas are operated by the well-informed Riaan Pienaar of Coastal Safaris ☏ 028-435-7148 or 082-331-6819.

ACCOMMODATION

Agulhas Guest House

Main Rd ℡028-435-7650,
ⓦ www.agulhas.de.
The smartest accommodation
in town is a relatively grand
stone building perched
halfway up a hillside with
eight rooms varying in level
of luxury from ones with just
showers to sea-facing suites
with large rooms and huge
baths. ❹–❺

Oupos

258 Main Rd ℡028-435-6132.
A small house where the guest
rooms face the sea, run by a
friendly, elderly Afrikaner
couple who adore children. ❷

Sea House B&B

Van Breda St ℡028-435-6542,
ⓔ pfm@isat.co.za.
Informal B&B bang in front
of the tidal pool with three
rooms in a thatched two-
storey house. ❸

The Southernmost

Corner of Van Breda and
Lighthouse streets ℡028-435-
6565, ⓔ cowper@isat.co.za.
As its name implies you'll find
the most southerly beds in
Africa for rent here. Kids and
mobile phones not welcome.
B&B rooms ❷ and
backpacker accommodation
❶.

ELIM

A good reason to venture along the network of dirt roads
that crisscrosses the **Whale Coast interior** is to visit **Elim**,
a Moravian mission station 40km northwest of Agulhas,
founded in 1824. The whole village is a National
Monument of streets lined with thatched, whitewashed
houses and fig trees. There's nothing twee about this extra-
ordinarily undeveloped and untouristy place whose facilities
amount to a couple of tiny stores where coloured kids play
video games.

ELIM

●

275

The **tourist information** bureau near the church in
Church Street (Mon–Sat 9am–12.30pm & 1.30–5pm;
☎028-482-1806) has brochures about the area and can
advise visitors about **accommodation** at the guest house,
which was due for completion in early 2002, as well as
arranging for you to have a cup of tea or a **snack** at the *Old
Mill Tea Room* (booking ahead necessary).

Tours of the village start at the tourist information
bureau and take in the oldest house in the settlement, the
restored old water mill where wheat is still ground into
flour, the church and the memorial commemorating the
emancipation of slaves in 1834. This is the only such
monument in South Africa and its presence reflects the fact
that numerous freed slaves found refuge in mission stations
like Elim.

ARNISTON

After the cool deep blues of the Atlantic to the west, the
tepid azure of the Indian Ocean at **Arniston** is truly startling, and it's made all the more dazzling by its white dunes
interspersed with rocky ledges. This is one of the best
places to stay in the Overberg and is refreshingly under-
developed compared with Hermanus and places closer to
Cape Town. The village is known to locals by its Afrikaans
name, **Waenhuiskrans** (Wagon-house Cliff), after a huge
cave 1.5km south of town which trekboers reckoned was
spacious enough to accommodate a wagon and span of
oxen. The English name derives from a British ship, the
Arniston, which hit the rocks here in 1815.

Shallow seas that are treacherous for vessels give Arniston
the safest swimming waters along the Whale Coast. Apart
from sea bathing, **Kassiesbaai**, a collection of starkly beautiful limewashed cottages now collectively declared a National
Monument, and occupied by coloured fishermen, is the

principal attraction of this unspoilt hamlet. Unfortunately, you can't stay in the cottages; all the holiday accommodation is in the adjacent new section of town, which has managed miraculously to blend in with the spirit of the old village.

ACCOMMODATION

Arniston Hotel

🕾 028-445-9000,
🅦 www.arnistonhotel.com.
Luxurious and well-run hotel in a central position along the seafront. The only place in the village offering sea views from some rooms. ❺

Arniston Seaside Cottages

Signposted from the R316 into town, along the street behind the *Arniston Hotel* 🕾 028-445-9772, ⓔ cottages@arniston-online.co.za.
Limewashed, fully equipped self-catering cottages in a mock-Arniston style. ❸

Southwinds

Huxham St, just behind the hotel 🕾 & ⓕ 028-455-9303, ⓔ southwinds@kingsley.co.za.
Three double B&B suites looking onto a courtyard garden. ❸

Waenhuis Caravan Park

Along the main road into Arniston 🕾 028-445-9620.
Either pitch your own tent or stay in small, four-bed en-suite bungalows. Bring your own bedding and towels. ❶

EATING

Arniston Hotel

See above.
Two eating spots with sea views: the bar does pub lunches and you can get more formal and expensive dinners in the dining room.

Waenhuis

Du Preez St (a continuation of the national road).
The only other place in the village, decorated to resemble a fishermen's tavern, which serves up fish'n'chips and other seafood.

ARNISTON

DE HOOP NATURE RESERVE

De Hoop Nature Reserve (daily 7am–6pm; R13) is one of the wilderness highlights of the Western Cape and, although the reserve makes an easy day-outing from Hermanus, you'll find it's more rewarding to come for a night or more, especially as this is reckoned to be the best place in South Africa to see **southern right whales**.

The breathtaking coastline is edged by bleached sand dunes that stand 90m high in places, and rocky formations that at one point open to the sea in a massive craggy arch. The **flora and fauna** are impressive too, encompassing 86 species of mammal, 260 different birds and 1500 varieties of plants. If you're here for a couple of days in whale-watching season, chances are you'll be in luck, with occasional reports of a score or more in evidence at one time: July to September is the best time.

Inland, rare **Cape mountain zebra**, **bontebok** and other antelope congregate on a plain near the reserve accommodation. Apart from **swimming** and strolling along the length of the white sandy beach, there are **hiking** and **mountain-biking trails**, but you'll need to bring your own bike as there's nowhere here to rent one. A 70km trail recently opened in the reserve consisting of three days, hiking along the coast and two days along the Potberg Mountains. Overnight huts are provided along the way and numbers are limited to twelve people. Book through De Hoop (see below).

Practicalities

Accommodation is limited to a **campsite** (❶) and two-bedroomed **self-catering cottages** (❷), which come with a cooker, fridge and kitchen utensils but you'll need to bring your own bedding, or rent some from the office. The choicest places to stay are the three luxury thatched cottages (❸) on the lip of the estuary, also with two bedrooms and a large comfortable living room. Booking should be made through the Manager, De Hoop Nature Reserve, Private Bag X16, 7280 Bredasdorp (☎028-542-1126, ℻028-542-1679). Overnight visitors must report to the reserve office, about 4km into the reserve, by 4pm. Be sure to stock up on supplies before you come – the nearest shop is 15km away, in the hamlet of Ouplaas. De Hoop is very popular and usually booked up at weekends. There is also good **private B&B accommodation** just outside the entrance gate at *Buchu Bushcamp* (☎028-542-1602, ⓔebushcamp@sdm.dorea.co.za; ❸) in six open-plan timber and thatch chalets as well as a **restaurant** where guests can get meals. Its major attraction is that the owner is an environmental conservationist who is extremely knowledgeable about the local flora and fauna and takes tours.

DE HOOP NATURE RESERVE

The Winelands

An hour's drive east of Cape Town, the Winelands provide perfect touring country. As well as wine sampling and wonderful scenery, you'll find some of South Africa's best restaurants, both in the towns and tucked away on estates at the end of oak avenues. Dutch colonial heritage reaches its height here, with impressive gabled homesteads lying dazzling white among vineyards and slatey mountains. The district takes in Cape Town's earliest European satellite settlements, at Stellenbosch, Paarl, Franschhoek and Somerset West, each with its own established wine route. Any of these towns makes an easy day-trip from Cape Town and you can comfortably include visits to three local wineries in your outing. If you want to extend your explorations to two or more of the towns and their wine routes it's advisable to overnight in the region – a thoroughly relaxing way to take in the scenery, sample some great food and meander through the vineyards.

Without private transport, your most sensible option is to head for **Stellenbosch**, which is served by regular trains from Cape Town. The most satisfying of the Winelands towns, it offers beautiful streetscapes, a couple of decent museums and good visitor facilities. Outside Cape Town, it's also the best place to pick up a tour of some of the wineries.

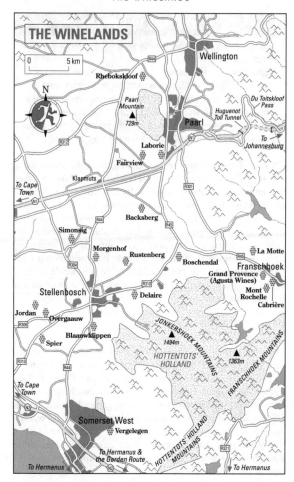

THE WINELANDS

0   5 km

N

Wellington

Rhebokskloof

Paarl
Mountain
729m

Du Toitskloof
Pass

Paarl

Huguenot
Toll Tunnel

To
Johannesburg

Laborie

Fairview

R312

R44

R1

R301

Klapmuts

To Cape
Town

N1

R44

Backsberg

R45

Simonsig

Morgenhof

La Motte

Rustenberg

Boschendal

Franschhoek

R304

Grand Provence
(Agusta Wines)

Stellenbosch

R310

Delaire

Mont
Rochelle

Jordan

Cabrière

R306

Overgaauw

Blaauwklippen

JONKERSHOEK MOUNTAINS

Spier

1494m

R310

HOTTENTOTS
HOLLAND

1363m

R44

FRANSCHHOEK Mountains

To Cape
Town

N2

Somerset West

Vergelegen

To Hermanus &
the Garden Route

HOTTENTOTS-HOLLAND
MOUNTAINS

R321

N2

To Hermanus

To Hermanus

VISITING THE WINELANDS

With over 150 estates in the Winelands, the big question is which ones to visit. The selection below covers wineries that feature beautiful architecture or scenery, or do something other than – of course – produce fine wine. Summer is the best time to visit: days are longer (as are opening hours), the vines are in leaf and you can enjoy time outdoors. Several estates offer lunch, while some allow picnics in their grounds. Most estates charge between R5 and R10 for a wine-tasting session.

One of the region's scenic highlights is the drive along the R310 through the heady **Helshoogte Pass** between Stellenbosch and **Paarl**, a workaday farming town. Smallest of the Winelands towns, **Franschhoek** has the most magnificent setting, at the head of a narrow valley, and with two dozen or more restaurants, it has established itself as the culinary capital of the Cape. By contrast, the sprawling town of **Somerset West** has a single but outstanding draw – **Vergelegen**, the most stunning of all the Wineland estates, which can be easily tacked onto a tour of the Stellenbosch wine route.

STELLENBOSCH

Dappled avenues of 300-year-old oaks are the defining feature of **STELLENBOSCH**, 46km east of Cape Town – a fact reflected in its Afrikaans nickname, Die Eikestad (Oak City). Seventeenth-century buildings, sidewalk cafés, water furrows and a European town layout centred on the Braak, a large village green, make it a pleasant place to wander around. The city (in name only) is the undisputed heart of the Winelands, having more urban attractions than either Paarl or Franschhoek, while at the same time being at the hub of the largest and oldest of the Cape **wine routes**.

Stellenbosch (Stel's Bush) was named in 1679 by **Simon van der Stel**, one of his first actions after arriving at the Cape in November 1679 to take over as VOC commander. It thus became the first of several places dotted around the Cape, including Simonsberg overlooking Stellenbosch, which the governor was to name after himself or members of his family. Soon he settled the area with **free burghers** – company employees freed from their contracts so they could farm independently and supply produce to the VOC. It developed fast, and in 1702 the Danish traveller Abraham Bogaert admired how it had "grown with fine dwellings, and how great a treasure of wine and grain is grown here". Eight years on, some of those fine thatch-roofed houses were destroyed by fire, but were soon rebuilt, and by the end of the eighteenth century there were over a thousand houses and some substantial burgher estates in and around Stellenbosch, many of which are still standing.

The authoritative and widely available *John Platter's South African Wine Guide*, updated annually, provides ratings of the produce of every winery in the country, as well as informed commentary on the estates.

Getting there and around

Coming to Stellenbosch **by car** gives you the freedom to explore the surrounding wineries at your leisure. The drive from Cape Town takes under an hour along either the N1 or N2. Metrorail **trains** (information ☏021/449 2991) commute between Cape Town and Stellenbosch roughly every two hours during the day, and take about an hour. Infrequent (and expensive) intercity buses from Cape Town pass through Stellenbosch, calling at the train station; again it's around an hour's journey.

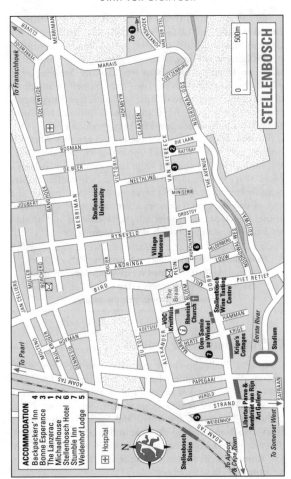

STELLENBOSCH

STELLENBOSCH

500m

To Franschhoek

To Paarl

To Airport & Cape Town

To Somerset West

CLUVER
VERFLICHD
MERRIMAN
JONKERSHOEK
To
VAN DER STEL
MARAIS
SOETEWEIDE
COETZENBURG
HOFMEYR
CLAASEN
NOORDWAL-OOS
BOSMAN
DIE LAAN
RATTRAY
VAN RIEBEECK
DE BEER
VICTORIA
NEETHLING
THE AVENUE
MINISERIE
JOUBERT
BANGHOEK
Stellenbosch University
MERRIMAN
DROSTDY
RYNEVELD
HELDERBERG
SUIDWAL
NOORDWAL-WES
JAN CELLIERS
MULLER
BORCHERD
CROZIER
Village Museum
ANDRINGA
PLEIN
CHURCH/KERK
LOUW
PIET RETIEF
BIRD
DORP
Stellenbosch Wine Tasting Centre
HAMMAN
Eerste River
DU TOIT
HOFMAN
PAUL KRUGER
MOLTENO
DENNESIG
KOETSIEF
ALEXANDER
MARKT
HERTE
BLOEM
TUIN
The Braak
Rhenish Church
VOC Kruithuis
Oom Samie se Winkel
Krige's Cottages
KRIGE
Stadium
ADAM TAS
ADAM TAS
PAPEGAAI
HEROLD
STRAND
Libertas Parva & Rembrandt van Rijn Art Gallery
WEIDENHOF
SAFRAAN
ADAM TAS
Stellenbosch Station

N

ACCOMMODATION

Backpackers' Inn	4
Bonne Esperance	3
The Lanzerac	1
Michaelhouse	2
Stellenbosch Hotel	6
Stumble Inn	7
Weidenhof Lodge	5

✚ Hospital

The busy **tourist information** bureau, about 1km from the station at 36 Market Street (Mon–Fri 8am–6pm, Sat 9am–5pm, Sun 9.30am–4.30pm; ☎021-883-3584, ⓦwww.istellenbosch.org.za), can provide basic information on local attractions, and can supply you with the *Discover Stellenbosch on Foot* leaflet, which describes a walking tour covering a daunting 62 sites.

The centre of Stellenbosch is small enough to explore on foot, but if you need to get further afield, contact Tazzis (☎072-210-7882), who provide transport in **tuk-tuks** that roam around collecting and dropping off passengers. They also offer excursions to wineries for around R25 per person per farm.

The Village Museum

Head north up Ryneveld Street, and at no. 18 you'll encounter Stellenbosch's highlight, the enjoyable **Village Museum** (Mon–Sat 9.30am–4.45pm, Sun 2–4.45pm; ☎021-887-2902, ⓦwww.museums.org.za/stellmus; R10), which cuts a cross-section through the town's architectural and social heritage by displaying four authentic adjacent dwellings from different periods.

Earliest of the houses is the homely **Shreuderhuis**, a vernacular cottage built in 1709, with a small courtyard garden filled with aromatic herbs, pomegranate bushes and vine-draped pergolas. Across the garden, **Blettermanhuis**, built in 1789 for the last Dutch East India Company-appointed magistrate of Stellenbosch, is an archetypal eighteenth-century Cape Dutch house, built on an H-plan with six gables. **Grosvenor House**, opposite, was altered to its current form in 1803, and reflects the growing influence of English taste after the British occupation of the Cape in 1795. The Neoclassical facade, with fluted pilasters supporting a pedimented entrance, borrows from high fashion

STELLENBOSCH

then current. The more modest **O.M. Bergh House**, across the road, is a typical Victorianized dwelling that was built in the same period as Blettermanhuis, but was "modernized" in the mid-nineteenth century on a rectangular plan, with a simplified facade without gables.

Dorp Street

From the Village Museum, head back south to **Dorp Street**, Stellenbosch's nicely preserved historic axis, well worth a stroll to take in the gabled buildings, oaks and roadside water furrows. Heading west along the street, you'll spot the **Stellenbosch Wine Tasting Centre** on your right, and next door **Oom Samie se Winkel**, a jampacked Victorian-style general dealer. On your left, look out for **Krige's Cottages**, an unusual terrace of historic town houses at nos. 37–51, built as Cape Dutch cottages in the first half of the nineteenth century. Victorian features were later added, resulting in an interesting hybrid, with gables housing later attic windows and decorative Victorian verandahs with filigree ironwork fronting the elegant simplicity of Cape Dutch facades.

Strand Street

A left turn into Strand Street brings you to **Libertas Parva**, a fine example of an H-plan Cape Dutch manor, and home to the **Rembrandt van Rijn Art Museum** (Mon–Fri 9am–12.45pm & 2–5pm, Sat 10am–1pm & 2–5pm; free); it doesn't actually display any Rembrandts, but is named for its owners, the Rembrandt van Rijn Tobacco company. The gallery, instead, has a small but stimulating collection of South African art, including a wonderful 360-degree panorama of Cape Town rendered in pen, ink and watercolour by Josephus Jones in 1808; *The*

Conservationists, Ball, an acerbic triptych by William Kentridge, a leading light among the current generation of South African artists; and a number of Irma Stern paintings and drawings (see p.101).

Stellenbosch wineries

Stellenbosch was the first locality in the country to wake up to the marketing potential of a **wine route**, which it launched in 1971. The tactic has been hugely successful and now draws tens of thousands of visitors from all over the world. This is the most extensive wine route in South Africa, offering some of the Cape's best reds and, overall, the greatest diversity of wines. The wineries are along a series of roads that radiate out from Stellenbosch, all signalled by wine-route signposts along the main road.

Blaauwklippen

4km south of Stellenbosch along the Strand Rd (R44) ⓣ 021-880-0133, ⓔ mail@blaauwklippen.com. Tasting & sales Mon–Fri 9am–5pm, Sat 9am–1pm; R10. Although big enough to take tour buses, Blaauwklippen isn't overly commercialized. Apart from the usual Cape Dutch buildings at the foot of the Simonsberg, there's a horse-carriage museum and a little shop selling soft drinks and knick-knacks. A ploughman's-style "coachman's lunch" is served (Mon–Sat) on the verandah. It's one of a handful of South African wineries producing Zinfandel, a flagship red wine.

Delaire

6km east of Stellenbosch along the R310 ⓣ 021-885-1756, ⓦ www.delaire.co.za. Tasting & sales Mon–Sat 10am–5pm; R10. For the Winelands' best views, head for Delaire on the Helshoogte Pass. The drive up from the pass through the slopes of the vineyard-covered hillside brings you to the tasting room with views through oaks across the Groot Drakenstein and Simonsig mountains and down into craggy valleys. After a number of pedestrian years, the output of this winery in the sky is starting to soar: its Chardonnay '97 was rated the New World's best white by the UK's Decanter magazine.

Jordan

4km west of Overgaauw along Polkadraai Rd (the R306) Ⓣ 021-881-3441, Ⓔ jordanw@cybertrade.co.za. Tasting & sales Mon–Fri 10am–4.30pm, Sat 9.30am–2.30pm; R7.50 (refundable against purchases).

Part of the new wave of Cape wineries, with a high-tech cellar, modern tasting room and friendly service. The drive there is half the fun, taking you into a *kloof* bounded by vineyards; the vines get a whiff of the seas from both False Bay and Table Bay, which has obviously done something for their outstanding Cabernet Sauvignon, Sauvignon Blanc and Blanc Fumé.

Morgenhof

Turn off 4km north of Stellenbosch, along Klapmuts Rd (R44 north) Ⓣ 021-889-5510, Ⓦ www.morgenhof.com. Tasting & sales May–Oct Mon–Fri 9am–4.30pm, Sat 10am–3pm; Nov–April Mon–Thurs 9am–5.30pm, Fri 9am–5pm, Sat & Sun 10am–5pm; tasting R10.

A French-owned chateau-style complex overlooked by the vine-covered Simonsberg, Morgenhof has a light and airy tasting room with a bar. Delicious light lunches are served outside, topped off with ice cream on the summery lawns. Among the numerous top-ranking wines worth sampling here are the Merlot, Cabernet Sauvignon,

---

Moddergat Road (the R310) heads southwest out of Stellenbosch parallel to the train tracks, branching off 5.5km later onto Polkadraai Road (the R306).

Pinotage, Sauvignon Blanc, Chardonnay and Chenin Blanc.

Overgaauw

1km after the Polkadraai turn-off along Polkadraai Rd (the R306) ☏ 021-881-3815. Tasting & sales Mon–Fri 9am–12.30pm & 2–5pm, Sat 10am–12.30pm; free.

Notable for having the only Victorian tasting room in the Winelands, with an atmosphere that's elegant and understated but convivial. A pioneering estate that turns out reds and ports of excellent quality, Overgaauw was the first in the country to produce Merlots and is the only one to make Sylvaner, a well-priced dry white.

Rustenberg

Ida's Valley, 4.5km northeast of Stellenbosch along the R310 ☏ 021-809-1200, ⓦ www.rustenberg.co.za. Tasting & sales Mon–Fri 9am–4.30pm, Sat 9am–12.30pm; free.

One of the closest wine estates to central Stellenbosch is also one of the most alluring. To get there, join the R310 from the R44 to Paarl, just north of town. After just under 2km along the R310 to Franschhoek, turn into Ida's Valley for a further 2km, which, after a drive through orchards, sheep pastures and tree-lined avenues, brings you to the estate. An unassuming working farm, Rustenberg's romantic pastoral atmosphere stands in counterpoint to its high-tech tasting room. The first vines were planted here in 1692, but the viniculture looks to the future. Most of their wines under the Rustenberg label are excellent, but also look out for highly drinkable and less expensive reds and whites under the Brampton brand, their second label.

Simonsig

Turn off to left, 4km north of Morgenhof along Klapmuts Rd (R44 north), then 2km down Kromme Rhee Rd ☏ 021-888-4900, ⓦ www.simonsig.co.za. Tasting & sales Mon–Fri 8.30am–5pm, Sat 8.30am–4.30pm; R5; cellar

STELLENBOSCH

tours Mon–Fri 10am & 3pm, Sat 10am; R10.

The outdoor tasting area under vine-woven pergolas gives majestic views back towards Stellenbosch, of hazy blue mountains and vineyards. There's no restaurant, but you can picnic at tables in a courtyard area, cooled by a fountain. Their huge choice of reds and whites offers some of the best value for money around. Among the stars are the Pinotage "Red Hill", Tiara claret, Chardonnay and Kaapse Vonkel, which broke ground some three decades ago by becoming the first commercial fermented-in-the-bottle South African "champagne".

Spier Cellars
7km southwest of Stellenbosch along the R310 ☎ 021-881-3351, Ⓦ www.spier.co.za.
Tasting & sales daily 9am–5pm, R6; cellar tours & tasting Mon–Fri 10am, noon & 3pm; R17.50.
A great family outing in a beautiful spot, with the requisite Cape Dutch buildings set around an ornamental lake, edged with lawns and picnic tables. Note that you can't bring your own food: you'll find Portuguese rolls and picnic foods in their Farmstall deli, and cheetahs roaming around in pens nearby. Pony rides for kids and much more besides: the amphitheatre is a major venue for opera, pop and classical music concerts, the *Taphuis Grill* and *Jonkershuis Restaurant* dish up good fare and the wines aren't bad either, especially the Cabernet Sauvignon and Chardonnay.

For more on cheetah encounters and pony rides at Spier, see p.235.

STELLENBOSCH

ACCOMMODATION

Backpackers' Inn

De Wet Centre, corner of Bird and Church streets ℡ 021-887-2020, Ⓔ bacpac1@global.co.za. Central, squeaky clean and family-friendly hostel. Dorms and doubles ❶

Bonne Esperance

17 Van Riebeeck St ℡ 021-887-0225, Ⓦ www.bonneesperance.com. Colonial elegance in a terrific two-storey Victorian villa with a lovely front garden and swimming pool and standard or luxury rooms. ❹

The Lanzerac

Jonkershoek Rd, 1km east of town ℡ 021-887-1132, Ⓦ www.lanzerac.co.za. Pure Winelands luxury, with elegant whitewashed buildings surrounded by vineyards and mountains. ❾

Michaelhouse

29 Van Riebeeck St ℡ 021-886-6343. B&B with cast-iron decor, a hint of the ethnic and a garden terrace with trellised vines. Room with shower ❸, with bath ❹.

Stellenbosch Hotel

Corner of Dorp and Andringa streets ℡ 021-887-3644, Ⓦ www.stellenbosch.co.za/hotel. Smart town-centre hotel housed in an atmospheric nineteenth-century National Monument. ❺

Stumble Inn

12 Market St ℡ & Ⓕ 021-887-4049, Ⓔ stumble@iafrica.com. Old established hostel in two Victorian houses, with friendly staff. Dorms and camping and doubles ❶

Weidenhof Lodge

24 Weidenhof St ℡ 021-886-4679, Ⓔ weidenhoflodge@hotmail.com. Good-value and popular self-catering mini-apartments with showers, kitchens and TVs. ❷

STELLENBOSCH

EATING AND DRINKING

De Akker
90 Dorp St.
Good spot for pub lunches and late nights (it hots up after 11pm) in a buzzing joint enjoyed both by students.

Decameron
50 Plein St ☎ 021-883-3331.
One of the best restaurants in town, offering southern Italian food, including pasta, pizzas and gnocchi, as well as first-rate seafood. Daily 11am–11pm.

The Fishmonger
Sanlam Building, Ryneveld St ☎ 021-887-7835.
Superb seafood restaurant, centrally located, with outdoor seating, but not cheap. Daily lunch and dinner.

La Masseria
Blaauwklippen Rd off the R44 ☎ 021-880-0266.
Good Italian food in an informal venue which is great for kids, and if you get there for Sunday lunch or a dinner, you may find yourself listening to the patron's songs and joining in yourself. Lunch Tues-Sun 12.30-5pm, dinner (booking only) Fri and Sat.

Lanzerac Manor & Winery
Lanzerac Hotel, Jonkershoek Rd ☎ 021-887-1132.
The light lunches on the terrace or in the pub here are less intimidating than this grand historic homestead's formal restaurant.

D'Ouwe Werf
30 Church St ☎ 021-887-1608.
In a beautiful courtyard with vines, this restaurant offers traditional Cape cuisine, including Karoo lamb, *bobotie* and oxtail brewed in red wine sauce tea.

Rustic Café
43a Bird St ☎ 021-883-3545.
Cosy and popular evening place with bean bags, couches and music that does cheap to moderately priced pizzas, nachos and salads. Open every evening.

STELLENBOSCH

Spice Café

Church St ☏ 021-883-8480.
Friendly folk and a central
location, with a relaxing
garden setting and play area
for kids, where you can get
fresh cakes, sandwiches, salads
and Mediterranean-based
meals. Mon–Fri 9am-5pm,
Sat 9am-2pm, Sun 10am-
2pm.

The Terrace

Shop 12, Drostdy Centre
☏ 021-887-1942.

Centrally located bar-cum-
restaurant overlooking the
Braak, where you can get
pub lunches, burgers and
light meals.

Volkskombuis & De Oewer

Aan-de-Wagenweg, off Dorp St
☏ 021-887-2121.
On the banks of the Eerste
River, this lunch and dinner
venue serves up Cape cuisine
and *boerekos* at acceptable
prices. Closed Sun evening.

VERGELEGEN

Vergelegen (daily 9.30am–4pm; ☏ 021-847-1334; R10,
plus R5 for wine tasting), on the Lourensford Road, off the
N2 in Somerset West, was the estate visited by the British
queen during her 1995 state visit to South Africa – a good
choice, as there's enough to occupy an easy couple of
hours. Although it's not on the official Stellenbosch wine
route, a trip here can easily be combined with one to
Stellenbosch, just 14km to the north. The **interpretive
centre**, across the courtyard from the shop at the building's
entrance, provides a useful history and background to the

Vergelegen's chintzy Lady Phillips Tea Garden (booking
essential ☏ 021-847-1346) serves quiches and homemade
pies accompanied by vegetables from the estate's gardens.
The less formal Rose Terrace offers outdoor light lunches
and wine by the glass.

VERGELEGEN

estate, which you can absorb in about ten minutes. Next door, the **wine-tasting centre** offers a professionally run sampling with a brief talk through each label.

The seventeenth-century **homestead**, which was restored in 1917 by Lady Florence Phillips, wife of a Johannesburg mining magnate, can also be visited. Its pale facade with a classical triangular gable and pilaster-flanked doorways is reached through an octagonal garden that dances with butterflies in summer. Massive grounds planted with chestnuts and camphor trees and ponds around every corner make this one of the most serene places in the Cape.

Vergelegen is synonymous with a notorious episode of corruption and the arbitrary abuse of power at the Cape in the early years of Dutch East India Company rule. It was built by **Willem Adriaan van der Stel**, who became governor in 1699 after the retirement of his father Simon. Willem Adriaan got hold of the land by illegally using his position and VOC slaves to build Vergelegen, and he appropriated Company resources to farm vast tracts of land in the surrounding areas. When this was brought to the notice of the VOC in the Netherlands, Willem Adriaan was sacked and Vergelegen was ordered to be destroyed to discourage future miscreant governors. It appears that the destruction was never fully carried out and only a section at the back was razed, the front remaining intact till the first rethatching, when the house was given its first rudimentary gables. The heavily moulded central gable was probably added in the 1770s and the end gables towards the close of the eighteenth century. The bold Neoclassical wine-cellar gable dates from 1816.

Getting there

Vergelegen is best reached **by car** – in fact, this is the only real option, unless you are taking a **tour** (see p.28). From Cape Town, take the N2 east past the International Airport, and leave the freeway at exit 43, signposted to Somerset West. This will bring you onto the R44, which you should follow into town. Once in Main Street, you'll see the turn-off to Lourensford Road (if you hit the town centre you've missed the turnoff), which you should follow for just over 3km to Vergelegen, off to the right.

PAARL

Although **Paarl** is attractively sited in a fertile valley brimming with historic houses and churches, at heart it's a parochial *dorp*, lacking either the sophistication of Stellenbosch or the new-found trendiness of Franschhoek. A prosperous farming centre, it earns its keep from agricultural light industry – grain silos, canneries and flour mills – on the north side of town, and the cornucopia of grapes, guavas, olives, oranges and maize grown on the surrounding farms. Metrorail and Spoornet **trains** from Cape Town pull in at Paarl's Huguenot Station in Lady Grey Street at the north end of town, near to the central shops.

Paarl was founded in 1657, just five years after the establishment of the VOC refreshment station on the Cape Peninsula, when a party under **Abraham Gabbema** pitched up in the Berg River valley in search of the legendary gold of Monomotapa. They obviously had treasure in mind: waking after a rainy night to the sight of the silvery dome of granite that dominates the valley, they dubbed it Peerlbergh (pearl mountain), which in its modified form, **Paarl**, became the name of the town.

THE HISTORY OF AFRIKAANS

Afrikaans is South Africa's third language after Zulu and Xhosa, spoken by fifteen percent of the population. English is the mother tongue of only nine percent of South Africans, and ranks fifth in the league of the eleven official languages.

Signs of the emergence of a new Southern African dialect of Dutch appeared as early as 1685, when H.A. van Rheede, a Dutch East India Company official from the Netherlands, complained about a "distorted and incomprehensible" Dutch being spoken in the Drakenstein valley around modern-day Paarl. By absorbing English, French, German, Malay and indigenous words and expressions, the language continued to diverge from mainstream Dutch, and by the nineteenth century was widely used in the Cape by both whites and coloureds, although regarded by the elite as unsuitable for literary or official communication. The first attempts by Dominee Stephanus du Toit and the Genootskap van Regte Afrikaners (League of True Afrikaners) to have Afrikaans recognized as a separate language made little impact outside Paarl, but pressure grew, and in 1925 it was recognized with English as one of South Africa's two official languages.

When the National Party took power in 1948, its apartheid policy went hand in hand with promoting the interests of its Afrikaans-speaking supporters. Afrikaners were installed throughout the civil service and filled most posts in the public utilities. Despite the fact that there were more coloured than white Afrikaans speakers, the language quickly became associated with the apartheid establishment. This had electrifying consequences in the 1970s, when the government attempted to enforce Afrikaans as the medium of instruction in African schools. The policy led directly to the Soweto uprising in 1976, which ironically marked the beginning of the end for Afrikaner hegemony in South Africa.

Thirty years later, Cape governor Simon van der Stel granted strips of lands on the slopes of Paarl Mountain to French Huguenot and Dutch settlers. In the twentieth century the town became significant for the two competing political forces that forged modern South Africa. **Afrikanerdom** regards Paarl as the hallowed ground on which their language movement (see box opposite) was born in 1875, with the launching of *Die Patriot*, the first white Afrikaans newspaper; it has a missable museum and the Taal ("Language") Monument to honour the fact. For the **ANC**, Paarl will be remembered as the place from which Nelson Mandela made the final steps of his long walk to freedom, when he walked out of **Victor Verster Prison** in 1990.

Paarl museum

Paarl Museum (Mon–Fri 10am–5pm, Sat 10am–1pm; R5), 303 Main Street, is housed in a handsome thatched Cape Dutch building with one of the earliest surviving gables (1787) in the "new style", characterized by triangular caps. The contents don't quite match up to the exterior, but include some reasonably enlightening panels on the architecture of the town, and several eccentric glass display cases of Victorian bric-a-brac. A token "Road to Reconciliation" display features press cuttings covering Paarl during the apartheid years. Among these you'll find passing mention that Nelson Mandela spent time here as a "guest" – his last years in jail, in fact (see below).

Victor Verster prison

Victor Verster Prison, Nelson Mandela's last place of incarceration, stands 9km south of the N1 as it cuts through Paarl. It was through the gates at Victor Verster (not

PAARL

●

Robben Island or Pollsmoor as many people suppose) that Mandela walked to freedom on February 11, 1990, and it was from here that the first images of him in 27 years were broadcast around the world. Under the draconian apartheid Prisons Act, he couldn't be quoted and no pictures of him (nor of other members of the banned anti-apartheid opposition) could be published until 1990. This meant that until he stepped out of Victor Verster, few South Africans had any idea of Mandela's appearance.

Mandela was moved here in 1988 when the apartheid government realized that he had to be part of the solution to the massive crisis facing the country, yet couldn't be seen by its supporters to be going soft on the ANC leader. A pretext arrived in August 1988, after Mandela was rushed to Tygerberg Hospital suffering from tuberculosis. When he was released three months later he was quietly moved under guard to a warder's cottage at Victor Verster, rather than back to a prison cell. He developed an affection for this temporary accommodation and later used its layout as the basis for his new house in his home town of Qunu.

The jail looks like a rather upmarket boys' school, fronted by rugby fields beneath hazy mountains, but there's still something bizarre about seeing a prison sign nonchalantly slipped in among all the vineyard and wine-route pointers. Since it's still a prison and you can't go inside, the usual tourist thing is to have yourself snapped standing in front of the gates.

Paarl wineries

Paarl was historically known as a region producing **fortified wines**, but as the demand for these diminished it established itself as a significant producer of fine **table wines**. There are over three dozen wineries on the Paarl wine route, including the three listed here, which are all photogenic and fun places to spend time.

Fairview

Take the R101 (the southwest extension of Main Rd) out of town, turning right at the Fairview sign and continuing for about 2.5km ⊤ 021-863-2450, ⊛ www.fairview.co.za.
Wine & cheese tasting & sales Mon–Fri 8.30am–5pm, Sat 8.30am–1pm; R10.

On the southern fringes of town, Fairview is a real crowd-pleaser, with much more than just wine tasting on offer. Your arrival is marked by a spiral tower for the goats to climb, the emblem of the estate. Fairview is an innovative family-run place with interesting tastings, public milking of its exotic goats and a deli that sells picnic fodder – cold meats as well as goat, sheep and cow cheeses made on the estate. It can get a bit hectic when the tour buses roll in, so try to phone ahead to find out when they're expected. The first-rate wines here include Shiraz-Merlot, Merlot and Chardonnay – all fabulous and all good value.

Laborie

Taillefert St, town centre ⊤ 021-807-3390, ⊛ www.kwv-international.co.za.
Tasting & sales Daily 9am–5pm; R8.

This is one of the most impressive Paarl wineries, made all the more remarkable for being right in town. The beautiful manor is fronted by a rose garden, acres of close-cropped lawns, historic buildings and oak trees – all towered over by the Taal Monument. There's a truly wonderful tasting room balcony, looking out over the vineyards trailing up Paarl Mountain. Try the Chardonnay, Sauvignon Blanc and the Pineau de Laborie, the world's first pot-stilled eau de vie made entirely from Pinotage grapes – delicious and well priced. They also produce a nice Cap Classique, a champagne-style sparkling wine.

Rhebokskloof

Take a left turn from Jan Philips, and continue for 2km ⊤ 021-863-8386, ⊛ www.rhebok-skloof.co.za.

Tasting & sales Mon–Fri 9am–5pm, free; formal tasting and cellar tour (book in advance) R7.

A highly photogenic wine estate, overlooking a shallow kloof that borders on a mountain nature reserve, Rhebokskloof has a growing reputation for its restaurant.

Although wine tasting is free, for a small charge you can book a formal tasting (24hr in advance) that includes a talk on wine, a video and a cellar tour. The Cabernet Sauvignon, Pinotage and Merlot are well worth sampling.

Rhebokskloof is a good choice if you find yourself at a loose end over a public holiday: it's one of the very few estates open every day of the year.

ACCOMMODATION

Lemoenkloof
396a Main St ⓣ 021-872-3782, ⓔ lemoenkloof@adept.co.za. Well-run guest house in an 1820s National Monument, with a TV and fridge in every room. ❹

Nantes Vue
56 Mill St ⓣ 021-872-7311. Good-value doubles decorated with artistic flair in a Cape Dutch National Monument. ❸

Roggeland Country House
Roggeland Rd, Dal Jospehat Valley ⓣ 021-868-2501, ⓦ www.roggeland.co.za. Good service, outstanding food and informality at a family-run inn in a wonderful eighteenth-century Cape Dutch homestead. Half-board. ❼

EATING AND DRINKING

Bosman's Restaurant
Grande Roche Hotel, Plantasie St ⓣ 021-863-2727.

PAARL

One of the best and priciest restaurants in the country, offering superb European cuisine with elaborate service. Lunch & dinner daily.

Kostinrichting Coffee Shop

19 Pastorie St.

Conveniently close to the museums, this is a good spot for tea, cakes, toasted sandwiches and salads.

Laborie Restaurant & Wine House

Taillefert St ⊤ 021-808-7429.

Seasonal *à la carte* and traditional Cape cuisine set-menu lunches every day, plus dinners. Closed Sun & Mon.

Roggeland Country House

Roggeland Rd, Dal Jospehat Valley ⊤ 021-868-2501.

Imaginative set menu that changes frequently, inspired by the regional produce of Paarl and accompanied by a selected wine. Daily lunch & dinner.

Wagon Wheels Steakhouse

57 Lady Grey St ⊤ 021-872-5265.

Better than average steakhouse with surprisingly tasty sauces and seafood alternatives. Lunch Tues–Fri, dinner Tues–Sat.

FRANSCHHOEK

It's only relatively recently that **Franschhoek** (79km from Cape Town, 33km from Stellenbosch and 29km from Paarl), has emerged from being the dowdy *dorp* of the Winelands to become the culinary capital of the Western Cape. Its late Victorian architecture, combined with bland modern bungalows, can't match the elegance of Stellenbosch, but the terrific setting, hemmed in on three sides by mountains and with vineyards down every other backstreet, has created a place people from the capital drive out to just for lunch.

A CORNER THAT IS FOREVER FRANCE

Between 1688 and 1700, about two hundred **French Huguenots**, desperate to escape religious persecution in France, accepted a VOC offer of passage to the Cape and the grant of lands. Conflict between the French newcomers and the indigenous **Khoi** followed familiar lines, with the white settlers gradually dispossessing the herdsmen, and forcing them either further into the hinterland or into servitude on their farms. The establishment of white dominance was swift, and by 1713 the area was known as *de france hoek* (French corner). Because of explicit Company policy, French speaking died out within a generation, but many of the estates are still known by their French names. The town Franschhoek itself occupies parts of the original farms of La Cotte and Cabrière and is relatively recent, having been established around a church built in 1833.

Since eating and drinking is what Franschhoek is all about, there's little point in making the effort to get here without trying at least one or two of its excellent **restaurants**. In town, these are concentrated along Huguenot Road, but there are a number of excellent alternatives in the more rustic environment of the surrounding wine estates; booking is essential. Franschhoek's cuisine tends to be French-inspired, but not exclusively so, and salmon trout is a local speciality.

There's no public **transport** to Franschhoek or in the town itself. The only way to get here is by car; head east out of Cape Town along the N1 and take the southbound turnoff onto the R45 or R301, both of which lead to Franschhoek.

- -

Restaurants are listed on pp.306–7. For coffee or a sandwich, head for one of the many cafés in town, or book a picnic hamper at one of the wineries.

- -

The Town

Away from the wining and dining, Franschhoek's attractions are limited to hiking, horse-riding and cycling in the valley, or visiting the Huguenot Monument and adjacent museum, which together occupy a prime position at the head of Huguenot Road, where it forms a T-junction with Lambrecht Street. The **Huguenot Monument** consists of three skinny interlocking arches symbolizing the Holy Trinity, while the rather unexciting **Huguenot Museum** (Mon–Fri 9am–5pm, Sat 9am–1pm & 2–5pm, Sun 2–5pm; R4) covers Huguenot history, culture and their contribution to modern South Africa.

Franschhoek wineries

Franschhoek's **wineries** are small enough and sufficiently close together to make it a breeze to visit two or three on foot, by mountain bike or even on horseback. Heading north through town from the Huguenot Monument, you'll find virtually all the wineries signposted off Huguenot Road and its extension, Main Road.

Boschendal

16km west of Franschhoek and almost equidistant from Stellenbosch at the junction of the R45 and R310 ☏021-874-1031, Ⓦwww.boschendal.com. Tasting & sales April–Sept Mon–Fri 8.30am–4.30pm, Sat 8.30am–12.30pm; Oct–March Mon–Sat 8.30am–4.30pm, Sun 9.30am–12.30pm; R5.

If you have time for only one estate around here, Boschendal is the obvious choice. It's geared to absorbing busloads of tourists, who lap up its impressive Cape Dutch buildings, tree-lined avenues, choice of restaurants and cafés (see p.306) and – of course – its wines. Now owned by the massive Anglo-American Corporation, one of the huge

FRANSCHHOEK

multinationals which has moved from mining to dominate the South African economy, Boschendal is one of the world's longest-established New World wine estates, dating back to 1685, when its lands were granted to Huguenot settler Jean Le Long. The Cape Dutch manor was built in 1812 by Paul de Villiers and his wife, whose initials appear on the front gable. Wine tasting takes place at the Taphuis, where you can sit indoors or sip under shady trees. The range of wines is extensive and generally of an impressive standard.

Cabrière

Berg Rd, close to the Huguenot Memorial ☎021-876-2630, ⓦwww.cabriere.co.za. Sales Mon–Fri 8.30am–5pm, Sat 11am–1pm; cellar tours Mon–Fri 11am & 3pm; R15; Sat 11am; R20.

Cabrière Estate is reached through groves of fruit trees that lead up to the homestead and tasting room. The winery is notable for its Pinot Noir,

and the colourful presence on Saturdays of winegrower Achim von Arnim guarantees an eventful visit; his speciality is slicing off the neck of a bottle of bubbly with a sabre.

Grand Provence

1km west of the centre of town. Daily 10am–6pm; R5 ☎021-876-3195, ⓔorders@agustaw-ines.co.za.

The winery which produces Agusta wines is one of the most casual and friendly, where you can sit in comfy armchairs in a tasting room with a traditional *rietdak* (cane and mud ceiling). The estate is best known for Angels' Tears, a fruity blend of Chenin Blanc and Muscat d'Alexandrie grapes, whose name derives from the legend of a French village where angels came at night to taste the new vintage and wept for joy at its brilliance. Although the wine is highly drinkable, come for the genial ambience rather than to hear heavenly sighs.

La Motte

6km west of town along the R45
ⓣ 021-876-3119,
ⓦ www.la-motte.com.
Tasting & sales Mon–Fri
9am–4.30pm, Sat 9am–noon;
R5.

La Motte presents a supremely cool front, with a superb designer tasting room that looks onto the cellar through a sheer wall of glass. This was the estate that put to rest once and for all the long-held notion that Franschhoek was a poor region for producing red wines. Their wines are almost all uniformly excellent and the stunning Millennium red blend sells out quickly.

Mont Rochelle

Daniel Hugo Rd, next door to
Cabrière ⓣ 021-876-3000,
ⓔ montrochelle@wine.co.za.
Tasting & sales Mon–Sat
10am–4pm, plus Sept–April Sun
11am–1pm; R5; cellar tours
Mon–Sat 11am, 12.30pm &
3pm; R10 including tasting.

Next door to Cabrière, Mont Rochelle has one of the most stunning settings in Franschhoek and an unusual cellar in a converted nineteenth-century fruit-packing shed, edged by eaves decorated with fretwork, stained-glass windows and chandeliers.

A great way to do wine tasting is to get on a horse and ride to three different wine farms, through Mont Rochelle Equestrian Centre (ⓣ 083-300-4368). Their three-cellar ride (about two-and-a-half hours) costs roughly R150, which takes in Clos Cabrière, Grand Provence and Mont Rochelle.

ACCOMMODATION

Chamonix Guest Cottages

Uitkyk St ⓣ 021-876-2498,
ⓦ www.chamonix.co.za.

Fully equipped, self-catering cottages surrounded by vineyards on a wine farm. ❷

Le Ballon Rouge Guest House

12 Reservoir Rd ⓣ 021-876-

FRANSCHHOEK

2651, Ⓦ www.ballon-rouge.co.za.
Small B&B in a Victorian
town house with brass
bedsteads and floral fabrics.
Rooms lead onto a verandah
overlooking a side street.

4 La Gileppe

Corner Huguenot Rd and De
Wet St Ⓣ 021-876-2146,
Ⓦ www.lagileppe.co.za.
High quality B&B in a
restored and immaculately
maintained Victorian house.
③—④

Paradise Cottages

Robertsvlei Rd
Ⓣ & Ⓕ 021-876-2160.
Among the most inexpensive
rooms in the valley, in old,
basic accommodation on a
farm. ①

Le Quartier Français

Corner of Berg and Wilhelmina
streets Ⓣ 021-876-2151,
Ⓦ www.lequartier.co.za.
The most luxurious place in
Franschhoek, with two suites
(one with its own pool) and
fifteen huge rooms arranged
around herb and flower
gardens. ⑧

Reeden Lodge

Off Cabrière St Ⓣ 021-876-
3174, Ⓔ reeden@telkomsa.net.
Four lovely self-catering
cottages on a farm, set along
a river near Cabrière Estate.
Minimum charge for three
people. ②

EATING AND DRINKING

Boschendal

Junction of the R45 and R310 to
Stellenbosch Ⓣ 021-874-1252.
Three choices for lunch: pricey
but substantial daily buffet in
the main restaurant, which will
set you up for the rest of the
day; light sit-down lunches at
Le Café; or deluxe picnic
hampers daily under the shady
pines from *Le Pique Nique*.
Booking essential. Daily.

Bread & Wine

Môreson Farm, Happy Valley
Rd, off the R45
Ⓣ 021-876-3692.
Enjoy a *meze*-style lunch
spread and the estate's own
wines in a courtyard
surrounded by orchards and
vineyards. Closed Mon.

FRANSCHHOEK

Chez Michel

Huguenot Rd, just north of *Le Quartier Français* and opposite the post office ☎021-876-2671.
Congenial bistro patronized by locals, in a Victorian house. Lunch Tues–Sun, dinner Tues–Sat.

Frandeli

Co-op Building, Huguenot Rd.
Licensed deli that serves delicious, filled focaccias and bagels accompanied by beer or wine to eat in or take away. Picnic baskets supplied. Daily for breakfast & lunch.

Gideon's Famous Pancake House

50 Huguenot Rd ☎021-876-2227.
Tasty savoury or sweet pancakes with a touch of Cape Muslim flavours. Pavement tables where you can also get sandwiches and salads.

Haute Cabrière Cellar Restaurant

Franschhoek Pass ☎021-876-3688.
Bunker-like venue with interesting mix-and-match menu – no starters or main courses – planned around Cabrière wines. There's a helipad on the roof should you wish to fly in. Lunch daily, dinner summer only.

Le Quartier Français

16 Huguenot Rd ☎021-876-2151.
No-holds-barred formal meals with a local flavour and an imaginative edge at the place that made Franschhoek synonymous with Cape-Provençal food.

FRANSCHHOEK

CONTEXTS

CONTEXTS

309

A brief history of Cape Town

C ape Town's history is complex and what follows is
only a brief account of major events in the city's
past. For more detailed coverage on both Cape
Town's and South Africa's history in general, see the list in
"Books", p.348.

Hunters and herders

Rock art provides evidence of human culture in the
Western Cape dating back nearly 30,000 years. The artists
were hunter-gathers, sometimes called bushmen but more
commonly **San**, a relatively modern term from the Nama
language with roots in the concept of "inhabiting or
dwelling", to reflect the fact these were South Africa's
aboriginals. San people still maintain a tenuous survival in
tiny pockets, mostly in Namibia and Botswana, making
theirs the longest-existing culture in the subcontinent. At
one time they probably spread throughout sub-Saharan
Africa, having pretty well perfected their **nomadic
lifestyle** – the men hunting and the women gathering –

leaving them considerable time for artistic and religious pursuits. People lived in small, loosely connected bands comprising family units and were free to leave and join up with other groups.

About two thousand years ago, this changed when some groups in territory north of modern South Africa laid their hands on fat-tailed sheep and cattle from northern Africa, thus transforming themselves into **herding communities**, known as **Khoikhoi** or simply Khoi. The introduction of livestock had a revolutionary effect on social organization and introduced the idea of ownership and accumulation. Animals became a symbol of both wealth and social status, and those who were better at acquiring and holding onto their herds gradually became wealthier. Social divisions developed, and political units became larger, centring around a chief, who had important powers, such as the allocation of pasturage.

The Cape goes Dutch

Portuguese mariners, under the command of **Bartholomeu Dias**, first rounded the Cape in the 1480s, and named it Cabo de Boa Esperanza, the **Cape of Good Hope**. Marking their progress, they left an unpleasant set of calling cards all along the coast – slaves they had captured in West Africa and had cast ashore to trumpet the power and glory of Portugal with the aim of intimidating the locals. Little wonder then, that the first encounter of the Portuguese with the indigenous Khoikhoi along the Garden Route coast was not a happy one. It began with a group of Khoikhoi stoning the Portuguese for taking water from a spring without asking permission, and ended with a Khoikhoi man lying dead with a crossbow bolt through his chest. It was another 170 years before any European settlement was established in South Africa.

In 1652, a group of white employees of the **Dutch East India Company** (VOC or Verenigde Oostindische Compagnie), which was engaged in trade between the Netherlands and the East Indies, pulled into Table Bay to set up a refreshment station to revictual Company ships trading between Europe and the East. There were no plans at this time to set up a colony; in fact, the Cape post was given to the station commander **Jan van Riebeeck** because he had been caught with his hand in the till. Van Riebeeck dreamed up a number of schemes to keep "darkest Africa" at bay, including the very Dutch solution of building a canal that would cut the Cape Peninsula adrift. In the end he had to satisfy himself with planting a **bitter almond hedge** (still growing in Cape Town's Kirstenbosch Gardens) to keep the natives at arm's length.

Despite van Riebeeck's view that the indigenous Khoikhoi were "a savage set, living without conscience", from the start the Dutch were dependent on them to provide livestock, which were traded for trinkets. As the settlement developed, van Riebeeck needed more **labour** to keep the show going, and bemoaned the fact that he was unsuccessful in persuading the Khoikhoi to discard the freedom of their herding life for the toil of ploughing furrows for him. Much to his annoyance, the bosses back in Holland had forbidden van Riebeeck from enslaving the locals, and refused his request for slaves from elsewhere in the Company's empire.

Creeping colonization

Everyone at the Cape at this time was under stringent contract to the VOC, which effectively had total control over their activities and movements – a form of indentureship. But a number of Dutch men were released from their contracts in 1657 to farm as **free burghers** on land granted by the Company; they were now at liberty to pursue their own economic activities, although the VOC still controlled the market and set prices for produce. This annexation of the lands around the mud fort, which preceded the construction of the more solid Castle of Good Hope, ultimately led to the inexorable process of **colonization**.

The only snag was the land granted didn't belong to the Company in the first place, and the move sparked the first of a series of **Khoikhoi–Dutch wars**. Although the first campaign ended in stalemate, the Khoikhoi were ultimately no match for the Dutch, who had the tactical mobility of horses and the superior killing power of firearms. Campaigns continued through the 1660s and 1670s and proved rather profitable for Dutch raiders, who on one outing in 1674 rounded up eight hundred Khoikhoi cattle and four thousand sheep.

Meanwhile, in 1658, van Riebeeck had managed successfully to purloin a shipload of **slaves** from West Africa, whetting an insatiable appetite for this form of labour. The VOC itself became the biggest slave owner at the Cape and continued importing slaves, mostly from the East Indies, at such a pace that by 1711 there were more slaves than burghers in the colony. With the help of this ready workforce, the embryonic Cape colony expanded outwards and trampled the peninsula's Khoikhoi, who by 1713 had lost everything. Most of their livestock (nearly 50,000 animals) and most of their land west of the Hottentots Holland Mountains had been gobbled up by the VOC. Dispossession, and diseases like smallpox, previously unknown in South Africa, decimated their numbers and shattered their social system. By the middle of the eighteenth century, those who remained had been reduced to a condition of miserable servitude to the colonists.

Kaapstad

During the early eighteenth century, Western Cape Khoikhoi society disintegrated and **slavery** became the economic backbone of the colony, which was now a rude colonial village of low, whitewashed, flat-roofed houses. Passing through in 1710, Jan van Riebeeck's granddaughter, Johanna, commented contemptuously that the settlement was "a miserable place. There is nothing pretty along the shoreline, the Castle is peculiar, the houses resemble prisons" and "one sees here peculiar people who live in strange ways".

Dutch global influence began to wane in the early 1700s, but by mid-century the Cape settlement had developed an independent identity and some little prosperity based on its pivotal position on the European–Far East trade route. People now began referring to it as "**Kaapstad**" (Cape Town), rather than "the Cape settlement", and by 1750 it had a thousand buildings, with over 3000 **diverse inhabitants**. Some of these were indigenous Khoikhoi people, but the largest number were VOC employees, dominated by an elite of high-ranking Dutch-born officials. The lower rungs were filled by the poor from all over Europe, including Scandinavia, Germany, France, England, Scotland and Russia, while slaves came from East Africa, Madagascar, India and Indonesia. There was also a transient population from passing ships, which by the second half of the century were largely manned by Indian, Javanese and Chinese crews. If nothing else, the constant **maritime traffic** injected some life into this intellectual desert, which couldn't boast a single printing press, let alone a newspaper. Entertainment consisted mainly of carousing, whoring and gambling.

Britain takes the Cape

By the 1790s the VOC was more or less bankrupt, and its control over the restive Cape burghers had become decidedly tenuous. As Dutch maritime influence declined, Britain and France were tussling for domination of the Indian Ocean. The outbreak of the French Revolution in 1789 and the establishment of a Francophile republic in the Netherlands a few years later made the **British** distinctly jittery about their strategic access to Cape Town. In August 1795, Rear-Admiral George Keith Elphinstone was sent in haste with four British sloops of war to secure Cape Town; by mid-September the ragtag Dutch garrison had capitulated.

The British occupation heralded a period of **free trade** in which exports from the Cape lifted off as tariffs were slashed, with the result that Cape wines, the largest Cape export, were meeting ten percent of British wine consumption by 1822. The tightly controlled and highly restrictive Dutch regime was replaced with a more tolerant government, which brought immediate **freedom of religion**, the abolition of the slave trade in 1808, and the **emancipation** of slaves in 1834.

Although British-born residents were a minority during the first half of the nineteenth century, their influence was huge, and Cape Town began to take on a British character through a process of cultural, economic and political dominance. **English** became the language of status and officialdom and by 1860 there were eight newspapers, six of them in English. A vibrant press fed a culture of **liberalism** which led Capetonians to thwart British attempts to transport convicts to the Cape (see box on p.44) – the first time since the American Revolution that an outpost of empire had successfully defied Whitehall. This gave the colonists the confidence to demand **self-government** and, in 1854, males, regardless of race, who owned property worth £25 or more won the right to vote for a lower house of parliament, which was based in Cape Town. A significant development of the second half of the nineteenth century was the rapid growth of **communications**, both within Cape Town, and also into the interior, which reinforced the city's status as the principal centre of a Cape Colony that by now extended 1000km to the east. The road from Cape Town to Camps Bay across Kloof Nek was started in 1848, a telegraph line between Cape Town and Simon's Town was laid in 1860, but most significant of all was the introduction of steam. The first **rail line** from central Cape Town to Wynberg was completed in 1864, opening up the southern peninsula to the development of **middle-class suburbia**.

From backwater to breakwater

The development of an urban infrastructure wasn't enough to lift Cape Town from its backwater provinciality. That required the discovery in 1867 of the world's largest deposit of **diamonds** around modern-day Kimberley. Coinciding with this, the city's breakwater was started and the **harbour** was completed just in time to accommodate the massive influx of fortune-hunters, immigrants and capital into Cape Town en route to the diggings. More significant still was the **discovery of gold** around Johannesburg in the Boer-controlled South African Republic in the 1880s, which gave Cape Town a new significance as the gateway to the world's richest mineral deposits.

From the 1870s, growing middle-class self-confidence was reflected in the erection of grand **Victorian frontages** to the city centre's shops, banks and offices. Echoing Victorian London, this prosperous public facade hid a growing world of poverty, inhabited by immigrants, Africans and coloureds who made up a cheap labour force. The degradation and vice that thrived in Cape Town's growing slums were disquieting to the Anglocentric middle class, which would have preferred Cape Town to be like a respectably homogenous Home Counties town, rather than a cultural melting pot.

As the twentieth century dawned, the authorities attempted to achieve a closer approximation to the white middle-class ideal by introducing laws to stem **immigration**, other than from Western Europe, while other statutes sought to protect "European traders" against competition from other ethnic groups. Racial segregation wasn't far behind, and an outbreak of bubonic plague in 1901 gave the town council an excuse to establish **Ndabeni**, Cape Town's first black location, near present-day Pinelands.

Industrialization and segregation

Apart from contributing to Cape Town's development as a trading port, the discovery of gold had more significant consequences for the city. By the end of the nineteenth century, a number of influential capitalists, among them **Cecil John Rhodes** (prime minister of the Cape from 1890 to 1897), were convinced that it would be a good idea to annex the two Boer republics to the north to create a unified South Africa under British influence. In 1899 Britain marched on the Boer republics, in what was rashly described by Lord Kitchener as a "teatime war", but became known internationally as the **Anglo-Boer War**, Britain's most expensive campaign since the Napoleonic Wars. Eventually, three years later, the Anglo-Boer War ended with the Boers' surrender. What followed was nearly a decade of discussions, at the end of which the two Boer republics (the South African Republic and the Orange Free State) and two British colonies (the Cape and Natal) were federated in 1910 to become the **Union of South Africa**, Cape Town gaining a pivotal position as the **legislative capital** of the country.

Africans and coloureds, excluded from the cosy deal

between Boers and Brits, had to find expression in the workplace, flexing their collective muscle on the docks in 1919, where they formed the mighty **Industrial and Commercial Union**, which boasted 200,000 members in its heyday. Cape Town began the process of becoming a modern industrial city and, with the building of the South African National Gallery, promoted itself as the urbane cultural capital of the country. Accelerated **industrialization** brought an influx of Africans from the rural areas and soon Ndabeni was overflowing. Alarmed that Africans were living close to the city centre in District Six and were also spilling out into the Cape Flats, the authorities passed the **Urban Areas Act**, which compelled Africans to live in what were named locations and empowered the city council to expel jobless Africans – measures that preceded apartheid by 25 years. In 1927, the new location of **Langa** (which ironically means "sun") was opened next to the sewage works. Laid out along military lines, with barrack-style dormitories for the residents, it was surrounded by a security fence.

World War II

During the 1930s, Cape Town saw the growth of several fascist movements, the largest of which was the **Greyshirts**, whose favourite meeting place was the Koffiehuis (coffee house) next to the Groote Kerk in Adderley Street. Its members included Hendrik Verwoerd, a Dutch-born intellectual who became a fanatical Afrikaner Nationalist and South African prime minister from 1958 to 1966. When **World War II** broke out there was a heated debate in parliament, which narrowly voted for South Africa to side with Britain against Germany. Members of all South African communities volunteered for service, the ANC (founded in 1912) arguing that their support should be linked to full citizenship for blacks. Afrikanerdom was deeply divided and **Nazi sympathizers**, among them John Vorster (Verwoerd's successor as prime minister), were jailed for actively attempting to sabotage the war effort. *Die Burger*, Cape Town's Afrikaans-language newspaper, backed Germany throughout the war.

The war brought hardship, particularly to those at the bottom of the heap, leading to an increased influx of Africans and poor white Afrikaners from the countryside to the cities. This changed the demography of the city of Cape Town, which lost its British colonial flavour and, for the first time in 150 years, had more black (mostly coloured) than white residents. To accommodate the burgeoning African population, Langa was extended and new townships were built during and after the war at **Nyanga** and **Guguletu**.

By the end of hostilities, Cape Town was a mixed bag of ad hoc official **segregation** in some areas of life while in others, such as on buses and trains, there was none. Coloureds in the Cape, in contrast with residents of the former Boer republics, still had the franchise provided they qualified on the grounds of property ownership.

Apartheid and defiance

In postwar South Africa, ideological tensions grew between those pushing for universal civil rights and those whites who feared black advancement. In 1948 the **National Party** came to power, promising its fearful white supporters that it would reverse the flow of Africans to the cities. In Cape Town it introduced a policy favouring coloureds for certain unskilled and semi-skilled jobs, admitting only African men who already had work and forbidding the construction of family accommodation for Africans – hence turning the townships into predominantly male preserves.

During the 1950s, the National Party began putting in place a barrage of laws that would eventually constitute the structure of apartheid. Early **onslaughts on civil rights** included: the Coloured Voters Act, which stripped coloureds of the vote; the Bantu Authorities Act, which set up puppet authorities to govern Africans in rural reserves; the Population Registration Act, which classified every South African at birth as "white, Bantu or coloured" (see p.329); the Group Areas Act, which divided South Africa into ethnically distinct areas; and the Suppression of Communism Act, which made anti-apartheid opposition (communist or not) a criminal offence. Africans, now regarded as foreigners in their own country, had at all times to carry **passes** – one of the most hated symbols of apartheid.

The ANC responded in 1952 with the **Defiance Campaign**, whose aim was the granting of full civil rights to blacks. A radical young firebrand called **Nelson Mandela** was appointed "volunteer-in-chief" of the campaign, which had a crucial influence on his politics. Up to that point he had rejected political association with non-Africans, but the campaign's interracial solidarity brought him round to the conciliatory inclusive approach for which he is now famous. The government swooped on the homes of the ANC leadership, resulting in the detention and then banning of over a hundred ANC organizers. Unbowed, the ANC pressed ahead with the **Congress of the People**, held near Johannesburg in 1955. At a mass meeting of nearly three thousand delegates, four organizations – representing Africans, coloureds, whites and Indians – formed a strategic partnership.

From within the organization, a group of Africanists criticized co-operation with white activists, leading to the formation in 1958 of the breakaway **Pan Africanist Congress** (PAC) under the leadership of the charismatic **Robert Mangaliso Sobukwe** (see p.88). Langa township became a stronghold of the PAC, which organized peaceful **anti-pass demonstrations** in Gauteng and Cape Town on March 21, 1960. Over a period of days, work stayaways spread to all Cape Town's locations, achieving a temporary nationwide suspension of the pass laws – the calm before the storm. As the protests gathered strength, the government declared a **State of Emergency**, sent the army in to crush the strike, restored the pass laws and banned the ANC and PAC. Nelson Mandela continued to operate clandestinely for a year until he was finally captured in 1962, tried and imprisoned – together with most of the ANC leadership – on **Robben Island**.

Soweto and the Total Strategy

With resistance stifled, the state grew more powerful, and for the majority of white South Africans, business people and foreign investors, life seemed perfect. The panic caused by the 1960 uprising soon became a dim memory and confidence returned. For black South Africans, poverty deepened – a state of affairs enforced by apartheid legislation.

In 1966 the notorious **Group Areas Act** was used to uproot whole coloured communities from many areas, including District Six, and to move them to the soulless **Cape Flats** where, in the wake of social disintegration, gangsterism took root. It remains one of Cape Town's most pressing problems (see box on p.114). Compounding the injury, the National Party stripped away coloured representation on Cape Town city council in 1972.

The **Soweto Revolt** of June 16, 1976, signalled the start of a new wave of anti-apartheid protest, when black youths took to the streets against the imposition of Afrikaans as a medium of instruction in their schools. The protests spread to Cape Town where, as in Gauteng, the government responded ruthlessly by sending in armed police, who killed 128 and injured 400 Capetonians.

Despite naked violence, protest spread to all sections of the community. The government was forced to rely increasingly on armed police to impose order. Even this was unable to stop the mushrooming of new liberation organizations, many of them part of the broadly based **Black Consciousness movement**. As the unrest rumbled on into 1977, the government responded by banning all the new black organizations and detaining their leadership.

From the mid-1960s to the mid-1970s, Prime Minister **John Vorster** had relied on the police to maintain the apartheid status quo, but it became obvious that this wasn't working. In 1978 he was deposed in a palace coup by his minister of defence, **P.W. Botha**, who conceived a complex military-style approach he called the **Total Strategy**. The strategy was a two-handed one of reforming peripheral aspects of apartheid, while deploying the armed forces in unprecedented acts of repression. In 1981, as resistance grew, Botha began contemplating change and moved Nelson Mandela and other ANC leaders from Robben Island to Pollsmoor Prison in mainland Cape Town. At the same time he poured ever-increasing numbers of troops into the townships.

In 1983, Botha concocted what he believed was a master plan for a so-called **New Constitution** in which coloureds and Indians would be granted the vote – in racially segregated chambers with no executive power. The only constructive outcome of this project was the extension of the Houses of Parliament to their current size.

Apartheid suffers a stroke

As President Botha was punting his ramshackle scheme in 1983, 15,000 anti-apartheid delegates met at Mitchell's Plain on the Cape Flats, to form the **United Democratic Front (UDF)**, the largest opposition gathering in South Africa since the Congress of the People in 1955. The UDF became a proxy for the banned ANC, and two years of strikes, boycotts and protest followed. As the government resorted to increasingly extreme measures, internal resistance grew and the international community turned up the heat on the apartheid regime. The Commonwealth passed a resolution condemning apartheid, the US and Australia severed air links, Congress passed disinvestment legislation and finally, in 1985, the Chase Manhattan Bank called in its massive loan to South Africa.

Botha declared his umpteenth **state of emergency** and unleashed a last-ditch storm of tyranny. There were bannings, mass arrests, detentions, treason trials and torture, as well as assassinations of UDF leaders by sinister hit squads. At the beginning of 1989, **Mandela** wrote to Botha from prison describing his fear of a polarized South Africa and calling for negotiations. An intransigent character, Botha found himself paralyzed by his inability to reconcile the need for radical change with his fear of a right-wing backlash. When he suffered a stroke later that year, his party colleagues moved swiftly to oust him and replaced him with **F.W. de Klerk**.

Faced with the worst crisis in South Africa's history, President de Klerk realized that repression had failed. Even South Africa's friends were losing patience, and in September 1989 US President George Bush told de Klerk that if Mandela wasn't released within six months he would extend US sanctions. Five months later, de Klerk announced the unbanning of the ANC, PAC, the Communist Party and 33 other organizations, as well as the release of Mandela.

On February 11, 1990, Cape Town's history took a neat twist when, just hours after being released from prison, **Nelson Mandela** made his first public speech from the balcony of City Hall to a jubilant crowd spilling across the Grand Parade, the very site of the first Dutch fort.

APARTHEID SUFFERS A STROKE

Democracy

Four protracted years of negotiations followed, leading eventually to South Africa's current constitution. Following the country's first-ever democratic elections in 1994, Mandela became South Africa's president. One of the anomalies of the 1994 election was that while the most of South Africa delivered an **ANC landslide**, the Western Cape, supposedly the most liberal region of the country, returned the **National Party** as its provincial government.

This indicated that politics in South Africa were not divided along a faultline that divided whites from the rest of the population as many had assumed; the majority of coloureds had voted for the very party that had once stripped them of the vote, regarding it with less suspicion than the ANC.

During the ANC's first term, affirmative action policies and a racial shift in the economy led to the rise of a **black middle class**, but even so this represented a tiny fraction of the African and coloured population, and many people felt that transformation hadn't gone far enough.

Into the new millennium

Despite several years of non-racial democracy, Cape Town in the twenty-first century largely remains a divided city, with whites and a few middle-class blacks enjoying a leafy existence in the suburbs along the two coasts and the slopes of Table Mountain, while most Africans live in deprived townships. On the **Cape Flats**, some progress has been made in bringing electricity to the shanty towns, but the shacks are still there – and spreading.

The **2000 local elections** proved just how divided a city Cape Town still is. The ANC had hoped that its campaign for better service delivery in poorer areas would capture the hearts and minds of the city's African and coloured township dwellers and allow it to wrest control of the Western Cape and Cape Town city council from the National Party, now restyled as the **New National Party** (NNP) and putting forward coloured candidates in an attempt to distance itself from its shabby apartheid past.

In the run-up to the election the liberal Democratic Party, which for decades had been the only vociferous parliamentary opposition to the apartheid government, joined its NNP former enemy to form the **Democratic Alliance** (DA) under the leadership of the Democratic Party's chief Tony Leon, with the NNP's Martinus van Schalkwyk as deputy. The DA's slogan for the 2000 campaign was "Keep the ANC Out", which many read as a thinly disguised reversion to the National Party's apartheid-era catchphrase of "Swart Gevaar" (Black Peril), only this time the tactic aimed, not to preserve "white purity", but to unite coloured and white voters against Africans. The tactic worked and the alliance won control of the city and the province. The NNP's Gerald Morkel and Peter Marais, both of them coloured, became the Western Cape provincial premier and Cape Town mayor respectively.

Peter Marais – described by the *Mail and Guardian* as "a buffoon of note," who "offers voters a curious mixture of American evangelism and H.F. Verwoerd" – proved to be a populist and erratic city leader, whose arbitrary behaviour, particularly the street-renaming debacle (see box on p.45) led to his sacking in 2001 by the DA leader, Tony Leon. This in turn led to the swift collapse of the alliance, with Marais opting to stay with the NNP, while Morkel threw in his lot with the Democratic Party.

In a curious twist to the saga, the NNP now chose to enter an alliance with the ANC. Formerly the bitterest of adversaries – the NNP's predecessors had, after all, locked up the ANC's leadership on Robben Island – they made unlikely bedfellows. Stranger still, the ANC welcomed them. A senior ANC cabinet minister Steve Tshwete went on record saying: "There is a closer affinity between the ANC and the NNP than with any other party in this country." In the farcical follow-up, the NNP in alliance with the ANC retained control of the province but the DA held onto Cape Town, with Morkel and Marais swapping jobs. At the end of 2001 Marais was the provincial premier and Morkel Cape Town mayor. This proved, if nothing else, how resourceful Western Cape politicians can be in preserving their jobs. What remains to be seen is whether they can apply those resources to dealing with Cape Town's problems.

INTO THE NEW MILLENNIUM

The language
of colour

I t's very striking just how un-African Cape Town looks – and sounds. The dominant language of the city is **Afrikaans**, a close relative of Dutch and the only "European" language to evolve outside Europe. Although English is universally spoken and understood, Afrikaans is the mother tongue of a large proportion of the city's **coloured** residents, as well as a good number of whites. The term "coloured" is fraught with confusion, but in South Africa doesn't have the connotations and meaning it does in Britain and the US. It refers to South Africans of mixed race, as opposed to indigenous Africans or whites of European ancestry. This comes as a surprise to most visitors, who assume that it's all black and white in South Africa, when in fact issues of ethnicity and language are extremely complex.

Slavery and the coloureds

Most brown-skinned people in Cape Town (over fifty percent of the population), and many others throughout the country, are coloureds, with origins in the **slave society** of the seventeenth to early nineteenth centuries. Halfway between East and West, Cape Town drew its population from Africa, Asia and Europe, and traces of all three continents are in the genes, language, culture, religion and cuisine of South Africa's coloured population.

Because Cape slave society was predominantly domestic (distinct from the plantation slavery of the Americas), there was always close contact between masters and slaves. Proximity and uneven power relations made sex between masters and female slaves common, and the offspring of these unions were usually themselves slaves – the first coloureds. Proximity also meant a huge degree of convergence between owners' and slaves' culture, one result of which was the creolized version of Dutch that became Afrikaans.

Afrikaans and apartheid

In the late nineteenth century, Afrikaans-speaking whites, fighting for an identity, sought to create a "racially pure" culture by driving a wedge between themselves and coloured Afrikaans speakers. They reinvented Afrikaans as a "white man's language", eradicating the supposed stigma of its coloured ties by substituting Dutch words for those with Asian or African roots. In 1925, the white dialect of Afrikaans became an official language alongside English, and the dialects spoken by coloureds were treated as comical deviations from correct usage.

For Afrikaner nationalists this wasn't enough, and after the introduction of apartheid in 1948, they attempted to codify perceived racial differences. Under the **Population Registration Act**, all South Africans were classified as white, coloured or Bantu (the apartheid term for African). The underlying assumption was that these distinctions were

AFRIKAANS AND APARTHEID

based on objective criteria. For apartheid it seemed fairly clear who was "Bantu" and who was white, but the coloureds posed particular problems. First, they weren't homogenous so, to accommodate this, the **Coloured Proclamation Act** of 1959 defined eight categories of coloured: Cape Coloured; Malay (Muslim); Griqua; Chinese; Indian; Other Indian; Other Asiatic; and Other Coloured. For reasons of expediency related to trade, Japanese people were defined as "honorary white".

The second difficulty surrounding coloureds was the fact that their appearance spans the entire range, from those who are indistinguishable from whites to those who look like Africans. A number of coloureds managed successfully to reinvent themselves as whites, and apartheid legislation made provision for the racial reclassification of individuals. Between 1983 and 1990, nearly five thousand "Cape Coloureds" were reclassified as "White" and over two thousand Africans were reclassified as "Cape Coloured". Notorious tests were employed – one, for example, where a pencil would be placed in a person's hair and twirled; if the hair sprang back they would be regarded as coloured, but if it stayed twirled they were white.

This wasn't simply a matter of semantics; it was fundamental to what kind of life you could have. There are numerous cases of families in which one sibling was classified coloured, while another was termed white and then could live in salubrious white areas, enjoy good employment opportunities (a lot of jobs were closed to coloureds) and have the right to send their children to better schools and universities. Many coloured professionals, on the other hand, were evicted from houses they owned in comfortable suburbs such as Claremont, which were overnight declared white.

One city, many cultures

With apartheid over, residential boundaries are shifting and so is the thinking on ethnic terminology. Some people now reject the term "coloured" because of its apartheid associations, and refuse any racial definitions, while others are proudly reclaiming the term and acknowledging their distinct culture, with its slave roots.

Formal attempts have been made to foster cultural interaction and to forge a more integrated city. In 1999, the *Cape Times* launched a highly popular "**One City, Many Cultures**" campaign, which featured regular articles highlighting the richness of Cape Town's different ethnic and religious groups. To the same end, the city's local government has been restructured, and its 69 racially segregated bodies rationalized into six councils, deliberately linking the wealthy and the disadvantaged and bringing black, white and coloured areas under common administrations for the first time ever.

Architecture and urban planning

Cape Dutch style developed in the countryside from the seventeenth to the early nineteenth century, and is so distinctively rooted in the Winelands that it has become an integral element of the landscape. The dazzling limewashed walls look stunning in the midst of glowing green vineyards, while the thatched roofs and elaborate curvilinear gables seem to echo the undulations of the surrounding mountains. The style was embraced in the twentieth century as part of white South African identity, and elements appear on the facades of many **suburban homes**.

A less attractive twentieth-century development was the attempt to replan Cape Town as a segregated city, one result being the growth of a new architectural vernacular of tin and cardboard shanties that began to appear on the edges of the city under apartheid, and have proliferated rapidly in the post-apartheid era.

The Cape Dutch vernacular (1652–1850)

The **Posthuys** (1673) in Main Road, Muizenberg, is

CAPE DUTCH ARCHITECTS

Many of the Cape's nineteenth- and twentieth-century buildings were anonymously designed and built, but between 1750 and 1850 – the golden century of Cape architecture – three men were associated with some of the most highly regarded buildings in the colony.

Anton Anreith (1754–1822) was born near Freiburg in Germany, and is believed to have been apprenticed to a Rococo master-sculptor. He joined the Dutch East India Company's army as a private in 1776, but soon became a carpenter, later earning the commission to reconstruct the facade of the Lutheran Church in Strand Street. In 1786, he became the VOC's master-sculptor and was probably responsible for the Kat balcony at the castle.

Hermann Schutte (1761–1844) was born in Bremen and apprenticed to an architect in Germany for seven years. After joining the VOC as a stone mason, he came to the Cape in 1790 and worked on the Robben Island quarries, losing an eye and a hand in a blasting accident. Discharged from the VOC, he became a private building contractor, benefiting from numerous commissions from the influential Louis Michel Thibault. Schutte designed the Groote Kerk in Adderley Street and is believed to have built the Green Point Lighthouse, the first along the South African coast.

Louis Michel Thibault (1750–1815), born near Amiens in France, was premier student at l'Academie Royale d'Architecture in Paris, before joining the Dutch East India Company as Lieutenant of Engineers. Effectively the colony's principal military engineer and government architect, he designed most of the major public buildings in Cape Town, including the Good Hope Masonic Lodge, which served as the parliamentary debating chamber before 1884, the current facade of the Slave Lodge and the imposing gables at Groot Constantia.

THE CAPE DUTCH VERNACULAR (1652–1850)

thought to be the oldest colonial dwelling in South Africa. A rude thatch-roofed cottage consisting of a single rectangular space, its tiny windows served as a defence against feared attacks by the Khoisan, as well as protection from the fierce winds that lash the peninsula. One of the few surviving examples of the so-called "**longhouse**", it represents the primitive language from which a rich vernacular **Cape Dutch** architecture evolved during the first two hundred years of colonial settlement.

Although there were important developments in the internal organization of Cape houses during this period, their most obvious element is the **gable**. End-gables were a common device of medieval northern European and particularly Dutch buildings, but central gables set into the long side of roofs were more exceptional. They were to become the quintessential feature of the Cape Dutch style. Large numbers of buildings in central Cape Town had gables during the eighteenth century, but they had disappeared from the urban streetscape by the 1830s to be replaced by buildings with flush facades and flat roofs.

Arson appears to have been a major reason for these developments. There was a succession of town fires believed to have been started by slaves, including one that razed Stellenbosch in 1710 and Cape Town's **great fires** of 1736 and 1798, leading to a series of measures that shaped the layout of central Cape Town as well as the design of its houses. Flat roofs, clad in fireproof materials, became compulsory on all VOC buildings, as exemplified by the **Town House** (1755) off Greenmarket Square. After the 1798 conflagration, alarmed officials studied reports from London's Great Fire of 1666 and introduced legislation based on lessons learned from there. To retard the spread of flames, narrow alleys were provided between houses, there was a total ban on thatched roofs, and any protrusions on building exteriors – including shutters – were banned. This led to the flush facades and internal shutters that typify early nineteenth-century Cape town houses. With the disappearance of pitched roofs, the urban gable withered away, surviving symbolically in some instances as minimal roof decoration, one example being the **Bo-Kaap Museum** (1763–68) in Wale Street, which sports a wavy parapet.

In an inverse evolution, **rural homesteads** developed from the plain longhouse to become increasingly elaborate over time. As landowners became wealthier, the size of homesteads grew and the house plan became more complex. The spread of fire from one building to another wasn't a major consideration in the countryside, nor were VOC building regulations. Consequently the pitched roof survived here, and with it gables, which became the hallmark of country manors, and an important element of the facade, positioned above the front door to provide a window that would let light into the loft. Because they were just above the front door, they could also provide protection for the entrance against burning thatch. From these functional origins, gables evolved into important symbols of wealth, with landowners vying to erect the biggest, most elaborate and most fashionable examples.

The British century (1800–1900)

The Cape Town the British occupied at the turn of the nineteenth century was a tightly gridded urban space reflecting the Dutch obsession with control. As the century progressed, Britain's growing global dominance and the development of an indigenous middle class became increasingly associated with a **laissez-faire** philosophy. By the late nineteenth century, this had contributed to Cape Town's rapid and unruly expansion.

Under the governorship of **Lord Charles Somerset** (1814–26), an official process of Anglicization included the enforcement of English as the sole language in the courts, but equally important was his private obsession with architecture, which saw the demolition of the two Dutch wings of **Tuynhuys** in Government Avenue. Imposing contemporary English taste, Somerset reinvented the entire garden frontage with a **Colonial Regency** facade, characterized by a verandah sheltering under an elegantly curving canopy, supported on slender iron columns.

During the second half of **Queen Victoria**'s reign, British influence made its greatest and most lasting impact on the shape and appearance of Cape Town. After the 1870s, as the city expanded on an unprecedented scale, the whole gamut of Victorian building types was erected across the peninsula, from town halls, post offices and dwellings to government buildings, shops and banks. In the city centre, the **Standard Bank** (1880) in Adderley Street, a hefty masonry structure with a central dome topped by a jingoistic statue of Britannia, expressed the pre-eminence of Empire and the solidity of capital, while the **Houses of Parliament** (1884) in Government Avenue were the ultimate statement of Cape Town's status as a colonial centre, using the language of a pedimented portico supported on a series of three-storey Corinthian columns – elements drawn from Imperial Roman architecture. Less monumental but no less typically Victorian was the transformation of **Long Street** from a thoroughfare dominated by plain flat-roofed one- and two-storey Georgian dwellings to a street of elaborately articulated roofscapes and intricately textured **wrought-iron** balconies.

In the 1880s and 1890s, Cape Town experienced an explosion of **speculative building**. While the town houses of Observatory, Woodstock, Sea Point and Green ·Point have a uniquely local flavour, they are still recognizably Victorian, with local adaptations that include verandahs and balconies edged with intricate ironwork to shelter their facades from the elements.

Imperial architecture and identity (1892–1910)

The process of defining Cape Town's architectural identity as British Imperial but still distinctly African reached its climax at the turn of the century. Closely associated with the figure of **Cecil John Rhodes**, the megalomaniac diamond magnate who became prime minister of the Cape in 1890, this architecture projected a feudal vision of a British landed gentry in Africa, lording it over the landscape from their stately homes. Rhodes, as a director of the British South Africa Company, had overseen the privatized colonization of Southern and Northern Rhodesia (now Zimbabwe and Zambia), and in his personal capacity owned vast tracts of land in the Rhodesias as well as in Cape Town.

In the Mother City, he is connected with numerous architectural projects and monuments. He commissioned **Herbert Baker**, a young English architect schooled in the **British Arts and Crafts Movement**, to build **Groote Schuur** (1898), his home on Klipper Road in Rondebosch. Baker used recognizable Cape elements such as gables, curving multi-paned windows and steeply pitched roofs, while other aspects relate to quite different traditions: for example the barley-sugar chimneys suggest Tudor prototypes and the gargoyles are replicas of totemic bird figures pillaged by Rhodes from Great Zimbabwe.

The style synthesized by Baker became known as the **Cape Dutch Revival**, and was again used by the architect at **Rust en Vrede** (1902), Rhodes' seaside residence in Main Road, Muizenberg. The Cape Dutch Revival has become well established in South African architectural parlance: it became popular in the twentieth century to use Cape Dutch elements, particularly gables, in suburban houses, no matter how inappropriate their scale or context.

Monuments from the same period are also concerned

with European domination of Africa. The **Van Riebeeck Statue** (1899), commissioned by Rhodes, stands in a prominent position at the bottom of Adderley Street, brazenly proclaiming colonial conquest. Rhodes himself, after his death in 1902, became a symbol of Britain's imperial destiny in Africa, and the **Cecil John Rhodes statue** (1908) in the Gardens has the entrepreneur pointing north with the inscription "Your hinterland is there", a reference to his dream of Africa from Cape to Cairo under the Union Jack.

Although that particular dream was never realized, Cape Town had established itself as a recognizably British city by the start of the twentieth century. Its coming of age was embodied in the **City Hall** (1905) in Darling Street – the first building that represented the city as a whole, as opposed to the municipal halls that existed in each suburb.

Modernism and modernization (1910–1948)

The search for a new kind of architectural identity was prompted by the unification of South Africa in 1910, which brought together the white communities (predominantly Afrikaners and those of British extraction) while excluding blacks. During the 1920s and 1930s, architects briefly flirted with the **Art Deco** style, which was used for a number of office blocks in the city centre such as **Shell House** (1929), now the *Holiday Inn*, on Greenmarket Square.

But issues of design were frivolities compared with Cape Town's real planning crisis. This centred around what to do with the rapidly growing urban population, the accompanying **slums** and the lingering desire of many whites for Cape Town to be a modern European-style city.

Under the guise of slum clearance, Africans were compelled in the 1920s to live in segregated **locations**, which owed more in concept to the Anglo-Boer War **concentration camps** than they did to the Modern Movement. **Langa** (1927), for instance, used industrial-style organization to create a rationally gridded area, deliberately divided into quarters by a pair of wide crossroads to permit easy access for troops. African locations were sited adjacent to factories, leaving little doubt that their real purpose was to serve the needs of industry. In contrast, whites were served up American-style suburbs, such as **Pinelands** (1923), which aimed to create a leafy environment close to the city centre. Spaciously laid out, it consisted of detached houses set in large gardens. Although coloureds didn't do quite so well, they usually fared better than Africans; after the removals of the 1960s and 1970s better-off families were accommodated in free-standing houses such as the ones you pass as you drive south to Muizenberg on the M4, through areas like Heathfield. However, closer to the coast alongside the M5, the dispiriting and decaying ranks of low-rise tenements in the ironically unfragrant suburb of Lavender Hill are far more typical of Cape Flats mass housing.

Pressures on housing were paralleled by pressures on Cape Town's harbour, with the **Victoria and Alfred basins** unable to cope with increased shipping during the first half of the twentieth century. Just before World War II, work was begun on the **Duncan Dock** (1938–43), which literally transformed Cape Town's **Foreshore** – 2km of land north of the Castle of Good Hope were reclaimed from the sea. The huge empty space between the city centre and the docks opened up a golden opportunity to define physically the role of Cape Town as a busy international port, the "**gateway to Africa**". The French architect E.E. Beaudouin was commissioned for the job and drew up plans in 1947 for an area of parks and grand boulevards, with an axis leading directly from the harbour up to the Gardens and the Houses of Parliament. Implementation of the plan took place under the National Party when it came to power in 1948, but, unfortunately, the resulting development is monumental and dehumanizing.

Grand apartheid, grand plans (1948–1994)

The government's "**grand apartheid**" scheme literally entailed redrawing the map of South Africa. While implementing unprecedented levels of ethnic segregation, the regime attempted to gain international acceptance through the construction of what appeared to be a modern and efficient capitalist country. At the Foreshore, a landscape of teeming roads and vast car parks was created, desolate spaces being punctuated by bland glass, concrete towers and monumental buildings. Among them was the hugely expensive government-financed **Nico Malan Theatre** (1971), named after a local National Party administrator but now called the Artscape Centre. The docks were enclosed by a security fence, denying free flow between it and the city, and a pair of flyover freeways erected in the 1950s and 1970s cast a gloomy shadow over it all.

Freeways were part of the modernization of Cape Town, providing rapid access to the heart of the city, but they could also – as in the case of the **M5** – be used as a concrete instrument of apartheid. A potent physical barrier, the motorway roughly marked Cape Town's racial divide, with the whites-only southern suburbs to the west, and the Cape Flats, to which coloureds and Africans were removed during the 1960s and 1970s, to the east. Apartheid's contribution to low-cost housing was the so-called "**matchbox house**", a bland facebrick cube with basic cooking and sleeping facilities and no internal running water. Lacking parks, public buildings and places of entertainment, the townships they occupied were featureless and Orwellian.

The townships reflected the fact that under apartheid Africans were regarded as foreign guest workers in Cape Town, their "real" place of residence being in one of the supposedly independent Bantustans, 1000km or more from the city. But, ultimately, laws proved unable to withstand the demographic pressures that were bringing people from impoverished rural areas throughout the country. In Cape Town, **Crossroads** squatter camp, adjacent to the airport along the N2, was first settled by "illegal" African families in the 1970s. By the mid-1980s it was estimated that between forty and eighty thousand people were living on this 2.5 square kilometre plot in corrugated-iron and timber shacks. Despite waves of pass arrests and brutal police raids in which shanties were flattened and their contents torched, the squatter population continued to grow. Realizing that it faced an immovable force, the government attempted to control the urbanization process, and in 1983 announced the creation of a new mega-township called **Khayelitsha**, close to Crossroads; the following year it scrapped the faltering influx-control laws. Far from eradicating Crossroads, which was its intention, Khayelitsha existed beside it, dwarfing its predecessor with a population that swelled to around half a million by the 1990s; fourteen percent of the population lived in brick houses and the remainder in shacks, making corrugated iron, timber and plastic the evolving vernacular style of the Cape Peninsula.

As the squatter camps lining the road from the airport to the city became Cape Town's real "gateway to Africa", the authorities revived the idea of a public face for the city that would link the central business district to the harbour. In 1988, work began on revitalizing the derelict Victoria and Alfred basins, which were turned into the **V & A Waterfront**, a development that sought to bring about a kind of Victorian Disneyland, incorporating the working harbour. Authentic examples of Victorian heritage such as the **Clock Tower** (1883) stand alongside modern buildings that pay homage to Victorian styles. The **Victoria Wharf** draws its inspiration from innovative nineteenth-century steel-ribbed structures, but here amounts to an oversized shell providing cover for a massive shopping mall. The Waterfront Development initially drew fire from the ANC, which saw it as a sanitized preserve, cut off from the realities of Cape Town life.

Democracy (1994 and beyond)

In the decade after South Africa's first democratic elections, the **Waterfront development** began expanding into the Duncan Dock to its east and linking up with the seaside suburbs to its west, establishing itself as Cape Town's urban focus. Thanks to their proximity to the Waterfront, areas such as Mouille Point, Green Point and De Waterkant enjoyed a new-found desirability, with their once-sleazy Georgian and Victorian alleys being rapidly gentrified.

Despite its initial misgivings, even the ANC found itself coming to terms with the Waterfront. Their association with it changed from simply using an old shed as the embarkation point for Robben Island, to construction of the prestigious and hugely symbolic three-storey **Nelson Mandela Gateway** (2001), occupying the Waterfront's prime site and centrepiece of the new Clock Tower Precinct. A monument to the defeat of apartheid, the Gateway houses a museum and the departure jetty for Robben Island trips.

On the Foreshore, adjacent to the west side of the Waterfront, work began on the **Cape Town International Convention Centre**, due for completion during the second half of 2003. It aims to provide the Mother City with a world-class conference facility, while its position between the city centre and Duncan Dock will help revitalize the desolate and windswept spaces of the Foreshore. From the end of Heerengracht, the city's oldest thoroughfare, a **canal** will connect the Convention Centre with the Waterfront by water-taxis and -buses. According to the scheme's developers, the idea is to create a number of major pedestrian walkways linking key open spaces – the Grand Parade, Greenmarket Square, the area around the station, Artscape and the Convention Centre – to the proposed Harbour Square at the edge of the Duncan Dock.

Books

or a country with a relatively small reading public, South Africa generates a huge number of **books**, particularly politics and history titles. Some of the South African published books may be tricky to find outside the country, but almost all those listed below are in print and should be available from the larger bookshops listed on p.207. Publishers of each book are given, where available, in the United Kingdom (UK), the United States (US) and South Africa (SA). University Press is abbreviated as UP.

Fiction

Andre Brink *A Chain of Voices* (Vintage, UK). Superbly evocative tale of Cape eighteenth-century life, exploring the impact of slavery on one farming family, right up to its dramatic and murderous end.

J.M. Coetzee *Disgrace* (Vintage, UK; Viking Penguin, US). A subtle, strange novel set in a Cape Town university and on a remote Eastern Cape farm, where the lives of a literature professor and his farmer daughter are violently transformed. Bleak but totally engrossing, this won the Booker Prize in 1999. See the box opposite for more on Coetzee.

Rayda Jacobs *The Slave Book* (Kwela, SA). A carefully researched historical novel

J.M. COETZEE

To read a J.M. Coetzee novel is to walk an emotional tightrope from exhilaration to sadness, with a sense throughout of being guided by a strong creative intellect and an exceptionally careful observer of human experience.

Coetzee's taut, measured style strikes some readers as cold and bloodless; he is relentlessly unsentimental, and plots tend to end on an unsettling note. But despite his reputation as a "difficult" writer, Coetzee never fails to involve us absolutely in the fates of his characters; in the words of Nadine Gordimer, Coetzee "goes to the nerve-centre of being".

Born in Cape Town in 1940, and trained as a linguist and computer scientist in South Africa and the US, Coetzee began to write fiction in the early 1970s. *Dusklands* and *In the Heart of the Country*, his first two novels, were dense and often over-wrought dissections of settler psychology, but his prose reached a soaring maturity with *Waiting for the Barbarians* (1980), in which an imaginary desert landscape is the setting for a chilling exploration of the dynamics of imperial power.

In 1983, *The Life and Times of Michael K*, following the wanderings of a reclusive refugee across a future South Africa ravaged by civil war, won the Booker Prize. The novel ends with a passage of extraordinary beauty and subtlety, and stands as a postmodern masterpiece that now bears ironic testimony to South Africa's actual future. After *Michael K* came the novels *Foe, Age of Iron* and *The Master of Petersburg*, an anthology of criticism, *White Writing*, and a moving childhood memoir, *Boyhood*.

When Coetzee won an unprecedented second Booker Prize for *Disgrace* in 1999, he became famous beyond literary circles for the first time. This has meant exasperation for soundbite-hungry media hounds, since Coetzee abhors publicity – he chose not to attend the Booker Prize award ceremony and is notoriously cagey in social interactions.

FICTION

●

dealing with love and survival in a slave household in 1830s Cape Town, on the eve of the abolition of slavery.

Ashraf Jamal *Love Themes For the Wilderness* (Kwela, SA). The inhabitants of a bohemian sub-culture are lovingly observed in this funny and free-spirited novel set in mid-Nineties Observatory.

Pamela Jooste *Dance with a Poor Man's Daughter* (Black Swan, UK). The fragile world of a young coloured girl during the early apartheid years is sensitively imagined in this hugely successful first novel.

Alex La Guma *A Walk in the Night* (David Philip, SA). One of the truly proletarian writers that South Africa has produced, La Guma, before his long exile in Cuba, focused on the conditions of life in Cape Town, particularly the inner-city areas like District Six. His social realism is gritty yet poignant and it gives us many indelible portraits of Cape Town in the mid-century. A real historian of the city.

Sindiwe Magona *Mother to Mother* (Beacon, US; David

Philip, SA). Magona adopts the narrative voice of the mother of the killer of Amy Biehl, an American student murdered in a Cape Town township in 1993. The novel is addressed to Biehl's mother, and is a trenchant and lyrical meditation on the traumas of the past.

Mike Nicol *Sea-Mountain, Fire City: Living in Cape Town* (Kwela Books, SA). One of the most recent books in that rare category, a documentary on living in Cape Town at the beginning of the new millennium. Hinging his narrative on the apparently prosaic business of moving house from one part of the city to another, Nicol maps many of those fissures, not to say abysses, that make Cape Town the divided city that it is.

Richard Rive *Buckingham Palace, District Six* (David Philip, SA). The unique urban culture of District Six is movingly remembered in this short novel about the life of a now-desolate street and its inhabitants.

Jann Turner *Heartland* (Orion, UK). A white farmer's daughter and a black labourer's son are childhood companions on a Boland fruit farm; a betrayal occurs, and years later the boy returns from political exile, ready to stake his claim to the land. A hefty and ambitious popular novel.

Zoe Wicombe, *You Can't Get Lost in Cape Town* (David Philip, SA).The author of a book of pri-marily short stories with a compelling title, Wicombe is remarkable for her sense of realism and the subtle way in which she produces work where social concern is transparent, humour is demonstrable, and yet which consents to none of the heavy-handed treatment anti-apartheid protest literature usually follows.

Guides and reference books

David Biggs *The South African Plonk Buyer's Guide* (Ampersand Press, SA). Updated annually, this pocket guide seeks out great wines that won't break the bank.

Duncan Butchart *Wild About Cape Town* (Southern Books, SA). Compact, well-illustrated pocket guide to common animals and plants of the Cape Peninsula. Covers mountain, seashore and garden environments.

Richard Cowling and Dave Richardson *Fynbos: South Africa's Unique Floral Kingdom* (Fernwood Press, SA). Lavishly illustrated coffee-table book. A fascinating layman's portrait of the fynbos ecosystem.

Tony Jackman *Cape on a Plate* (Guides for Africa, SA). Snazzy and comprehensive annually updated pictorial guide to restaurants in the Cape Town area.

Trish Lane *Playing: More than 101 Things to do with Little People in the Cape* (International Motoring Productions, SA). Not a goblin-spotting handbook, but a very handy compilation of kids' activities and destinations.

Mike Lundy *Easy Walks in the Cape Peninsula* (Struik, SA). An

GUIDES AND REFERENCE BOOKS

invaluable, not-too-bulky book for casual walkers, offering plenty of possibilities for an afternoon's stroll.

Mike Lundy *Weekend Trails In The Western Cape* (Struik, SA). The best guide to outings in the Cape. Good maps, good advice and notes on flora and fauna.

John Platter *John Platter's South African Wine Guide* (The John Platter South African Wine Guide, SA). One of the best-selling titles in South Africa – an annually updated pocket book that rates virtually every wine produced in the country. No aspiring connoisseur of Cape wines should venture forth without it.

History, politics and society

Vivian Bickford-Smith, Elizabeth van Heyningen and Nigel Worden *Cape Town: The Making of a City* and *Cape Town in the Twentieth Century* (David Philip, SA). The first book is richly illustrated and exhaustively researched, and recounts the growth of Cape Town, from early Khoisan societies to the end of the nineteenth century. The second volume is a thorough and elegant account of modern Cape Town, which interweaves rich local history with international events.

Antjie Krog *Country of My Skull* (Vintage, UK; Random House, US). An unflinching and harrow-

ing account of the Truth and Reconciliation Commission's investigations. Krog, a respected radio journalist and poet, covered the entire process, and skilfully merges private identity with national catharsis.

Nigel Penn *Rogues, Rebels and Runaways* (David Philip, SA). A hugely entertaining collection of essays on deviant types in the eighteenth-century Cape. Tragicomic and written in a wry, engaging style.

Robert C-H Shell *Children of Bondage* (Wesleyan UP, US; Witwatersrand UP, SA). Definitive social history of Cape slavery in the eighteenth century – a compelling academic text that is accessible to the lay reader.

Allister Sparks *The Mind of South Africa* (Random House, US). An authoritative journalist and historian traces the rise and fall of the apartheid state; a lively, economical and serious work.

Desmond Tutu *No Future Without Forgiveness* (Rider, UK; Doubleday, US; Random House, SA). Tutu's gracious and honest assessment of the Truth Commission he guided. An important testimony from one of the country's most influential thinkers and leaders.

Frank Welsh *A History of South Africa* (HarperCollins, UK; Kodansha, US; Jonathan Ball, SA). Solid scholarship and a strong sense of overall narrative mark this recent publication as a much-needed addition to South African historiography.

Biography and autobiography

J.M. Coetzee *Boyhood* (Minerva, UK). A moving and courageous childhood memoir by South Africa's greatest novelist. Written in the third person, it depicts the thoughts of a young boy with profound attentiveness.

Adrian Hadland and Jovial Rantao *The Life and Times of Thabo Mbeki* (Zebra, SA). The definitive biography of an enigmatic and powerful man. Much lies ahead for South Africa's president; this book is a solid account of what went before.

Nelson Mandela *Long Walk to Freedom* (Abacus, UK; Little Brown, US). Superb best-selling autobiography of the former president and national icon, which is wonderfully evocative of his early years and intensely moving about his long years in prison. A little too diplomatic, perhaps, on his love life and on the inside story behind the negotiated settlement that spelt the end of apartheid.

Art

Marion Arnold *Women and Art in South Africa* (David Philip, SA). Comprehensive, pioneering study of women artists from the early twentieth century to the present.

Sue Williamson and Ashraf Jamal *Art in South Africa: The Future Present* (David Philip, SA). Stylish and beautifully designed appraisal of contemporary South African art, profiling an enormous range of innovative artists.

Poetry

Ingrid de Kok *Transfer* (Snail Press, SA). Technically adroit and always moving work from probably the most intelligent of South Africa's feminist poets.

Ingrid Jonker *Selected Poems* (Human & Rousseau, SA). One of the few Afrikaans-language poets to be in print in an English translation that does justice to her work. The poems display a remarkable rawness in depicting the outrage of 1960s apartheid,

as well as a grief-stricken lyricism from a poet who drowned herself off Sea Point in 1965.

Stephen Watson *The Other City* (David Philip, SA). No one better evokes Cape Town's changeable beauty, though Watson also writes of the heart and the great universal themes that make him a first-rate poet of the world, rather than just of his native city.

Music

espite the slow pace of the Cape Town **music** scene, which is a lot less lively than Jo'burg's, a steady stream of quality records has been produced, particularly by jazz artists (see box on p.192). A handful of adventurous independent recording studios for jazz, *kwaito* and hip hop music have sprung up in recent years, and the industry is expanding; see pp.191–200 for the lowdown on individual acts and live-music venues. Of the established labels, Melt 2000 is the most innovative and intelligent. All the titles mentioned here should be available at one of the music shops listed on p.208 or can be ordered through them.

Essential Cape Town sounds

Basil Coetzee *Monwabisi*. Smoky, intensely energetic jazz record from the greatest of Cape jazz saxophonists.

Dantai *Operation Lahlela*. R'n'B-flavoured *kwaito* from one of Cape Town's up-and-coming dance acts.

Jimmy Dludlu *Echoes From The Past*. Slick Capetonian jazz with some truly infectious licks and tunes.

Brenda Fassie *Nomakanjani*. The tempestuous queen of township pop produces a string of ballsy post-*kwaito* tunes on this winning album.

Paul Hanmer *Windows to Elsewhere*. A subtle, invigorating jazz album from a gifted pianist who extends the tradition of Abdullah Ibrahim.

Abdullah Ibrahim *African Marketplace*. Pianist-composer Ibrahim's best album – a wistful, nostalgic, other-worldly journey.

Winston Mankunku *Crossroads*. Sinuous, upbeat township jazz from the veteran Cape Town saxman.

Tim Parr *Still Standing*. Simplicity, emotion and melodic power make for a beautiful rock-reggae record by one of South Africa's greatest songwriters.

Prophets of da City *The Struggle Continues*. Unflinching political rhymes from one of the finest hip hop outfits to emerge from the Cape Flats.

Springbok Nude Girls *Surpass the Powers*. Brave anthemic rock from a charismatic band that merits international acclaim.

Essential South African sounds

Bayete *Mmalo We*. Smooth, mellow, joyous African pop: Bayete are the Rolls-Royces of South African music.

Gloria Bosman *Tranquillity*. A young and compelling jazz vocalist, Bosman juggles African and American styles with consummate ease. Paul Hanmer arranges and tickles the ivories.

Juluka *Universal Men*. Seminal late-Seventies album in which traditional Zulu folk music collides with Celtic-flavoured rock:

the results are spine-tinglingly brilliant.

Ladysmith Black Mambazo *In Harmony*. The evergreen maestros of *isicatamiya* fuse their rich voices to exhilarating effect.

Vusi Mahlasela *Silang Mabele*. Known as "The Voice", Mahlasela is a singer-guitarist whose songs are timeless and affecting.

Pops Mohamed *How Far have We Come?* An exciting celebration of traditional African instruments: *mbiras*, *koras*, mouth-bows and various percussion instruments are supplemented by bass and brass in this ethereal but funky album.

Moses Molelekwa *Genes and Spirits*. Pianist-arranger Molelekwa's second album is a tour de force of progressive African jazz – mobile, imaginative and atmospheric.

Tananas *Seed*. Enchanting instrumental grooves that fuse African, oriental and Middle Eastern idioms.

Glossary

ablutions communal washing facilities found at campsites.

African indigenous South African, who speaks a Bantu language – in Cape Town usually Xhosa (see also "black").

Afrikaner literally "African": a white person who speaks Afrikaans.

apartheid National Party's discriminatory policy of "racial segregation".

arvie afternoon.

baai Afrikaans suffix meaning "bay", used in place names such as Smitswinkelbaai.

bakkie light truck or van.

bergie a vagrant in Cape Town, often living on the slopes of Table Mountain.

biltong sun-dried salted strips of meat, chewed as a snack.

black collective term for Africans, Indians and coloureds.

boerekos farm house cooking

boerewors spicy lengths of sausage that are de rigueur at braais.

Boland southern part of the Western Cape.

bottle store off-licence or liquor store.

braai barbecue.

bredie vegetable and meat stew.

BSAC British South Africa Company; Cecil Rhodes' private company, which colonized the area of modern Zimbabwe and Zambia in the 1890s.

Cape Doctor the southeaster that brings cool winds during the summer months.

Cape Dutch eighteenth- and nineteenth-century style of architecture, the buildings being whitewashed and featuring gables.

Cape Dutch Revival twentieth-century style based on Cape Dutch architecture.

coloured person of mixed race.

dagga marijuana.

dassie hyrax.

dominee minister of the Dutch Reformed Church.

dorp country town or village.

free burgher VOC employee released from contract to farm independently on the Cape Peninsula and surrounding areas.

frikkadel fried onion and meat ball.

fynbos term used for vast range of fine-leafed species that pre-dominate in the southern part of the Western Cape (see p.107).

gogga creepy-crawly or insect.

Group Areas Act now defunct law passed in 1950 that provid-ed for the establishment of separate areas for each "racial group".

Hottentot outmoded term for indigenous Khoisan herders encountered by the first settlers at the Cape.

is it? really?

jislaaik! exclamation equivalent to "geez" or "crikey".

jol party.

just now in a while.

Kaapstad Afrikaans name for Cape Town.

Khoikhoi self-styled name of South Africa's original herding inhabitants.

kloof ravine or gorge.

koeksister deep-fried plaited doughnut, dripping with syrup.

kopje hillock.

kramat shrine of a Muslim holy man.

krans sheer cliff-face.

lekker nice.

location old-fashioned term for African township.

Madiba Mandela's clan name, used affectionately.

Malay misnomer for Cape Muslims of Asian descent.

mealie/mielie maize.

melktert traditional Cape custard pie.

MK Umkhonto weSizwe (Spear of the Nation), the armed wing of the ANC, now demobbed or incorporated into the national army.

Mother City nickname for Cape Town.

naartjie tangerine or mandarin.

nek saddle between two mountains.

Nkosi Sikilel 'i Afrika "God Bless Africa" the anthem of the ANC and now of South Africa.

pawpaw papaya.

protea national flower of South Africa and part of the fynbos kingdom.

robot traffic light.

rondavel thatched cottage, circular in plan.

rooibos tea indigenous herbal tea.

shebeen unlicensed tavern.

skelm villain.

skollie gangster, usually on the Cape Flats.

snoek large fish that features in many traditional Cape recipes.

sosatie spicy skewered mince.

stoep verandah.

Strandloper name given by the Dutch settlers to the indigenous people they encountered at the Cape (literally: "beachcomber").

tackies trainers/sneakers.

township urban areas set aside for Africans under apartheid.

trekboer itinerant Afrikaans farmer during the nineteenth century – particularly one leaving the Cape to escape British rule.

tsotsi villain.

vlei marsh.

VOC Verenigde Oostindische Compagnie, the Dutch East India Company.

Afrikaans street signs

derde third	perron station platform
doeane customs	polisie police
drankwinkel liquor shop	poskantoor post office
eerste first	regs right
geen ingang no entry	ry go
gevaar danger	sentrum centre
hoof main	singel crescent
hoog high	stad city
ingang entrance	stad sentrum city centre
inligting information	stadig slow
kantoor office	stasie station
kerk church	strand beach
kort short	swembad swimming pool
links left	verbode prohibited
lughawe airport	verkeer traffic
mans men	versigtig carefully
mark market	vierde fourth
ompad detour	vrouens women
pad road	vyfde fifth
padwerke voor roadworks ahead	

Index

Map entries are in colour

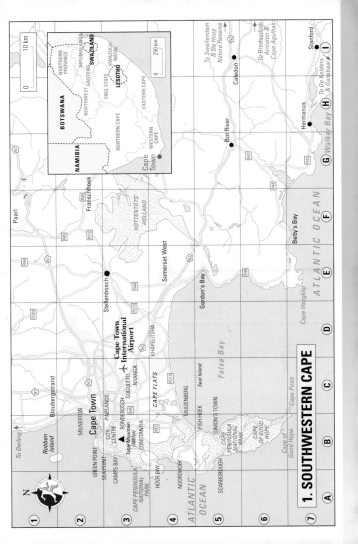

1. SOUTHWESTERN CAPE

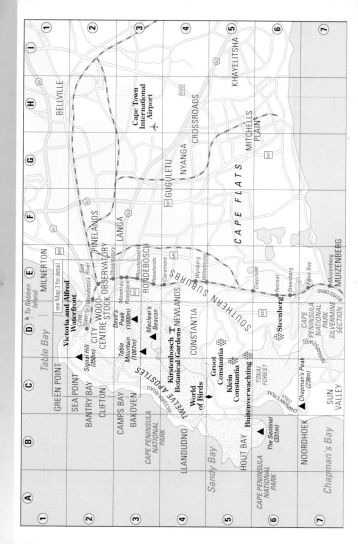

2. CAPE PENINSULA

Legend

- National road
- R300 Regional road
- M Metropolitan road
- Minor road
- Pedestrianized road
- Footpath/hiking route
- Railway
- Ferry route
- ◆ General point of interest
- Memorial
- Public gardens
- Vineyard
- Castle
- Mountains
- Mountain peak
- Lighthouse
- Airport
- Bus stop
- Parking
- Hospital
- Information point
- Post office
- Church
- Synagogue
- Mosque

ATLANTIC OCEAN

False Bay

Seal Island

KOMMETJIE
OCEAN VIEW
SCARBOROUGH
Olifantsbos
Gifkommetjie

St James ST JAMES
KALK BAY
Kalk Bay FISH HOEK
Clovelly
Fish Hoek GLENCAIRN
Sunny Cove
Glencairn
SIMON'S TOWN
Simon's Town

Boulders

CAPE PENINSULA NATIONAL PARK BOULDERS BEACH SECTION

CAPE PENINSULA NATIONAL PARK CAPE OF GOOD HOPE SECTION

Miller's Point
Smitswinkelbaai
Bordjiesrif
Buffels Bay

Cape of Good Hope

Cape Point (238m)
Cape Point

N

0   5 km

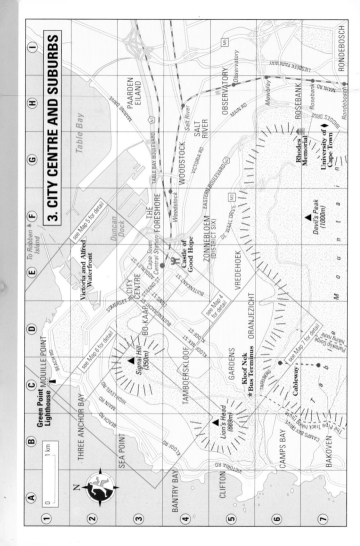

3. CITY CENTRE AND SUBURBS

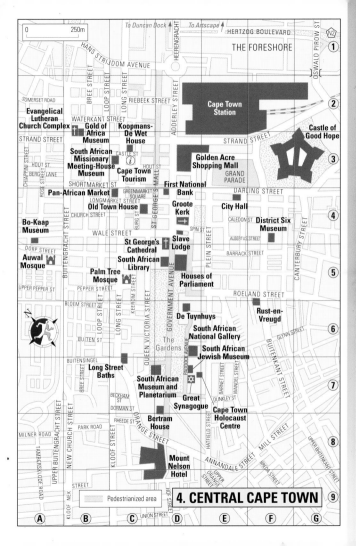

4. CENTRAL CAPE TOWN

To Duncan Dock
To Artscape

HERTZOG BOULEVARD

THE FORESHORE

0   250m

OSWALD PIROW ST

N2

HANS STRIJDOM AVENUE

HEERENGRACHT

BREE STREET

LOOP STREET

LONG STREET

RIEBEEK STREET

ADDERLEY STREET

SOMERSET ROAD

WATERKANT STREET

STRAND STREET

Cape Town Station

STRAND STREET

Castle of Good Hope

Evangelical Lutheran Church Complex

Gold of Africa Museum

Koopmans-De Wet House

CHIAPPINI ST

HOUT ST

BERG LANE

STRAND STREET

South African Missionary Meeting-House Museum

CASTLE ST

Cape Town Tourism

HOUT ST

Golden Acre Shopping Mall

GRAND PARADE

SHORTMARKET STREET

First National Bank

DARLING STREET

ROSE STREET

Pan-African Market

GREENMARKET SQUARE

LONGMARKET STREET

ST GEORGE'S MALL

BURG ST

Groote Kerk

City Hall

CALEDON ST

District Six Museum

CANTERBURY STREET

Old Town House

CHURCH STREET

SPIN ST

Bo-Kaap Museum

BUITENGRACHT STREET

WALE STREET

ALBERTUS STREET

DORP STREET

St George's Cathedral

Slave Lodge

BARRACK STREET

Auwal Mosque

South African Library

PLEIN STREET

UPPER PEPPER ST

Palm Tree Mosque

KEEROM STREET

PEPPER STREET

Houses of Parliament

BLOEM STREET

LOOP STREET

LONG STREET

ROELAND STREET

N

De Tuynhuys

Rust-en-Vreugd

BUITEN ST

QUEEN VICTORIA STREET

GOVERNMENT AVENUE

South African National Gallery

GLYNN STREET

BUITENKANT STREET

BUITENSINGEL

The Gardens

South African Jewish Museum

BREE STREET

LONG STREET

Long Street Baths

South African Museum and Planetarium

PADDOCK AVENUE

Great Synagogue

BECKHAM ST

DORMAN ST

BARNET STREET

WANDEL STREET

Cape Town Holocaust Centre

MILNER ROAD

PARK ROAD

Bertram House

ORANGE STREET

HATFIELD STREET

DUNKLEY ST

MILL STREET

UPPER BUITENKANT STREET

TAMBOERSKLOOF ROAD

NEW CHURCH STREET

UPPER BUITENGRACHT STREET

KLOOF STREET

Mount Nelson Hotel

ANNANDALE STREET

UPPER ORANGE STREET

BREDA STREET

KLOOF NEK

UNION STREET

RHEEDE STREET

Pedestrianized area

A   B   C   D   E   F   G

1 2 3 4 5 6 7 8 9

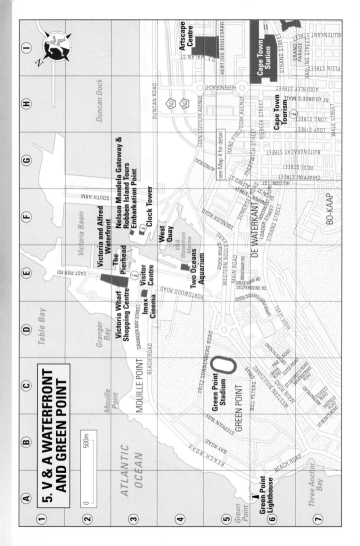

5. V & A WATERFRONT AND GREEN POINT

0   500m

N

ATLANTIC OCEAN

Table Bay

Mouille Point

Granger Bay

Victoria Basin

Duncan Dock

South Arm

EAST PIER RD

Victoria and Alfred Waterfront

The Pierhead

Victoria Wharf Shopping Centre

Imax Cinema

Visitor Centre

Two Oceans Aquarium

West Quay

V&A Waterfront Marina

Nelson Mandela Gateway & Robben Island Tours Embarkation Point

Clock Tower

see Map 4 for detail

Artscape Centre

Cape Town Station

Cape Town Tourism

MOUILLE POINT

GRANGER BAY STREET

BEACH ROAD

PORTSWOOD ROAD

DOCK ROAD

WESTERN BOULEVARD

MAIN ROAD

BRAEMAR RD

VESPERDENE RD

EBENEZER ROAD

ALFRED ST

SOMERSET ROAD

HUDSON STREET

CHIAPPINI STREET

ROSE STREET

PRESTWICH STREET

NAPIER STREET

WATERKANT STREET

DE WATERKANT

STRAND STREET

LOADER STREET

BO-KAAP

HIGH LEVEL

BUITENGRACHT STREET

LOOP STREET

LONG STREET

WALE STREET

BREE STREET

BIEBECK STREET

ST GEORGE'S MALL

ADDERLEY STREET

COEN STEYTLER AVENUE

HEERENGRACHT

OSWALD PIROW STREET

N2

N2

DUNCAN ROAD

ALFRED ROAD

HERTZOG BOULEVARD

WALTER SISULU AVENUE

DE VILLIERS STREET

GRAND PARADE

PLEIN STREET

DARLING STREET

STRAND STREET

BUITENKANT STREET

Green Point Stadium

GREEN POINT

FRITZ SONNENBERG ROAD

STERNAN WAY

BEACH ROAD

BAY ROAD

BILL PETERS

WESTERN BOULEVARD

MASTER ROAD

MAIN ROAD

HELEN ROAD

PINE ROAD

THREE ANCHOR BAY ROAD

VARNEYS ROAD

HASTINGS ROAD

Green Point Lighthouse

Green Point

Three Anchor Bay